ROUTLEDGE LIBRARY EDITIONS:
CHINESE LITERATURE AND ARTS

Volume 8

THE CHINESE KNIGHT-ERRANT

THE CHINESE KNIGHT-ERRANT

JAMES J. Y. LIU

Routledge
Taylor & Francis Group
LONDON AND NEW YORK

First published in 1967 by Routledge & Kegan Paul Ltd

This edition first published in 2022
by Routledge
4 Park Square, Milton Park, Abingdon, Oxon OX14 4RN

and by Routledge
605 Third Avenue, New York, NY 10158

Routledge is an imprint of the Taylor & Francis Group, an informa business

British Library Cataloguing in Publication Data
A catalogue record for this book is available from the British Library

ISBN: 978-0-367-11183-0 (Set)
ISBN: 978-1-032-25779-2 (Volume 8) (hbk)
ISBN: 978-1-032-25781-5 (Volume 8) (pbk)
ISBN: 978-1-003-28498-7 (Volume 8) (ebk)

DOI: 10.4324/9781003284987

Publisher's Note
The publisher has gone to great lengths to ensure the quality of this reprint but points out that some imperfections in the original copies may be apparent.

Disclaimer
The publisher has made every effort to trace copyright holders and would welcome correspondence from those they have been unable to trace.

THE CHINESE KNIGHT-ERRANT

by

JAMES J. Y. LIU

London

ROUTLEDGE AND KEGAN PAUL

First published 1967
by Routledge & Kegan Paul Ltd
Broadway House, 68–74 Carter Lane
London, E.C.4

Printed in Great Britain
by Richard Clay (The Chaucer Press), Ltd
Bungay, Suffolk

CONTENTS

Contents

Note — The author wishes to thank Mr. A. C. Scott for his drawings of theatrical knights which decorate this volume.

DYNASTIC TABLE

HSIA 2183–1752 B.C.*
SHANG 1751–1112 B.C.*
CHOU 1111–256 B.C.

Period of the *Spring and Autumn Annals* (Ch'un-ch'iu) 722–481 B.C.
Period of the Warring States (Chan-kuo) 403–221 B.C.

CH'IN 221–207 B.C.
HAN 206 B.C.–A.D. 220

Western or Former Han 206 B.C.–A.D. 23
Hsin (usurpation of Wang Mang) A.D. 9–22
Eastern or Later Han A.D. 25–220

THREE KINGDOMS

Wei	220–265
Shu Han	221–264
†Wu	222–280

CHIN 265–419

Western Chin	265–316
†Eastern Chin	316–419

SOUTHERN AND NORTHERN DYNASTIES

SOUTHERN		NORTHERN	
†Sung	420–478	Northern Wei	386–534
†Ch'i	479–501	Northern Ch'i	550–577
†Liang	502–556	Northern Chou	557–580
†Ch'en	557–589		

SUI 589–618
T'ANG 618–907

FIVE DYNASTIES

Later Liang	907–922
Later T'ang	923–935
Later Chin	936–946
Later Han	947–950

* These dates are given according to Tung Tso-pin's *Chronological Tables of Chinese History* (Hong Kong, 1960).

† These are known as the Six Dynasties.

Dynastic Table

Later Chou 951–959

SUNG 960–1279

Northern Sung 960–1126

Southern Sung 1127–1279

YUAN (Mongol) 1280–1368

MING 1368–1644

CH'ING (Manchu) 1644–1911

INTRODUCTION

Recently, scholars in the West have come to realize the inadequacy of the popular image of traditional Chinese society as a monolithic one in which everyone conformed to a rigid Confucian code of behaviour. Several articles and papers dealing with various kinds of nonconformity in Chinese society have appeared, such as Professor F. W. Mote's on Confucian eremitism and Professor David Nivison's on 'protest against conventions and conventions of protest'. Another important illustration of the spirit of protest and nonconformity in China is knight-errantry. I first discussed this topic in January, 1961, in a lecture, which was subsequently published in the first number of the *Journal of the Hong Kong Branch of the Royal Asiatic Society* in the same year. Then, in March, 1963, I read a paper on 'the ideological affinities and antipathies of the knights-errant in ancient China' at the Fifteenth Annual Meeting of the Association for Asian Studies held in Philadelphia. The broad outlines adumbrated in my 1961 lecture have now been filled in with details, while the contents of the 1963 paper have been incorporated in the first chapter of the present work, which is an attempt at a comprehensive study of the tradition of knight-errantry in Chinese history and literature from the fourth century B.C. to the present day.

In writing this book I had in mind several kinds of readers: students of Chinese history and literature, those of comparative literature, and, last but certainly not least, the general reader with a taste for the unusual. I shall begin with discussions on the rise of the ancient knights-errant, their social origins, and the ideological bases of their behaviour; then give examples of knights from various periods of Chinese history, before proceeding to trace the development of the theme of knight-errantry in poetry, fiction, and drama, with special attention to the way historical facts were transformed into imaginative literature. It is hoped that the discussions on historical knights, together with the descriptions of chivalric literature, may throw some light on an aspect of Chinese civilization not well known to Western readers, and bring into focus certain heroic, romantic, and individualistic qualities which the common reader would not normally associate with the Chinese. Since the Chinese conception of chivalry naturally challenges comparison with the Western one, I have in the final chapter touched on some similarities as well as differences. To carry out exhaustive comparisons is beyond the limit of my knowledge and the scope of the book. I can only hope that this book may provide some stimulus and material for further comparative studies by more competent hands. The reader who is neither a sinologue nor a specialist in comparative literature may take the book simply as an entertaining anthology.

A word of explanation may be needed on the use of the word 'knight-errant'. The Chinese term thus translated is *yu-hsia* or simply *hsia* (in modern Pekinese pronunciation). *Yu* means 'wandering',[1] and *hsia* (earlier pronunciation *hsieh*) is etymologically cognate with the verb *hsieh*, 'to force' or 'to coerce'. The term is applied to the kind of men who roamed around the country and used force to right wrongs. By calling them 'knights-errant' I do not imply that they resembled the mediaeval European knights in every way; what they were like and how they differed from the Western knights it will indeed be part of my task to show. Meanwhile, the reader is asked to accept the term 'knight-errant' as a matter of convenience, for this is literally close enough to the original and seems to me by far the least misleading of several possible translations. (Other translations of the term are 'cavalier', 'adventurer', 'soldier of fortune', and 'underworld stalwarts'. The first carries courtly associations irrelevant to the *hsia*, while the others suggest mercenary motives which the *hsia* did not have.) No doubt some of the men and actions to be described in the following pages will strike many a Western reader as far from being chivalrous, but it would be extremely awkward if I were to use the transliteration *hsia* throughout the book or to use inverted commas every time I mention the word 'knight-errant' or 'chivalrous'. After all, translations are but approximations, even with such common words as 'gentlemanly' or 'beautiful': the qualities denoted by these English words may be quite different from those conveyed by their correlatives in Chinese, yet we cannot help using these words in translation. Thus, when I write 'knight-errantry', 'chivalrous', etc., they are to be understood to mean 'what the Chinese call knight-errantry', 'what is (or was) considered chivalrous in China', etc.

In giving examples of historical knights and of chivalric literature, I have tried to let the works concerned speak for themselves, so that the reader can form his own impressions based on material

[1] See Additional Note 1.

as close to the original as possible. Many biographies, anecdotes, poems, and short tales are translated in full, while long prose romances and dramatic works are generally summarized. In no case have I attempted to retell a story in a 'modern' fashion to make it more interesting, or to alter details that might offend Western sensibility so as to render them more palatable, for this is intended to be an objective study, not an apologia. On the other hand, I have not refrained from making critical comments on works cited or described.

A dilemma which I have had to face is this: as I am writing for the general reader as well as the specialist, I cannot assume every reader to be familiar with Chinese literary history, yet to go into details of the development of various literary forms and the lives of the various writers involved would result in a general history of Chinese literature instead of a study of chivalry. I have tried to solve this problem by giving only such information about literary history as seems necessary for an intelligent and intelligible discussion on particular works of chivalric literature.

To avoid cluttering the text with an unwieldy number of footnotes, I have relegated most bibliographical details, especially those concerning works in Chinese, to a list of Sources and References and a Bibliography at the end of the book (to which the attention of specialists is invited), while using footnotes mainly for the purposes of explanation or cross reference. However, some bibliographical references to Western works which the general reader may wish to consult are given in footnotes. Discussions on more technical points, of interest chiefly to sinologues, are to be found in the Additional Notes.

As a rule, names of persons are transliterated, not translated, except for nicknames like Hei-hsüan-feng, 'Black Whirlwird', or personal names with obvious meanings like Chin-feng, 'Golden Phoenix'. A person is usually called by only one name in this book, although in Chinese it is common to refer to a person by a variety of names. Since we are not concerned with institutional history, official titles and honorifics are somewhat freely translated. I have contented myself with using an English phrase that would give some indication as to the function and rank of the official in question, rather than transliterating or literally translating the Chinese title, which would require laborious explanations. Sometimes the same word, when used differently, calls for different translations. For instance, the word *kung*, when used to denote the highest rank of nobility outside royalty, is translated as 'Duke'; when applied loosely to an official, it is rendered as 'Lord' even if the official so designated is not a nobleman (after all, in English usage the word is not confined to members of the peerage); and when used as a term of affection and respect for an old man of any social status, it is translated as 'Grandfather'. Some liberty is also taken in translating names of administrative units such as *sheng*, *chün*, *chou*, and *hsien*. Since these terms often changed their meanings throughout history, it is not possible to be perfectly exact and consistent in translating them without giving long explanations, which would be out of place in a work of this kind. I have generally used 'province' for *sheng*; 'prefecture' for *chün* and *chou*; 'district' for *hsien*. Chinese weights and measures are freely translated when used in rhetorical phrases like *ch'ien-wan-li*, 'thousands of miles', which it would be sheer pedantry to translate as 'thousands and tens of thousands of *li*'. When actual figures are mentioned, I have sometimes converted them into rough equivalents in English, e.g. 'about twenty miles' for 'fifty or sixty *li*'. In the main text, book titles are both translated and transliterated at first mention to facilitate identification, but are subsequently referred to by their translations only. In the Additional Notes and the list of Sources and References, works are referred to by author or title, as explained at the beginning of the Bibliography.

Dates of persons are given at first mention only, and if a reader wishes to be reminded of the dates of a person later, all he has to do is to look up the index to find out where the first mention occurs. Dates of periods, however, are repeated whenever necessary so that the reader will be in no doubt as to how long ago the works under discussion were produced.

Chinese names and words are romanized according to the Wade-Giles system as given in *Mathews' Chinese–English Dictionary*, with the following modifications: the umlaut in *yuan*, *yueh*, and *yun* is omitted, so is the circumflex above the *e* in syllables containing *en* and *eng*; *yi* is used instead of *i*, to avoid mispronunciation (I have heard readers pronounce the last syllable in 'Po Chü-i' as *ai*) and possible confusion with the Roman numeral or the first person singular. Well-known place names are spelt according to the old Post Office system by which they are most widely recognized, e.g. Kiangsu instead of Chiang-su, Soochow instead of Su-chou.

Chinese characters are to be found in the glossary, unless already given in the Additional Notes.

I

THE HISTORICAL KNIGHT-ERRANT

THE RISE OF KNIGHTS-ERRANT

The knight-errant first appeared on the Chinese historical scene during the Warring States period (403–221 B.C.), against a background of political instability, social unrest, and intellectual ferment. Politically, the royal house of Chou had long lost control over its nominal vassals, who now called themselves kings and engaged in constant warfare with one another in their struggle for power.[1] Socially, the old aristocracy had declined, so that many impoverished nobles, as well as men of special talent and skill (ritualists, musicians, astrologers, etc.) formerly retained by the aristocracy, now became socially displaced persons who roamed from one state to another, offering their services to the feudal lords. Intellectually, it was a time of unprecedented and unsurpassed florescence, which saw the emergence of various schools of thought, such as Confucianism, Taoism, Legalism, and Mohism, each offering a different remedy for the prevailing chaotic conditions. Briefly, the Confucians advocated a return to the way of the legendary sage-kings of remote antiquity, who reputedly ruled by moral influence; the Taoists recommended non-action and the abolition of all political and social institutions; the Legalists emphasized the rule of law and the use of punishment as a deterrent to crime; the Mohists preached pacifism and universal love. While the thinkers were busy arguing with one another and trying to convert the feudal rulers to their respective ways of thinking, the knights-errant simply took justice into their own hands and did what they thought necessary to redress wrongs and help the poor and the distressed. They did not hesitate to use force, nor did they have much regard for the law. On the other

[1] The major powers of the period were the states of Ch'in, Ch'u, Yen, Ch'i, Han, Chao, and Wei.

hand, they usually acted on altruistic motives and were ready to die for their principles. Such was the beginning of knight-errantry in China.

THEIR SOCIAL ORIGINS

Regarding the social origins of the knights-errant, modern scholars have different opinions. One view is that they were of purely plebeian origin. Professor Feng Yu-lan suggested that the knights-errant were unemployed peasants and artisans who became professional warriors, and Professor Lao Kan, in an article on the knights-errant of the Han dynasty (206 B.C.–A.D. 220), remarked that they were commoners who took up knight-errantry as a profession. Another view is that they were men without property but not exclusively of lower social origin. Mr. T'ao Hsi-sheng described the rise of knights-errant thus:

> Bankrupt warriors, merchants, and craftsmen, together with unemployed peasants, formed a large social class. This class had no property, but it would not be accurate to call it the proletariate. . . . These wandering men without property despised labour. They formed the habit of wandering and idling. . . . Among them were many impoverished members of the old warrior class, who still had the tendency to fight, as well as ambition, organizing ability, and capacity for leadership.

According to him, this warrior class (*shih*) originally formed a middle class between the aristocracy and the serfs, a class that corresponded to the knighthood of mediaeval Europe. Thus, in T'ao's view, the knights-errant were not all of plebeian origin. Professor Yang Lien-sheng's view is similar to T'ao's, as can be seen from these remarks:

> The knights-errant may have been nobles themselves. But, since they had lost their old status, they tended to identify themselves with the commoners.
>
> These people were first recognised as a group during the period of the Warring States. At that time, the old feudal order had disintegrated, and many hereditary warriors had lost their positions and titles. As brave and upright individuals, and joined by strong sons of lower origin, they scattered throughout the country and made a living by offering their services (and even their lives) to anyone who could afford to employ them.

A third view is that the knights-errant were not a special social group, but simply men of chivalrous temperament. This view was expressed by Professor Tatsuo Masubuchi. Personally, I am inclined to the last view, and I believe that being a knight-errant was more a matter of temperament than of social origin and that knight-errantry was a way of behaviour rather than a profession. My reasons are as follows. In the first place, the historian Ssŭ-ma Ch'ien (*c.* 145–86 B.C.), in the section entitled 'Biographies of Knights-errant' of his *Records of the Historiographer* (*Shih Chi*), repeatedly used phrases like 'plebeian knights (literally, knights who wore coarse clothes)', 'knights from the villages', and 'knights from humble alleys',[1] all of which imply that there were other knights who were *not* commoners and did *not* come from the villages or humble alleys, for if all knights-errant had been commoners, there would have been no need to specify their social origins. Secondly, the historian compared the feudal princes who retained knights as their 'guests' (*k'ê*) with the plebeian knights, and pointed out that the latter deserved more praise because what they did was more difficult. This shows that he regarded the former also as knights-errant of a sort, though it was the latter that he particularly admired. Moreover, Pan Ku (A.D. 32–92), author of the *History of the Han Dynasty*, referring to the same feudal princes, said that 'relying on the influence of kings and dukes, they all became knights-errant'. It is therefore evident that scholars of the Han dynasty did not confine the term 'knights-errant' to a group of commoners. Even if we exclude these feudal lords as patrons of knights-errant rather than knights themselves, it would still not be true to say that all knights-errant depended on their chivalrous deeds for a living. As Mr. Masubuchi pointed out, one of the knights-errant described by Ssŭ-ma Ch'ien, Chu Chia (third century B.C.), bought slaves to work on his land and therefore must have been a landowner.[2] Another man, Ning Ch'eng (second century B.C.), after purchasing land and accumulating considerable wealth, began to behave as a knight-errant. It is true that his biography appears not among those of knights-errant but among those of harsh officials in the *Records of the Historiographer*, but the significant fact is that he acted as a knight-errant *after* he had become rich, which means he did not enrich himself by being a knight-errant, but rather used his wealth

[1] See below, p. 16. [2] See below, p. 36.

acquired by other means to carry out chivalrous deeds. In fact, it was more common for a knight-errant to give money away than to receive payment for his chivalry. Though he might receive cash gifts from friends and followers,[1] these were in the nature of voluntary contributions rather than payment for service rendered. In short, the knights-errant, or at least some of them, did not depend on chivalry for a living. They cannot, therefore, be considered professionals. Nor were they necessarily professional warriors. Men like Chu Chia were famed not for expert swordsmanship or military genius but for altruism and sense of justice. For these reasons, I suggest it is best to regard the knights-errant not as a social class or a professional group but simply as men of strongly individualistic temperament, who behaved in a certain way based on certain ideals.

THEIR IDEALS

The ideals which formed the basis of knightly behaviour may be discussed under the following headings:

(*a*) *Altruism* One of the most remarkable characteristics of the knights-errant is their altruism. They habitually helped the poor and the distressed, and often risked their own lives to save others. Their unselfishness extended not only to their friends but even to total strangers, so much so that the word *hsia* ('knightly' or 'chivalrous') has become associated in usage with the word *yi*, which is usually translated as 'righteousness' but, when applied to knights-errant, has quite a different meaning and comes close to 'altruism'.[2] As Feng Yu-lan pointed out, *yi*, in the sense understood by the knights-errant, means doing more than what is required by common standards of morality, or in other words behaving in a 'supermoral' way. For instance, 'to bestow a kindness and not to expect a reward is moral; to bestow a kindness and to reject any reward is supermoral'. Such behaviour is typical of the knights-errant, as we shall see later.

(*b*) *Justice* The altruistic behaviour of the knights sprang from a sense of justice, which they placed above family loyalty. For example, the knight-errant Kuo Hsieh let go the killer of his nephew because he thought the nephew had been in the wrong.[3] This respect for justice and insistence on 'fair play', together with

[1] See below, p. 39.

[2] See Additional Note 2.

[3] See below, p. 38.

their altruism, are well illustrated by the common description of a knight-errant as someone who, 'seeing an injustice on the road, pulls out his sword to help'. Such action was often necessitated by the failure of the government to administer justice. While the philosophers hoped in vain for a change of heart on the part of the rulers, the knights found a quicker and more direct way of achieving at least a limited kind of justice.

(*c*) *Individual freedom* Not only did the knights manifest their rebellious nature in openly defying the law while attempting to see justice done, but they also showed their non-conformity in daily life by living in what would nowadays be called a Bohemian manner and paying little attention to social conventions. For instance, Ching K'o (*ob.* 227 B.C.) associated with a dog butcher and a musician, and together they drank in public, singing and weeping in turn.[1] Another knight, Chü Meng (second century B.C.), was 'fond of gambling and other games favoured by unruly youths'.[2] Chi An (*ob.* 112 B.C.), who was fond of chivalry, was 'haughty by nature and lacked courtesy'. In short, these men were individualists who objected to any rigid regimentation. They had little respect for the law of the state or the conventions of behaviour of the society in which they lived. The only rules they recognized were those of their own moral code.

(*d*) *Personal loyalty* To a knight-errant, personal loyalty was more important than loyalty to one's sovereign or parents. Even when a knight died for a prince, it was not out of a sense of loyalty such as a subject owed his sovereign, but such as one man owed another who 'appreciated him' (*chih-chi*). This is clearly illustrated by the lives of such men as Hou Ying and Ching K'o.[3]

(*e*) *Courage* It required physical and moral courage of the highest order to be a knight-errant. The question of danger seems never to have entered the minds of knights-errant, who faced death with a cavalier attitude that almost suggests they did not much care for life.

(*f*) *Truthfulness and mutual faith* The knights-errant stressed truthfulness in word and in action. The historian Ssŭ-ma Ch'ien said of them: 'They always meant what they said, always accomplished what they set out to do, and always fulfilled their promises.'[4] Sometimes a knight would even go so far as to commit

[1] See below p. 25. [2] See below, p. 37. Also see Additional Note 3.
[3] See below, pp. 21–2, 32–3. [4] See below, p. 14.

suicide so as to show he would not betray a secret trust. Thus, Chi Shao-kung committed suicide so as not to reveal the whereabouts of Kuo Hsieh, who was being sought by the officials; T'ien Kuang did the same to show he would not divulge the secret entrusted to him by Prince Tan of Yen.[1]

(*g*) *Honour and fame* The knights' concern for truthfulness is connected with their sense of honour. Ssŭ-ma Ch'ien remarked that 'they disciplined their action and cherished their honour so that their fame spread all over the empire'.[2] Even Han Fei Tzŭ, the Legalist thinker who condemned them, said they 'established standards of integrity to distinguish their names'. If it be contended that the knights-errant were not entirely motivated by altruism in their action, then their only selfish motive was their desire for fame.

(*h*) *Generosity and contempt for wealth* In contrast to their desire for fame is their contempt for wealth. A knight-errant might receive handsome sums from friends without any embarrassment, as Kuo Hsieh did; or refuse an offer of household effects worth several million cash, as Chü Chang did.[3] It was not that they had no use for money; they simply did not have a strong sense of proprietorship, and either lived lavishly while sharing their luxury with friends, or lived modestly themselves while giving money to the poor.

Naturally, not all those who claimed to be knights-errant actually lived up to these ideals, no more than those who call themselves Confucians or Christians have lived up to their respective ideals. This can only be attributed to human frailty, but cannot be held against knight-errantry as such. On the other hand, I do not mean the knights-errant were by any means perfect. Even those who did live up to these ideals had serious shortcomings. For one thing, they were too eager to fight and too quick to take offence. Sometimes they would take measures of revenge out of all proportion to the offence, real or imagined. There is a story in the *Huai-nan Tzŭ* (a philosophical work compiled in the second century B.C.) about a group of knights-errant who passed a tall building where a rich man and his friends were having a party upstairs. It so happened that a kite flew past and dropped a dead rat which hit one of the knights on the head. The knights im-

[1] See below, pp. 40, 28. [2] See below, p. 16.

[3] See below, pp. 39, 41.

mediately jumped to the conclusion that this was thrown at them by the rich man as an insult. Thereupon they raided his house at night and killed his whole family.[1] Moreover, the knights-errant had a rather limited conception of justice. They thought in terms of individuals, not of society as a whole. Therefore, in spite of their altruism, their action could only benefit a few, but not the whole community. Finally, they had no respect for the law, so that they further disrupted social order, though at the same time they brought redress to personal wrongs. That is why they were condemned by men like Han Fei Tzŭ and Pan Ku, while highly praised by Ssŭ-ma Ch'ien. When all is said, their merits outweighed their defects. Even Pan Ku admitted that 'they were good-hearted and loved people in general; helped the poor and saved the distressed; were modest and not boastful'. Without the ideals mentioned above, they could not have behaved thus.

THEIR IDEOLOGICAL AFFINITIES AND ANTIPATHIES

These ideals show that, ideologically, the knights-errant had certain things in common with various schools of thinkers, while differing from each in other respects. Let us compare the knights-errant with four major schools—Confucians, Legalists, Mohists, and Taoists—in turn.

1. *Knights-errant and Confucians*

In many ways, the knight-errant forms a strong contrast to the Confucian scholar. First, the Confucians believed in degrees of love and duty—one must first love one's parents, and filial duty was more important than abstract justice. The knight-errant, on the other hand, considered the same principles of justice and moral duty applicable to relatives and strangers alike. As Professor Yang Lien-sheng has pointed out, the Confucians modified universalism with particularism, while the knights-errant acted on a universalistic principle. The Confucians and the knights-errant had different conceptions of *yi*: to the former it meant 'doing the right thing', to the latter, as we have seen, it meant 'doing more than required by common standards of morality'.[2] Thus, by Confucian standards, the knights-errant often went beyond the call of duty. This,

[1] This story also occurs in the Taoist book *Lieh Tzŭ*. See A. C. Graham, *The Book of Lieh Tzŭ* (London, 1961), pp. 172–3.

[2] See above, p. 4.

to the Confucian way of thinking, was not only unnecessary but also undesirable, for if one died for a stranger, what should one do for one's parents?

This difference between the Confucians and the knights-errant was connected with the former's emphasis on moderation in contrast to the latter's tendency towards extremism. The Confucians held up the 'golden mean' as the ideal of human conduct, while the knights-errant often went to extremes in their feeling and action. The latter's generosity, even their self-sacrifice, would have been condemned as excessive by the Confucians.

Another difference is that the Confucians taught 'forgiveness' (*shu*) and 'yielding' or 'deferring' (*jang*),[1] whereas the knights-errant made revengefulness a virtue and were usually too proud to yield to anyone.

Furthermore, the knights-errant had an absolute conception of truthfulness, while the Confucians had a relative one. The former insisted one must always be true in word and in action; the latter regarded such men as 'little men' (*hsiao-jen*), as pointed out by Professor Yang.

Next, whereas the Confucians aimed at order and stressed the need for the individual to conform to a rigid pattern of behaviour and to subjugate himself to the family, the knight-errant valued personal freedom above family solidarity. Consequently, the former attached great importance to ritual and social manners, but the latter paid scant attention to outward forms of conduct.

Finally, the Confucians were against the use of force, while the knights-errant often resorted to violence in their attempts to achieve justice. However, a word of warning may not be out of place here: though the Confucians were against violence, they were not physical cowards. The 'Six Liberal Arts' (*Liu-yi*) pursued by the ancient Confucian gentleman included archery and charioteering as well as ritual, music, writing, and arithmetic. The popular image of a Confucian scholar as an over-refined and effeminate bookworm came into being centuries later, and is in any case not true of all Confucian scholars even in later periods.

The differences mentioned above were due, I believe, not so much to social status as to temperament. It would be an over-simplification to say that Confucianism represented the morality of the gentlemen and knight-errantry that of the commoner.

[1] More colloquially, one might say 'one-downmanship'.

Rather, we might say that the former represented a type of men naturally inclined towards conservatism, moderation, and conformity, and the latter, a type of men naturally inclined towards individualism, revolt, and extravagance.

In spite of these differences, the Confucians and the knights-errant did have certain similarities. As Feng Yu-lan pointed out, both were faithful to the tasks entrusted them, even to death, and both showed personal loyalty based on a principle of reciprocity. To these may be added that both cherished honour and belittled wealth. We have already seen the knights' concern for honour and fame. The Confucian gentleman, too, thought it a cause for worry if he should end his days without achieving fame. And like the knights-errant, the Confucians also despised wealth. Confucius praised those who cared little for the material comforts of life but lived cheerfully in poverty, such as his favourite disciple Yen Hui. Indeed, Mencius's definition of a great man as one 'whom wealth and rank cannot corrupt, poverty and humble position cannot change, and authority and power cannot bend' would apply to the ideal Confucian scholar as well as the ideal knight-errant.

2. *Knights-errant and Legalists*

If the contrast between the Confucians and the knights-errant is great, that between the Legalists and the knights is even greater. The Legalists advocated the supremacy of the state and the suppression of the individual, while the knights-errant valued personal freedom above social security. The Legalists tried to maintain social order by governmental authority; the knights-errant had little respect for official authority. Furthermore, the Legalists stressed the importance of the law and the necessity for its strict enforcement: all those who transgressed against the law must be punished. This left little room for human sympathy and understanding in individual cases. The knights-errant, on the other hand, judged each case from a personal angle, not a legal one. Their sense of justice was based on human sympathy, not on an abstract concept of law.

In short, the Legalists and the knights-errant were diametrically opposed in basic outlook. The former looked at society from the ruler's point of view; the latter, from the private citizen's point of view. The Legalists were preoccupied with the art of government; the knights-errant were not only uninterested in government but also too impatient to be governed. In emphasizing individual dignity against the authority of the state and in preferring a humanistic conception of justice to a legal one, the knights-errant were at one with the Confucians. Both placed a moral code above the law, though the moral code of each was different. That is why the Legalist Han Fei Tzŭ included both in what he called the 'Five Vermin' of state and condemned them both: 'The Confucian scholars confuse the law with their writings, while the knights-errant violate the prohibitions by force. Yet the rulers of men treat both with courtesy. That is why there is disorder.' By contrast to the Legalist, the Confucian would now appear more congenial to the knight-errant, while the Legalist stood for everything that the knight abhorred.

3. *Knights-errant and Mohists*

The knights-errant and the Mohists, the followers of Mo Tzŭ, whose life span fell between 479 and 381 B.C. and who preached universal love, obviously had much in common. Indeed, it has been suggested by Professor Feng Yu-lan that the Mohists originated from the knights-errant. His theory may be summarized as follows. After the collapse of aristocratic government about the time of Confucius (551–479 B.C.), a new class of professional men came into being, known as the *shih*. At first this word simply meant any man of special talent or skill, and such men were kept by the aristocracy. After they lost their employment, they became what we may call free lances.[1] Those who specialized in ritual, music, and education were the 'scholars' (*ju*), of whom Confucius was one, and their moral code developed into Confucianism (*Ju-chia*, literally, 'scholasticism'). Those who specialized in warfare were the knights (*hsia*), and their moral code developed into Mohism.

Later, Feng modified his theory a little when he realized that there was no mention of the 'knights' (*hsia*) before the Warring States period and suggested substituting the term 'military experts' (*wu-shih*) for 'knights'. But his basic view remained unchanged. As he himself put it, 'What we need is some proof that before or during the time of Mo Tzŭ there were such men [whose profession was to help people in warfare]. . . . As for whether

[1] This account of the *shih* is somewhat different from T'ao Hsi-sheng's, as mentioned above on p. 2.

these men were called "knights", that is a separate question which has no great bearing on our main view [that the Mohists derived from professional warriors].' He then gave various examples of men who may be considered military experts. Thus, he succeeded in showing that there were professional warriors before and during the time of Mo Tzŭ, but did not succeed in showing that these warriors were the same kind of men as the 'knights-errant'. In fact, there is some evidence to the contrary. Ssŭ-ma Ch'ien remarked, 'About the plebeian knights-errant of antiquity, we have no means of obtaining information.'[1] This suggests he did not regard the warriors mentioned by Feng as knights-errant. Moreover, the historian also said, 'both the Confucians and the Mohists rejected them [the knights-errant] as being unworthy of mentioning'.[2] This could hardly have been the case had the Mohists been the spiritual heirs of the knights-errant. It seems safer, therefore, to regard the professional warriors before the Warring States period as the kind of men whose moral code may have influenced both the knights-errant and the Mohists, than to confuse these warriors with the knights-errant and say that Mohism derived from knight-errantry.

Although we cannot accept the view that the Mohists originated from the knights-errant, we can still acknowledge the similarities between the two. Both were inspired by an altruistic spirit and a strong sense of justice,[3] and both acted on a universalistic principle, as against the Confucian principle of degrees of love and duty. Both belittled wealth and shared what they had. Both were absolutely truthful and trustworthy.

On the other hand, there are considerable differences between the two. Professor Feng himself mentioned three differences: first, the knights-errant were professional fighters (who fought for anyone), while the Mohists fought for principles and would only fight for a weak state against a strong one; secondly, the Mohists were interested in government, while the knights-errant only had personal courage; thirdly, the knights-errant merely *practised* a kind of morality, while the Mohists not only practised it but also systematized, theorized, and universalized it. Since we do not accept the view that the knights-errant were professional warriors,

[1] See below, p. 16. [2] See below, p. 16.

[3] Mo Tzŭ's conception of *yi*, as seen in *Mo Tzŭ*, 47, is closer to 'altruism' and 'justice' than 'righteousness'.

we may disregard the first difference. The second one is certainly one of the main distinctions between the knights-errant and the Mohists. As for the last one, again it would probably be better to say that the Mohists inherited from the warriors of Pre-Warring-States times certain moral ideals which may have also influenced the knights-errant, rather than that the Mohists systematized the morality of the knights.

Further differences between the Mohists and the knights may be discerned. The Mohists led an austere and disciplined life; the knights-errant were often free and easy. The Mohists were a highly organized body of men, whose leader had the authority of life and death over the members; the knights-errant were only loosely associated on a voluntary basis. The Mohists, though they helped weak states in self-defence, were against fighting in principle; the knights were always ready for a fight. Basically, the Mohists were concerned with political and social equity, but the knights-errant were only concerned with personal justice.

4. *Knights-errant and Taoists*

It may seem at first sight rather far-fetched to link the quick-tempered, swashbuckling knights-errant with the other-worldly, contemplative Taoists, yet they did have certain things in common. Professor Lao Kan mentions several knights-errant of early Han, namely Ch'en P'ing, T'ien Shu, Chi An, and Cheng Tang-shih, who are said by Ssŭ-ma Ch'ien and Pan Ku to have studied Taoism. This shows there was some connection between Taoism and knight-errantry. However, when Professor Lao goes on to say that this connection arose because both the knights and the Taoists were commoners, I find it hard to agree. We have already seen that not all knights-errant were commoners, and even if they all had been, that would still not have been sufficient reason for them to embrace the teachings of Taoism, granted that Taoism is a philosophy of the commoners, which is rather begging the question. It seems to me one cannot account for a man's ideas and ideals entirely by his social origin. What is more likely is that certain aspects of Taoist philosophy appealed to the same temperament that found expression in chivalry.

What are these aspects of Taoism then? First, Taoism is individualistic and against conformity to social conventions. The Taoists advocated the principle of following Nature, instead of forcing oneself to fit some Procrustean bed. Thus, Chuang Tzŭ said, 'The duck's legs are short, but if we try to stretch them, the duck will feel pain. The crane's legs are long, but if we try to shorten them, the crane will grieve. Therefore, we should not shorten what is naturally long, nor stretch what is naturally short.' The knights-errant were actually practising this principle of following one's natural inclinations whether they fully realized its Taoist implications or not.[1]

Secondly, the Taoists, like the knights-errant, also had an anarchistic attitude towards government and law. For instance, Lao Tzŭ says, 'The more restrictions and prohibitions there are in the world, the poorer the people will be. . . . The more laws and ordinances are promulgated, the more thieves and bandits there will be.' Similarly, Chuang Tzŭ admonishes us: 'Reject saintliness and discard wisdom, and great bandits will cease; throw away jades and destroy pearls, and petty thieves will no longer rise; burn official tallies and seals, and the people will be plain and honest; break measures and weights, and the people will no longer quarrel.' This antipathy towards legal control and governmental authority would have appealed readily to the chivalrous temperament.

Of course, there are differences between the Taoists and the knights-errant. The Taoists recommended non-action, while the knights were only too eager for action. The Taoists sought a kind of absolute, spiritual freedom; the knights only strove for social freedom. The more mystical aspects of Taoism were altogether beyond the knights-errant: there is no evidence they were interested in Taoist metaphysics.

To sum up: the knights-errant had certain affinities with various schools of thinkers, but no actual affiliations with any. They were neither intellectuals nor politicians, but men of strong will and simple faith, who lived and died the way they wanted.

KNIGHTS-ERRANT OF THE WARRING STATES AND EARLY HAN PERIODS (*c.* 300–120 B.C.)

Having considered the social and intellectual backgrounds of knight-errantry, we may now look at some examples of knights-errant of the Warring States and early Han periods. Our best

[1] See Additional Note 4.

source of information is Ssŭ-ma Ch'ien's *Records of the Historiographer*, to which we owe much enlightenment on the nature of knight-errantry. In his general introduction to the whole work (which actually comes at the end, as is not uncommon in Chinese books), Ssŭ-ma Ch'ien writes:[1]

> To save people from distress and relieve people from want: is this not benevolence? Not to belie another's trust and not to break one's promises: such conduct a righteous man would approve. That is why I wrote the 'Biographies of Knights-errant'.

In the preamble to these biographies, he gives a more detailed exposition of the spirit of knight-errantry. He begins by comparing the fate of Confucian scholars with that of knights-errant, and points out that the former were often more fortunate, for whether they achieved worldly power and position or not, they still enjoyed some fame, while knights-errant usually remained in obscurity:

> Han Fei Tzŭ said, 'The Confucian scholars confuse the law with their writings, while the knights-errant violate the prohibitions by force.' Thus, he disapproved of both. Yet scholars are often praised by the world [while knights-errant remain unknown]. Among scholars, those who, by means of political skill, attained high official positions and aided their rulers, have had their achievements recorded in official history, and there is really no more to be said about them. As for scholars like Chi-tz'ŭ and Yuan Hsien,[2] they were commoners who stayed in their humble homes. They pursued learning and cherished the personal virtues of the gentleman. They refused to compromise their principles and come to terms with the world they lived in, and the world laughed at them. Therefore, to the end of their days, these men remained in poverty, living in bare rooms under thatched roofs, without even sufficient plain clothing and simple food. Now, they have been dead for over four hundred years, yet their disciples have kept their memory fresh. Now, as for the knights-errant, though their actions were not in accordance with the rules of propriety, they always meant what they said, always accom-

[1] I made my translations of passages from the *Shih Chi* before I saw Dr. Burton Watson's translation entitled *Records of the Grand Historian of China* (New York and London, 1961). Since my translations differ from his significantly in places, I have decided to let mine stand. Moreover, some of the examples of knights-errant given below are from sections of the *Shih Chi* not included in Dr. Watson's translation.

[2] Two disciples of Confucius.

plished what they set out to do, and always fulfilled their promises. They rushed to the aid of other men in distress without giving a thought to their own safety. And when they had saved someone from disaster at the risk of their own lives, they did not boast of their ability and would have been ashamed to brag of their benevolence. Indeed, there is much to be said for them. Besides, distress is something that anyone may encounter from time to time.

It is clear from the above paragraph that the author has more sympathy with the knights-errant than with the Confucian scholars, and that he understands how knight-errantry came into being as a matter of social necessity. After mentioning various ancient sages in distress, including Confucius, the historian comments:

> All these are regarded by scholars as virtuous and sagacious men, yet they encountered such distresses. How much more difficult is it, then, for men of average talents, living in a time of social disorder and moral decline? Can their misfortunes be numbered?

Ssŭ-ma Ch'ien then proceeds to justify the actions of the knights-errant by pointing out the relative nature of ethical standards:

> There is a saying among the common people, 'What do I know about benevolence and propriety? Anything that brings me profit is "good".' Thus, Po-yi regarded the founding of the Chou dynasty as disgraceful and starved himself to death on the Shou-yang Hill, but this did not affect the reputation of Kings Wen and Wu of Chou as sage-kings. Chih and Chiao[1] were violent and wrong-headed, yet their followers praised their unselfishness endlessly. From such instances we may perceive the truth of the saying, 'One who stole a hook is executed; one who stole a country becomes a marquis. Where a marquis resides, there benevolence and propriety dwell.'[2] Now, those pedantic and narrow-minded scholars who held to their limited understanding of propriety and isolated themselves for ever from the world, would they not have done better to have behaved like those others who lowered their tune to suit the common herd and moved with the crowd to obtain honours and power?

Here, the author's tone is a little contemptuous, both to the 'narrow-minded scholars' who remained in splendid isolation, and the worldly scholars who compromised their principles for power

[1] Two notorious bandits.

[2] This is from the *Chuang Tzu*, Chapter 10.

and glory. At heart he admires neither, but keeps his admiration for the knights-errant:

> However, some commoners established mutual faith and were praised a thousand miles around for their altruism. They would meet death without caring what the world thought of them. These men had their own good points, and what they did, they did not do lightly. Therefore, when a man was in trouble, he could entrust his life to such men. Are these not what we call 'virtuous, worthy, outstanding men'? If the knights-errant from the villages had been asked to compete with scholars like Chi-tz'ŭ and Yuan Hsien in wielding power to serve the world they lived in, their achievements would have been less great. But if it is considered necessary for men to accomplish what they set out to do and mean what they say, then how can one do without the principles of knight-errantry?

Having thus justified the knights-errant, the author expresses his regret that little is known about the knights-errant of antiquity. He then singles out for admiration knights who were commoners, as distinct from chivalrous noblemen who harboured knights as their guests. On the other hand, he carefully distinguishes knights-errant from mere local bullies:

> About the plebeian knights-errant of antiquity, we have no means of obtaining information. In more recent times, the princes of Meng-ch'ang, Ch'un-shen, P'ing-yuan, Hsin-ling, and others,[1] being royal kinsmen and relying on their landed wealth and high ranks, attached to themselves worthy men from all over the empire and spread their fame among the feudal lords. One cannot say these princes were not worthies. Yet what they did was like shouting in the direction of the wind: it is not that the sound travels faster than normal, but the speed of the wind carries it on.[2] As for the knights-errant who came from humble alleys, and who disciplined their action and cherished their honour so that their fame spread all over the empire, what they did was truly difficult. However, both the Confucians and the Mohists rejected them as being unworthy of mentioning. Consequently, the names of plebeian knights-errant who lived before Ch'in times have vanished—a fact that I deeply regret. As far as I know, since the rise of the Han dynasty, there have been

[1] In the original text, the name (Prince of) Yen-ling appears after the four princes. Since he belongs to an earlier age and is not particularly famous for retaining knights, the inclusion of his name here is probably a textual error. I have therefore omitted it in the translation.

[2] This is paraphrased from the *Hsün Tzŭ*, Chapter 1.

> many knights such as Chu Chia, T'ien Chung, Wang Kung, Chü Meng, and Kuo Hsieh. Although they often offended the laws of the times, in their private lives they showed unselfishness, integrity, and modesty, which well deserve our praise. Their fame was not built on nothing, and men did not follow them for no reason. As for those who formed cliques among their friends and clansmen, plotting together to enrich themselves and exploiting the poor, using force to bully the weak and indulging their desires to satisfy themselves, the knights-errant too regarded them as shameful. I am grieved that the ordinary people of the world do not realize this but hastily condemn men like Chu Chia and Kuo Hsieh with the bullies.

After this preamble, Ssŭ-ma Ch'ien gives an account of the lives of several knights-errant. Moreover, in other sections of the *Records of the Historiographer,* there are more examples of men who acted in a chivalrous way, even if they are not always called 'knights-errant' in so many words. The following accounts are translated from various parts of this monumental work. I have telescoped paragraphs from different biographies to make a more coherent story when necessary, and have omitted some minor details.

Prince Wu-chi (*ob.* 243 B.C.), *Hou Ying* (326–257 B.C.), *and Chu Hai*

Prince Wu-chi of Wei[1] was the youngest son of King Chao of Wei (reigned 295–277 B.C.) and half-brother of King An-hsi (reigned 276–243 B.C.). When King Chao died and King An-hsi came to the throne, the latter enfeoffed Wu-chi as Prince of Hsin-ling (in modern Honan province).

The Prince was kind by nature and humbled himself before knights. No matter whether they were worthy or not, he would treat them all with courtesy, and would not dare to behave haughtily because of his wealth and noble rank. Therefore, men from several thousand miles around vied with one another to come and attach themselves to him, so that he retained three thousand guests. At that time, the other feudal lords, realizing that the Prince was a worthy man and had many guests, dared not invade Wei for more than ten years.

Once, when the Prince and the King of Wei were playing backgammon, an alarm came from the northern frontier that the King

[1] The state of Wei occupied parts of modern Shansi and Honan.

of Chao[1] was invading Wei. The King of Wei put down his pieces and was about to summon the ministers for discussion, but the Prince stopped him, saying, 'The King of Chao is hunting, not coming to invade us.' And he went on playing as before. The King was afraid and could not keep his mind on the game. After a while, news came again from the north that the King of Chao was hunting, not invading Wei. The King of Wei was greatly astonished and asked the Prince, 'How could you know it?' The Prince replied, 'One of my guests can obtain the secrets of the King of Chao. Whatever he does, my guest reports to me. That is how I knew.' After this incident, the King of Wei was jealous and afraid of the Prince, and would not entrust State affairs to him.

There was a recluse in Wei named Hou Ying. In his seventieth year, because of poverty, he worked as the gate-keeper of Yi Men, the Eastern Gate of the capital Ta-liang (modern K'ai-feng). When the Prince heard of him, he went to visit Hou and wished to give him a handsome sum of money. Hou refused, saying, 'I have cultivated my personal integrity for several decades, and I will never receive money from Your Highness, poor gate-keeper as I am.' Thereupon the Prince prepared a great banquet and invited many guests. When they were seated, the Prince left with some attendants. He kept empty the seat of honour on the left in his carriage and went personally to the Eastern Gate to request Hou's presence. Holding his tattered clothes, Hou went straight to the carriage and took the seat of honour, without even making a show of declining, so as to test the Prince. The Prince, holding the reins, looked even more deferential. Then Hou Ying said to the Prince, 'I have a friend who is a butcher at the market-place. May I bother you to drive your carriage there?' The Prince drove the carriage to the market-place, and Hou came down to see his friend Chu Hai. He deliberately looked arrogantly left and right, and stood there talking for a long time, while secretly observing the Prince's reaction. The expression on the Prince's face became even milder. At that time, the generals, ministers, and royal clansmen of Wei, who were the Prince's guests, were all waiting for him to start the banquet. Simultaneously, the people in the market-place saw the Prince holding the reins for Hou Ying, while all the attendants privately cursed Hou. Seeing that the

[1] The state of Chao occupied parts of modern Hopei, Honan, and Shansi.

Prince still did not change his expression, Hou said good-bye to his friend and took to the carriage. On arriving home, the Prince led Hou to the seat of honour and introduced him in flattering terms to the guests. All the guests were astonished. When they became high-spirited with wine, the Prince rose and toasted Hou, wishing him long life. Hou took this opportunity to say to the Prince, 'Today I have made you suffer enough. I am only the gate-keeper of the Eastern Gate, yet Your Highness came personally in your carriage to fetch me before a crowd. It was not proper for you to visit me, yet you purposely visited me. However, I wished to make your name for you, so I kept you waiting for a long time at the market-place, and went to see my friend to observe your reaction. You became even more respectful. All the people in the market-place thought me a petty man and you a worthy lord who could humble himself before men.' So they stopped drinking, and from that moment Hou Ying was treated as a guest of honour.

Hou said to the Prince, 'The butcher I visited, called Chu Hai, is a worthy man, but the world cannot appreciate him. That is why he hides his light among butchers.' The Prince went several times to visit Chu, but the latter never returned the courtesy. The Prince wondered why.

In 257 B.C., King Chao of Ch'in[1] defeated the troops of Chao and besieged the capital of Chao, Han-tan (in modern Hopei). Prince Wu-chi's elder sister was married to the Prince of P'ing-yuan, younger brother of the former King of Chao. She wrote several times to the King of Wei and the Prince for help. So the King of Wei sent General Chin Pi with an army of a hundred thousand men to come to the rescue of Chao. The King of Ch'in sent a messenger to the King of Wei, saying, 'I am attacking Chao and expect the capital to fall any moment. If any other feudal lord dares to come to the rescue of Chao, I will divert my forces to attack him as soon as Chao is conquered.' The King of Wei became afraid and sent someone to stop Chin Pi, telling him to encamp at Yeh (on the border between Chao and Wei), thus nominally coming to aid Chao but actually waiting to see which side would win. The Prince of P'ing-yuan sent one messenger after another to Wei and reproached Prince Wu-chi: 'The reason why I attached myself in marriage to your family was that I thought you were full of noble altruism and could save people in

[1] The state of Ch'in occupied what is now Shensi province.

distress. Now, Han-tan may surrender to Ch'in any moment, yet no aid has come from Wei. Where is the proof you can save people in distress? Besides, even if you do not think much of me and will abandon me to surrender to Ch'in, have you no pity for your sister?' Prince Wu-chi was worried and several times spoke to the King. He also sent sophists[1] to try to persuade the King with every possible argument, but the King, frightened of Ch'in, would not listen. The Prince reckoned that he could never get the King's consent to act, but resolved he would not remain alive alone and let Chao perish. So he asked some of his guests to follow him, gathered together over a hundred carriages, and was about to go to meet the Ch'in army and perish with Chao.

When the Prince passed the Eastern Gate, he went to see Hou Ying and told the latter why he was going to meet the Ch'in army in this suicidal manner. Hou said, 'Courage to Your Highness! Your old servant cannot follow.' After the Prince had gone a few miles, he was unhappy and said to himself, 'I have treated Hou Ying with every possible kindness, as the whole world knows. Now I am about to die, yet he did not say anything to me as a farewell message. Could it be I have missed something?' So he turned his carriage back and went to see Hou again. Hou laughed and said, 'I knew Your Highness would come back! Your Highness is fond of keeping knights, as is known all over the empire. Now, faced with a disaster, you have no better plan than going to meet the Ch'in army, like throwing meat to a hungry tiger: what is the use? And what is the use of having guests then? However, Your Highness treated me with great kindness, but I did not send you off properly; that is why I knew you would come back.' The Prince bowed twice and asked his advice. Hou Ying then asked all attendants to be dismissed and said, 'I hear that half of the tally[2] that gave Chin Pi control over the army is constantly kept in the King's bedroom. Now Lady Ju is the King's favourite and often goes in and out of his bedroom. She should be able to steal it. I have heard that Lady Ju's father was murdered, and she grieved for three years, but no one, from the King downwards,

[1] *Pien-shih*, men who specialized in persuasion.

[2] The tally (*fu*) was cast in bronze in the shape of a tiger and consisted of two halves. One half was kept by the king, the other half given to the general. If the king had further orders, he would send his half to the general, who would put the two halves together to see if they tallied.

could find the murderer and avenge her father's death. At last she told you in tears, and you sent a guest to kill her enemy. He succeeded and presented the enemy's head to her. Lady Ju would be willing to die for you; only she has not had a chance. If you will but say the word, she will certainly do what you wish. Then, with the "tiger tally", you can take over the army from Chin Pi, save Chao in the north, and repel the Ch'in troops from the west. This is an enterprise worthy of the Big Five.'[1] The Prince followed his advice and asked Lady Ju, who did steal the King's half of the tally and give it to the Prince.

The Prince was about to leave, when Hou Ying said, 'When a general is leading an army outside, he can refuse to obey an order from the King in the national interest. Now, even if you show Chin Pi your half of the tally and it fits, he may refuse to obey but ask for further orders from the King. Then things would be dangerous. You had better take my friend, the butcher Chu Hai, with you. He is a very strong man. If Chin Pi will obey, all is well; if not, let Chu kill him.' On hearing this, the Prince wept. Hou asked, 'Is Your Highness afraid of death? Why are you weeping?' The Prince replied, 'Chin Pi is a tempestuous old general. I am afraid he will not obey and I shall have to kill him. That is why I am weeping. How can I be afraid of death?'

The Prince then asked Chu Hai to go with him. Chu laughed and said, 'I am a mere butcher, but Your Highness has visited me several times. The reason why I never returned the courtesy was that I thought petty courtesy was useless. Now you have an emergency; this is the time for me to repay you, even with my life.' So he joined the Prince.

Once more the Prince came to take his leave of Hou Ying. Hou said, 'I should follow you, but cannot because of my age. Allow me to count the days of your journey, and on the day you should reach the army, I will look towards the north and cut my throat to bid you farewell.' Thereupon the Prince left.

When he reached Yeh, he pretended to have an order from the King to replace Chin Pi. Chin Pi put the two halves of the tally together, but still had his doubts. Raising his hands and looking at the Prince, he said, 'I am leading an army of a hundred thousand men on the border. This is a heavy responsibility to the country.

[1] Five powerful feudal lords of an earlier age, namely the Dukes of Ch'i, Chin, Ch'in, and Sung, and the King of Ch'u.

Now you come all alone to replace me: how can that be?' He was about to refuse, when Chu Hai, who had hidden an iron hammer weighing forty catties in his sleeve, killed Chin Pi with it. The Prince then took control of the army and issued the following order: 'If father and son are both in the army, let the father go home; if two brothers are in the army, let the elder one go home; if only son, go home to look after your parents!' Thus he had eighty thousand choice soldiers left, with whom he attacked the Ch'in forces. The Ch'in army withdrew, so the siege of Han-tan was raised and the kingdom of Chao saved. The king of Chao and the Prince of P'ing-yuan came personally to the border to welcome Prince Wu-chi. The Prince of P'ing-yuan, carrying the bow-case and the quiver, led the way before Prince Wu-chi. The King of Chao bowed twice and said, 'Since ancient times, there has been no worthy man comparable to Your Highness!' At that time, the Prince of P'ing-yuan (who formerly was known as one of the four princes who retained knights) dared not compare himself with the others.

Prior to this, on the day when the Prince reached the army, Hou Ying really cut his throat while looking towards the north.

The King of Wei was angry with the Prince for having stolen the tally and killed Chin Pi, and the Prince knew this. So, having saved Chao, he sent a general to lead the army back to Wei, while he himself with his guests stayed in Chao. The King of Chao, out of gratitude, wished to enfeoff Prince Wu-chi with five towns. When the Prince heard this, he was proud and showed signs of self-satisfaction. Thereupon one of his guests advised him: 'Some things one must not forget, some things one must forget. If someone else has done Your Highness a kindness, you must not forget it; if Your Highness has done someone else a kindness, then I wish you would forget it. Moreover, what you did—forging the King's order and taking over the army from Chin Pi by force—was a meritorious deed to Chao, but hardly loyal to Wei. Yet Your Highness seems to be proud of it and to regard this as your merit. In my humble opinion, this is not worthy of you.' The Prince at once felt as ashamed of himself as if there had been no place to hide. When the King of Chao received the Prince, he swept the road and personally welcomed the Prince. Observing the duties of a host, the King led the Prince to the western stairway (the guest's approach to the hall). The Prince, walking sideways in humility, declined the honour and ascended the hall by the eastern stairway (the host's approach). Then he reproached himself, saying that he had betrayed Wei without having done anything meritorious for Chao. The King of Chao entertained him with wine till evening, but was too embarrassed to bring up the subject of offering the Prince five towns, since the latter was so humble. Eventually the Prince stayed in Chao, and the King of Chao offered him the town of Hao (in modern Hopei) as his 'bathing place'.[1] The King of Wei also offered Hsin-ling back to the Prince, but he remained in Chao.

The Prince had heard that in Chao there were two men of ability who chose to remain in obscurity. One was called Grandfather Mao, who lived among gamblers; the other was known as Grandfather Hsüeh, who worked in a wine shop. The Prince wished to see them, but they hid themselves and would not see him. Finally the Prince heard where they were and went on foot to see them. On meeting each other, they became great friends. When the Prince of P'ing-yuan heard of this, he said to his wife, 'At first I heard your brother was a paragon of virtue, now I hear he is associating with gamblers and wine-sellers. He is only a rash person!' When she told the Prince this, the latter asked permission to leave, saying, 'At first I heard the Prince of P'ing-yuan was a worthy man, and that is why I betrayed the King of Wei to save Chao, so as to satisfy the Prince. Now I see he makes friends merely to show his generosity, not to seek worthy men. Ever since I was in Ta-liang, I had already heard of these two men. When I came to Chao, I was afraid I could not get to know them. Even with someone like me, I was afraid they would not want to know me. Now the Prince of P'ing-yuan thinks it a shame to know them! He is not worthy to be a friend.' Thereupon Prince Wu-chi started to get his luggage ready for departure. When his sister told her husband, the Prince of P'ing-yuan, with hat off, apologized to Prince Wu-chi, and firmly asked him to stay. When the guests of the Prince of P'ing-yuan heard this, half of them left him to join Prince Wu-chi, and knights from other parts of the empire also came to follow the Prince.

The Prince stayed in Chao for ten years without going back.

[1] *T'ang-mu yi*, originally a place assigned by the king to a vassal for him to rest when coming to court; here used to mean a modest seat, not a proper fief.

When the King of Ch'in heard the Prince was in Chao, he sent troops eastward to attack Wei day and night. The King of Wei was worried and sent a messenger to ask the Prince back. The Prince, for fear the King was still angry with him, warned his retainers: 'If anyone dares to speak on behalf of the King's messenger, he dies.' Since all the retainers had disobeyed the King of Wei and followed the Prince to Chao, none of them dared to advise him to return. At that time, Grandfather Mao and Grandfather Hsüeh went to see the Prince and said, 'The reason why Your Highness is so much esteemed in Chao and so famous among the feudal lords is simply the existence of Wei. Now Ch'in is attacking Wei, yet you show no pity for Wei in this emergency. If the Ch'in army should take Ta-liang and raze your ancestral temple to the ground, how could you face the world again?' Before they had finished talking, the Prince changed colour and hastily gave orders to get the carriages ready for his return.

When the King of Wei and the Prince saw each other, they both wept, and the King gave him the seal of the generalissimo. In 247 B.C., the Prince sent messengers to all the other feudal lords, informing them of his appointment. On hearing this, they all sent generals with troops to help. The Prince, as Commander-in-Chief of the allied forces of five states, defeated the Ch'in army south of the Yellow River and drove the enemy out of the Han-ku Gate. The Ch'in troops dared not come out again, and the Prince's heroic fame spread all over the empire.

The King of Ch'in then bribed a former retainer of Chin Pi's with ten thousand catties of gold and made him slander the Prince before the King of Wei: 'The Prince was an exile abroad for ten years. Now he is the generalissimo of Wei, and the generals from the other states are all under his command. The other feudal lords have only heard of the Prince but not the King of Wei. The Prince himself wants to take this opportunity to ascend the throne, and the other feudal lords, who fear his authority, will support him.' Moreover, the King of Ch'in repeatedly sent messengers to Wei, pretending to have come to congratulate the new King and asking if the Prince had ascended the throne yet. The King of Wei, hearing such slander daily, could not help believing. Later, he ordered someone else to replace the Prince.

The Prince knew that he had been deprived of his power because of slander, so he asked for sick leave and refused to come to court. He had long drinking bouts with his guests at night, taking strong wine and dallying with many women. After indulging in wine, women, and song day and night for four years, he actually died of alcoholism. In that year (243 B.C.) the King of Wei also died. The King of Ch'in, on hearing of the Prince's death, sent an army to invade Wei and occupied twenty towns, which formed the new Eastern Prefecture of Ch'in. Eighteen years later, Ch'in captured the King of Wei of that time and slaughtered the people of Ta-liang.

Ching K'o (*ob.* 227 B.C.), *T'ien Kuang* (*ob.* 232 B.C.), *and Kao Chien-li* (*ob. c.* 221 B.C.)

Ching K'o was a native of the state of Wey.[1] He was fond of reading and swordsmanship, and offered his services to Prince Yuan of Wey, who did not make use of him. Later, when Ch'in invaded Wei (of which Prince Yuan of Wey had become a vassal) and established the Eastern Prefecture,[2] Prince Yuan was forcibly moved to another place. (If Prince Yuan had made use of Ching K'o, he might have been able to save his country.)

Once, while travelling through Han-tan, Ching K'o quarrelled with another knight called Lu Kou-chien while playing backgammon. Lu scolded Ching angrily. Ching K'o said nothing and left.

After further travelling, Ching K'o arrived in the state of Yen,[3] where he was commonly called Master Ching. He became very fond of a dog butcher and a musician named Kao Chien-li, who was an expert player of the zither (*chu*).[4] Being addicted to the cup, Ching K'o drank daily with these two at the market-place. When they became high-spirited with wine, Kao Chien-li would play his zither, which Ching K'o would echo with singing. Thus they enjoyed themselves together. But soon they would start to weep,

[1] I have spelt this name Wey to distinguish it from the larger state of Wei. The state of Wey was originally situated in modern Honan, later moved to Hopei.

[2] See last paragraph.

[3] The state of Yen occupied parts of modern Hopei, Manchuria, and northern Korea.

[4] A string instrument that came into being about this time and apparently passed out of use not long afterwards. It is variously described as having 5, 13, or 21 strings, and was played with the left hand and a bamboo stick held in the right hand.

as if nobody else had been around. Although Ching K'o associated with drinkers, he had a profound nature and was fond of studying. Wherever he travelled, he would always make friends with the worthy and distinguished men of the region. When he arrived in Yen, a knight living in retirement named T'ien Kuang treated him kindly, knowing him to be an outstanding man.

In 232 B.C., it so happened that Prince Tan, the heir apparent of Yen, who had been kept by the King of Ch'in as a hostage, escaped back to his native country. At first, Prince Tan was a hostage in Chao, where the reigning King of Ch'in, Ying Cheng, was born. As a young man Ying Cheng befriended Prince Tan, but after he became King of Ch'in and the latter became his hostage, he treated Prince Tan badly. Therefore the Prince bore a grudge against him and escaped home. After his arrival home, Prince Tan sought someone to avenge his wrongs on the King of Ch'in, but because his country was small he could not succeed. Later, Ch'in daily invaded Ch'i, Ch'u, and the three Chin states (Han, Chao, and Wei, who had partitioned the former state of Chin), and was about to reach Yen. The King of Yen and his subjects were all apprehensive of impending disaster. Prince Tan was worried and asked his tutor Chü Wu for advice. Chü Wu said, 'The King of Ch'in owns large territories all over the empire, and threatens Han, Wei, and Chao. He has the natural defence of the Sweet Spring Mountain [Kan-ch'üan] and the Valley Mouth [Ku-k'ou] in the north, the fertile valleys of the Ching and Wei rivers in the south, and the rich lands of Pa and Han; the mountains of Lung and Shu guard him on the right, the Han-ku Gate and Yao-pan Mountain on the left. His subjects are numerous, his soldiers fierce, and his arms plentiful. If he intends to expand further, then there will be no security south of the Great Wall and north of the river Yi [i.e. the kingdom of Yen]. Why do you want to "touch the dragon's reverse scale"[1] because of a personal insult?' Prince Tan asked, 'What should we do, then?' Chü Wu replied, 'Allow me to think it over.'

Some time later, a general of Ch'in, Fan Wu-chi, offended the King and escaped to Yen. Prince Tan received him and housed him. Chü Wu advised the Prince against this, saying, 'This will

[1] This expression is from the *Han Fei Tzŭ*, Chapter 4. Han Fei Tzŭ, comparing the King to the dragon, says that there is a reverse scale under the dragon's chin, which, when touched, so enrages the dragon that he will kill.

not do. The tyranny of the King of Ch'in, in his accumulated anger against us, is enough to make one shudder. How much worse when he hears General Fan is here? This is what you call "throwing meat in the path of a hungry tiger", which will bring irremediable catastrophe. Even if you had Kuan Chung and Yen Ying,[1] they could not help you. I wish Your Highness would quickly send General Fan to the Huns to remove this excuse for the King of Ch'in to invade us, then form an alliance with the three Chin states in the west, and with Ch'i and Ch'u in the south, while negotiating with the Khan of the Huns to the north. We can then hope to defeat Ch'in.' Prince Tan replied, 'Your plan, Grand Tutor, involves too much delay, but my mind is so full of worries that I can hardly wait a single moment. Besides, General Fan came to me in extremity and placed his life in my hands. I will never, because of the threat of the powerful Ch'in, desert a friend on whom I took pity and send him to the Huns. That would be the end of me. Will you please think it over again?' Chü Wu said, 'To act dangerously while seeking security, to create disaster while seeking blessing, to have shallow plans but deep grievances, to keep the friendship of one man while disregarding great calamities to the country—this is really a case of "encouraging hatred and aiding disaster". For if you throw a feather over the fire, nothing will be left. What more is there to be said when the King of Ch'in, ferocious as a vulture, gives vent to his fury? In our country there is a knight in retirement named T'ien Kuang, who is a man of profound wisdom and high courage. You may consult him.' The Prince asked, 'Would it be possible for me to become acquainted with Master T'ien through you, Grand Tutor?' Chü Wu replied, 'Yes, sir.'

Thereupon he went to see T'ien Kuang and said, 'The Crown Prince wishes to discuss affairs of state with you.' T'ien replied, 'I will do as you say.' So he went to the Prince. The Prince came out to meet him, walking backwards to show him the way (as a sign of great respect). Then he knelt down and dusted the mat for T'ien.[2] When T'ien Kuang had settled down and no attendants were about, the Crown Prince left his sitting mat (to show he dared not remain seated) and said, 'Yen and Ch'in cannot coexist.

[1] Two wise ministers of the state of Ch'i, who lived respectively in the seventh and sixth centuries B.C.

[2] In ancient China people sat on mats on the floor.

Will you ponder on this, sir?' T'ien replied, 'I have heard that when a fine horse is young, he can run a thousand miles a day, but when he is old, even a poor horse will outstrip him. Now, Your Highness has heard of what I was like in my prime, but you do not know that my vitality has gone. However, though I dare not presume to discuss affairs of state with you, my friend Ching K'o can be entrusted.' The Crown Prince asked, 'Would it be possible for me to be acquainted with Master Ching through you, sir?' T'ien replied, 'Yes, sir,' and immediately rose and hastened out. The Prince saw him to the door and warned him: 'What I have told you and what you have said concern great affairs of state. Please do not divulge them.' T'ien Kuang, bending his head and smiling, said, 'I promise.'

Bending low with age, he walked to Ching K'o's house and told him: 'Everyone in Yen knows that you and I are great friends. Now, the Crown Prince heard what I was like when in my prime, not realizing that my strength no longer measures up to my reputation. He favoured me with his presence and said, "Yen and Ch'in cannot coexist; will you ponder on this?" I, presuming to be a close friend of yours, mentioned you to the Prince. Will you go and see him at his palace?' Ching K'o replied, 'I will do as you say.' T'ien said, 'I have heard that an honest man does not arouse the distrust of others in his action. Now the Prince told me, "What I told you concerns great affairs of state; please do not divulge them." This shows he distrusts me. If one arouses the distrust of others, one is not a true knight of integrity.' Moreover, he wanted to commit suicide to force Ching K'o, so he said, 'Will you please hasten to the Prince and say I have died to show that I would not talk.' Thereupon he cut his own throat.

Ching K'o went to see the Crown Prince and told him T'ien Kuang had died, repeating T'ien's words. The Prince bowed twice, knelt down, and, moving forward on his knees, cried bitterly. Only after a while was he able to speak. He then said, 'The reason why I warned Master T'ien not to talk was to make sure this great enterprise would succeed. Now Master T'ien died to show he would not talk; how could this be what I intended?' When Ching K'o had settled down, the Prince left his sitting mat, bowed his head, and said, 'Master T'ien, not realizing my unworthiness, enabled me to come before you and be bold enough to express myself: this shows Heaven has taken pity on Yen and will not desert its orphan.[1] Now, the King of Ch'in has an avaricious mind and insatiable desires. Until he has conquered all the territories of the empire and subjected all the rulers within the seas, he will not be satisfied. At present, he has already captured the King of Han and annexed all his land. Moreover, he is sending troops to invade Ch'u in the south and Chao in the north. Wang Chien, with several hundred thousand men, is attacking Chang and Yeh [on the southern border of Chao], while Li Hsin is attacking Chao from T'ai-yuan [in modern Shansi] and Yun-chung [in Inner Mongolia]. Chao cannot resist Ch'in and will certainly surrender, and then disaster will reach Yen. Yen is a small and weak state and has already suffered several times from military difficulties. I reckon even with the power of the whole country we cannot resist Ch'in, while the other feudal lords are so afraid of Ch'in that they will not dare form an alliance with us. In my humble opinion, if we could get one of the bravest men of the world to go to Ch'in as an envoy and offer the King of Ch'in heavy profits, he, being greedy, will certainly give this man a chance to do what we want. If we could force the King of Ch'in to return all the lands he has conquered, all will be well. If not, then kill him. The generals of Ch'in are leading armies outside the country, so that if disturbance occurs inside, the new King and the generals will suspect each other. Taking advantage of this opportunity, we can then form an alliance with the other feudal lords, and will certainly defeat Ch'in. This is my highest wish, but I do not know to whom to entrust this mission. Will you ponder on it, Master Ching?' After a long time, Ching K'o said, 'This is a great affair of state; with my inferior abilities, I fear I am not worthy of such a mission.' The Prince came forward, bowing his head, and firmly asking Ching not to refuse. Only then did the latter agree. Thereupon the Prince honoured Ching as a minister of the upper rank, and housed him in a superior mansion. Every day the Prince came to visit him. He was supplied with rich food, and from time to time presented with rare objects. Whatever carriages, horses, or beautiful women took his fancy, the Prince obtained them for Ching K'o, so as to please him.

[1] Some commentators have doubted the appropriateness of the word 'orphan', since the Crown Prince's father was still alive. But it seems to me the word is used here merely as a rhetorical figure to emphasize the helpless condition of Yen.

After a long time, Ching K'o showed no sign of leaving. Meanwhile, the Ch'in general Wang Chien had conquered Chao, captured its king, and annexed its land. He was now moving his forces north to the southern border of Yen. Prince Tan, in fear, said to Ching, 'The Ch'in army may cross the river Yi any moment now. Then, even if I would like to attend on you indefinitely, how could it be possible?' Ching replied, 'Even if Your Highness had not spoken, I would have come to see you. If I now go to Ch'in without any token of good faith, it will be hard to get close to the King. Now, the King of Ch'in is putting up a reward of a thousand catties of gold and the revenue from ten thousand households for the capture of General Fan. If I could get General Fan's head, together with a map of the Tu-k'ang region of Yen [a fertile region], and offer them to the King of Ch'in, he would certainly be pleased and see me. Then I would be able to repay your favours.' The Prince said, 'General Fan came to me in extremity. I cannot bear to go against the principles of an honest man for the sake of personal interests. Will you think again, sir?' Ching K'o knew that the Prince could not bear to take General Fan's life, so he went in secret to see Fan himself and said, 'The King of Ch'in has certainly treated you with deep malice, general. Your parents and kinsmen have all been executed or taken as slaves, and now I hear he is putting up a reward of a thousand catties of gold and the revenue from ten thousand households on your head. What will you do?' Fan Wu-chi looked up to heaven, sighed, and said in tears, 'Whenever I think of it, it hurts me right to the marrow of my bones. But I do not know what to do.' Ching said, 'What would you say if I could tell you in a word how to remove the threat to Yen and avenge your wrongs?' Fan came forward and asked, 'What?' Ching said, 'I wish to have your head to present to the King of Ch'in, who will certainly be pleased and see me. I will grab his sleeve with my left hand and stab his chest with my right. Then your wrongs will be avenged and the disgrace of Yen of having been insulted removed. Would you agree, general?' Fan Wu-chi bared one arm, held his right wrist with his left hand (in great agitation), and said, 'This is what I have been gnashing my teeth and eating my heart out about day and night! Only now have I been enlightened!' Thereupon he cut his own throat. When the Crown Prince heard this, he rushed there and cried over the corpse in extreme grief. However, since there was nothing he could do now that the deed was done, he placed Fan's head in a box and sealed it.

The Crown Prince searched everywhere for a particularly sharp dagger, and eventually obtained one from Chao for a hundred pieces of gold. A workman was ordered to temper its edge with poison, and when it was tried on people, they all died as soon as a trickle of blood appeared. The Prince then ordered his men to get Ching K'o's luggage ready. He further ordered a brave youth named Ch'in Wu-yang as Ching K'o's deputy. This youth had killed someone at the age of thirteen, and no one dared to stare back at him.

Ching K'o was waiting for someone whom he wished to take with him. This man lived far away and had not yet arrived, but Ching was getting his luggage ready for him. After a while, Ching still had not set out. The Prince, thinking he was too late and suspecting he had changed his mind, asked him, 'Time is getting late; do you really mean to go, Master Ching? May I send Ch'in Wu-yang first?' Ching K'o angrily scolded the Prince: 'Why does Your Highness want to send a mere boy on such a mission of no return—and what is more, to carry a dagger and go to the dangerous, powerful Ch'in? The reason why I have been dallying is that I was waiting for a friend to go with me. Now, since you think I am too late, I beg to take my leave at once!' So he set out. The Prince and all his guests who knew about it came in white mourning clothes to see Ching K'o off. Soon they reached the river Yi, and, having poured a libation to the Spirit of the Roads, Ching K'o took to the road. Kao Chien-li played his zither, while Ching K'o echoed him with a song in the *Pien Chih* mode.[1] All those who heard it shed tears. Then Ching K'o came forward and sang:

> The wind whistles, whistles—ah, the river Yi is cold!
> The brave knight once gone—ah, will return no more!

Again, he sang in the *Yü* mode,[2] which was heroic in character, and all the men glared in anger, till their hair stood up, almost

[1] *Pien Chih* is the fourth note of the heptatonic scale, and the *Pien Chih* mode has been identified with the Greek Locrian by J. H. Levis in his *Foundations of Chinese Musical Art* (Peiping, 1936), p. 73. Cf. Additional Note 18.

[2] *Yü* is the sixth note of the heptatonic scale, and the *Yü* mode has been identified with the Dorian. (*Ibid.*)

pushing off their hats. So Ching K'o took to his carriage and left, without once looking back.

After arriving in Ch'in, Ching K'o bribed a favourite official of the King's with rich gifts. This official paved the way for him and spoke to the King: 'The King of Yen is truly shaken by Your Majesty's power and dare not resist your forces. He is willing to submit himself and all his subjects to Your Majesty's authority, be treated as a vassal, and pay tribute in the same way as the provinces under your direct control, so that he may be allowed to keep his ancestral temple. In trepidation he dare not speak for himself, but has respectfully sent an envoy, with the head of Fan Wu-chi and the map of Tu-k'ang, both sealed, to offer them to Your Majesty. The envoy is awaiting Your Majesty's pleasure.' On hearing this, the King was greatly pleased. So he put on his court dress and ordered a formal audience to be held, with nine ministers officiating at the ceremony, to receive the envoy from Yen at Hsien-yang Palace. Ching K'o, holding the box containing Fan Wu-chi's head, and Ch'in Wu-yang, holding that containing the map, proceeded one after the other according to etiquette. When they reached the steps leading to the throne, Ch'in Wu-yang changed colour and trembled in fear, at which the officials wondered. Ching K'o looked back at Ch'in Wu-yang and laughed; then went forward to apologize: 'The uncouth man from the northern barbarian regions has never seen the Son of Heaven. Therefore he is trembling in fear. Will it please Your Majesty to make some allowance for his ignorance so that he may complete his mission?' The King told Ching K'o, 'Bring us the map.' Ching took the map and presented it to the King, who gradually unrolled it (the map being in the form of a scroll). When it came to an end, the dagger appeared. Ching K'o grabbed the King's sleeve with his left hand, and, with the dagger in his right hand, tried to stab him. But before it reached him, the King pulled himself up in astonishment, breaking the sleeve off. The King tried to pull out his sword, but it being a long one, he only got hold of the sheath. In his hurry and confusion he could not pull out the sword at once, since it was firmly sheathed. Ching K'o chased the King, who ran round a pillar. The officials were all astounded and thrown into utter confusion by this sudden emergency. According to the laws of Ch'in, officials in attendance at court were not allowed to carry any arms, while the armed guards standing beneath the hall were not allowed to come up unless summoned by the King. In this emergency, there was no time to summon the guards: that was why Ching K'o was able to chase the King. The officials still had no weapons to attack Ching K'o with, so they fought him with their bare hands, while the royal physician tried to hit him with the medicine bag. The King was running round the pillar and did not know what to do in his confusion. An attendant shouted, 'King, push the sword back!' The King did so and was thus able to unsheath the sword. With this he struck at Ching K'o and broke his left thigh. Crippled, Ching threw his dagger at the King but missed, only hitting the wooden pillar.[1] The King struck again at Ching and inflicted eight wounds. Knowing he had failed, Ching K'o leant back against the pillar and laughed. Squatting on the floor, he cursed and said, 'The reason why I failed is that I wanted to take him alive and force him to sign a treaty so that I might report back to the Crown Prince.' Thereupon the officials came forth and killed Ching K'o. The King remained upset for a long time. Later, he rewarded and punished the officials according to their deserts. In particular, he gave two hundred *yi* (four thousand taels) of gold to the royal physician.

In his fury the King of Ch'in sent more troops to Chao and ordered General Wang Chien to invade Yen from there. In the tenth moon (of 226 B.C.), the capital of Yen, Chi (modern Peking) fell. The King of Yen and Prince Tan led their best troops to Liao-tung (in modern Manchuria). While the Ch'in general Li Hsin chased the King of Yen hard, a Prince of Chao sent a letter to the King of Yen, saying, 'The Ch'in army is chasing you so hard simply because of Prince Tan. If you will kill him and present his head to the King of Ch'in, I am sure the latter will withdraw his forces; then your country will be spared.' Later, General Li Hsin chased Prince Tan, who went into hiding. The King of Yen then sent a messenger to kill Prince Tan, and presented his head to the King of Ch'in.[2] But the Ch'in forces, instead of withdrawing, launched another attack. In 222 B.C. Ch'in vanquished Yen and captured the King of Yen. Next year, the

[1] See Additional Note 5.

[2] The original text has 'wanted to present his head to the King of Ch'in', but judging by the biography of the King of Ch'in, he actually received Prince Tan's head. The word 'wanted' therefore must be a textual error.

King of Ch'in conquered all China and styled himself August Emperor (Huang-ti).[1]

The Emperor of Ch'in chased the former retainers of Prince Tan and Ching K'o, who all ran away. Among them, the musician Kao Chien-li changed his name and became a hired labourer at Sung-tzǔ (formerly a town in the state of Chao, in modern Hopei). After a long time, he began to feel the strains of hard labour. When he heard a guest of the house playing the zither, he lingered about, unable to tear himself away, and said aloud, 'He is good in some places, not so good in others.' A servant of the house told the master, 'That labourer seems to understand music; he even presumes to criticize.' The master summoned him to come and told him to play. All those who heard him applauded, and he was given some wine to drink. Now Kao Chien-li thought to himself: I cannot go on hiding in fear like this for ever. So he withdrew, took out his own zither and fine clothes from his luggage, and reappeared after changing. Astonished, all the guests left their seats and treated him as an equal, while the master received him as a guest of honour. When he was asked to play and sing, everyone was moved to tears. The people of Sung-tzǔ took turns to entertain him, and the news reached the Emperor of Ch'in, who summoned him to the court. Someone recognized him and said, 'This is Kao Chien-li.' The Emperor, out of pity for him as a musician, spared his life but had him blinded. Whenever he was told to play, the Emperor approved. Gradually the Emperor allowed Kao to come closer, whereupon Kao filled his zither with lead and, when he came near the Emperor, tried to hit the latter with it, but missed. So the Emperor executed Kao Chien-li, and for the rest of his life never allowed former servants of the feudal lords to come near him again.

When Lu Kou-chien (who once quarrelled with Ching K'o) heard of Ching's unsuccessful attempt to assassinate the King of Ch'in, he said to himself, 'Alas, what a pity he did not perfect his swordsmanship! And how undiscerning of me not to have realized what kind of man he was! Formerly I scolded him, and he must have thought me an unworthy man!' (Otherwise Lu might have helped Ching K'o.)

[1] This shows his arrogance, for previous monarchs were only called 'King' (*wang*); even the legendary sage-kings of antiquity were called either 'August One' (*huang*) or 'Emperor' (*ti*) but not both together.

The Historical Knight-Errant

Chu Chia (*c.* 247–195 B.C.) *and Chi Pu*

Chu Chia was a contemporary of the first Emperor of the Han dynasty, Han Kao-tsu, and a native of Lu (the native state of Confucius, corresponding to parts of modern Shantung and Kiangsu). Most men of Lu followed Confucianism, but Chu Chia was known as a knight-errant. He sheltered from the law hundreds of chivalrous men and saved their lives. As for the ordinary people he had helped, they were innumerable. Yet he never boasted of his power or showed off his benevolence. Indeed, he would go so far as to avoid seeing someone again after having done the latter a favour, so as not to receive any reward or expression of gratitude. In helping people in distress, he always paid his attention first to the poor and humble. But he himself had no money to spare in the house, wore old and shabby clothes, had only one dish for each meal, and went out in a cart drawn by a bullock. He made it his special concern to rush to the aid of others, devoting more time to this than to his own affairs. In particular, he saved the life of General Chi Pu.

This Chi Pu was a native of Ch'u.[1] He indulged in chivalrous deeds and was well known in Ch'u. He was particularly famous for his truthfulness, so that the people of Ch'u had a saying, 'A promise from Chi Pu is worth more than a hundred catties of gold.' He led the troops of Hsiang Yü (King of Ch'u, rival of the King of Han who became the first Emperor of Han) and cornered the King of Han in battle several times. After the fall of Hsiang, the Emperor of Han put up a reward of a thousand pieces of gold for the apprehension of Chi Pu, and threatened to execute the whole family of anyone who should dare to conceal him. However, Chi Pu found refuge with a certain Mr. Chou of P'u-yang (in modern Hopei). Chou said, 'The Emperor of Han is searching hard for you, and soon the messengers will reach my house. If you, general, can trust me and follow my advice, I have a plan to offer you. If not, allow me to commit suicide first [to show that I will not betray you].' Chi Pu listened to his advice. Thereupon Chou shaved Chi's hair and put an iron collar round his neck to make him look like a convict, dressed him in coarse clothes, and put him in a big cart together with several dozens of domestic

[1] The state of Ch'u extended over Hupeh, Hunan, Anhwei, Chekiang, Kiangsu, as well as parts of Szechwan, Kwangsi, and Shensi.

slaves. Chou then took them to Lu and sold them to Chu Chia. Now Chu knew in his heart that one of the slaves was Chi Pu, so he bought the latter and put him to work in the fields. He then warned his son, 'Let this slave attend to the fields as he likes, and he must have the same food as you.' After that, he took a fast and light carriage and went to Lo-yang to see the Marquis of Ju-yin (Hsia-hou Ying). The Marquis entertained Chu with food and wine for several days, during which time the latter found opportunity to ask, 'What great crime has Chi Pu committed that the Emperor is searching for him so hard?' The Marquis replied, 'Chi Pu cornered His Majesty for Hsiang Hü several times; that is why His Majesty bears a grudge against him and is determined to catch him.' Chu Chia asked, 'In your view, what kind of man is Chi Pu?' 'A worthy man,' replied the Marquis. Then Chu said, 'Every subject serves his own Lord. When Chi Pu served Hsiang Yü, that was his duty. Can all the former servants of Hsiang be exterminated? Now, His Majesty has recently won the empire, but he is searching for one man because of a personal grudge. Why does he take such a narrow view of the world? Moreover, given a worthy man like Chi Pu, if you drive him too hard, he will either go north to join the Huns or go south to serve the Yueh barbarians. To bear a grudge against a hero and drive him to join an enemy state—that is why Wu Tzŭ-hsü whipped the corpse of King P'ing of Ch'u.[1] Why don't you look for an opportunity to speak to the Emperor and explain this?' The Marquis knew in his heart that Chu Chia was a great knight-errant, and guessed that he was harbouring Chi Pu, so he promised to do as Chu suggested. After a while, he really found opportunity to speak to the Emperor along the lines Chu Chia indicated. Thereupon the Emperor pardoned Chi Pu. After Chi Pu had received official honours, Chu Chia refused ever to see him again. Because of what he did for Chi Pu, Chu Chia's fame spread all over the Empire, and men longed to make his acquaintance. For instance, T'ien Chung of Ch'u, who was a well-known knight-errant and swordsman, treated Chu Chia as his father and regarded himself as inferior.

[1] Wu Tzŭ-hsü's father and brother were killed by King P'ing of Ch'u. Later Wu borrowed troops from the state of Wu and defeated Ch'u. By then King P'ing had already died, so Wu Tzŭ-hsü dug his body out of his tomb and whipped it three hundred times.

Chü Meng (second century B.C.)

Chü Meng was a native of Lo-yang. Most men there engaged in commerce, but he distinguished himself as a knight-errant and was known to the nobles. When the Princes of Wu and Ch'u rebelled (against Emperor Ching in 154 B.C.), the Marquis of T'iao (Chou Ya-fu) was Grand Marshal and came hastily to Honan prefecture. When he obtained the services of Chü Meng, he was delighted and said, 'The Princes of Wu and Ch'u want to overthrow the dynasty, yet they did not ask for Chü Meng; I know they will not succeed!' At a time when the empire was in turmoil, the Marshal was as pleased to have got Chü Meng as if he had conquered an enemy state.

Chü Meng's behaviour was very much like Chu Chia's, but he was fond of gambling and other games favoured by unruly youths. Yet, when his mother died, about a thousand carriages came from far away to attend the funeral.

Once Chü Meng visited Yuan Yang, a high official, and the latter received him kindly. Some rich man asked Yuan, 'I hear Chü Meng is a gambler; why do you associate with him, general?' Yuan replied, 'Though he is a gambler, when his mother died a thousand carriages came to attend the funeral, which shows he must have some outstanding qualities. Moreover, anyone may encounter distresses. In an emergency, if you go and knock on the door to ask for help, Chü Meng and Chi Hsin [younger brother of Chi Pu] are the only men in the world who can be relied on not to make excuses.'

After Chü Meng's death, his family did not even have ten pieces of gold to spare.

Kuo Hsieh (ob. c. 127 B.C.)

Kuo Hsieh was a native of Chih (in modern Honan province). His maternal grandfather was an expert physiognomist. His father was a knight-errant who was executed by Emperor Wen (reigned 179–157 B.C.). Kuo Hsieh was small in person but energetic and brave, and was a teetotaler. In his youth, he was spiteful and killed many people who had offended him. He avenged the private wrongs of his friends at the risk of his own life, concealed those on the run from the law, robbed people and even tombs, and illegally coined money. All these crimes he committed countless times, but he either managed to escape or was pardoned because of an amnesty. As he grew older, he reformed his ways. He became modest and exerted self-control; he repaid grievances with kindness; he gave liberally but expected little from others. Yet at heart he became even more fond of chivalrous deeds, and remained revengeful, ever ready to retaliate a slight offence. Many unruly young men who admired him would avenge his wrongs without letting him know it, while he on his part would save someone else's life without boasting about it afterwards.

Once, Kuo Hsieh's sister's son, relying on Kuo's influence, forced another man to drink beyond his capacity. The latter grew angry, killed the young man, and ran away. Kuo's sister, angry that the killer had escaped, said, 'My brother is known for his altruism, yet now he can't even find the murderer of my son!' So she left her son's body in the road and refused to bury it, so as to shame Kuo Hsieh. Eventually Kuo found out who the killer was, and the latter, in desperation, came to see him voluntarily and told him the whole truth. Kuo said, 'It was my nephew's fault; you were quite right to kill him.' So he let the killer go and quietly buried his nephew. All those who heard about this admired him for putting fairness above family loyalty, and more and more men came to follow him.

Whenever he went out, all men made way for him. But one day a man remained squatting and stared at him to his face. Kuo sent someone to find out this man's name. Meanwhile, some of Kuo's followers wanted to kill this man, but Kuo said, 'If I am not respected in my native district, there must be something lacking in me. What fault of his is that?' After he found out the man's name, he told the district clerk in charge of compulsory service: 'This man is someone I cannot do without. When it is his turn for service, exempt him.' So several times this man was passed over when it was his turn for service. He wondered why and found out that it was Kuo who had arranged for his exemption. Thereupon he went to Kuo and apologized in great humility. The unruly young men of the district, when they heard this, admired Kuo even more.

Two families in Lo-yang engaged in a feud, and, in spite of the efforts of a dozen or so local influential men to mediate between them, refused to be reconciled. Finally, Kuo was appealed to. He came to Lo-yang and saw the two hostile families by night, and they reluctantly allowed themselves to be persuaded by him to stop the feud. Kuo said to them, 'I hear that many gentlemen of Lo-yang have tried to make peace between you, but you would not listen. Now, fortunately, you listened to me. But why should I usurp the rights of the worthy gentlemen of another district?' So he slipped away at night, saying, 'There is no need to entertain me now. When I am gone, let the local gentlemen mediate between you, then follow their advice.' (In this way, not only did he bring a family vendetta to an end, but also saved the 'face' of the local influential men who had failed to do so.)

In spite of his great influence, Kuo behaved modestly and dared not ride in a carriage when he went to the district office. Sometimes he travelled to other prefectures on other people's business, and if a thing could be settled, he would settle it; if not, he would still try to find a compromise to the satisfaction of all concerned. Only then would he accept any hospitality. Therefore, men respected him and competed with one another to be of service to him. Often, the local unruly youths as well as chivalrous men from neighbouring districts came to visit him, and it was a common sight to see more than ten carriages outside his house at night. These men often asked to be allowed to house some of Kuo's guests to share his burden.

In 127 B.C., Emperor Wu ordered all those who owned more than three million cash to move from all parts of the empire to Mao-ling, near the capital Ch'ang-an, so as to keep a strict eye on potential rebels. Kuo's family did not have so much, but his name was included in the list of those to be moved. General Wei Ch'ing, half-brother of the Empress, spoke on Kuo's behalf to the Emperor: 'Kuo Hsieh is a poor man and should not be forced to move.' The Emperor replied, 'A commoner who has enough influence to make a general speak for him cannot be poor.' So Kuo's family had to move, and his friends contributed more than ten million cash towards his removal expenses. Meanwhile, Kuo Hsieh's brother's son killed the local clerk who first put Kuo's name in the list. After the Kuo family moved, the clerk's father was also murdered. When the family of the murdered sent a messenger to report to the throne, the messenger too was killed. The Emperor then ordered Kuo's arrest, whereupon he left his family at Hsia-yang (in modern Shensi) and fled alone to Lin-chin (on the border between Shensi and Shansi). There, a man named

Chi Shao-kung, who did not know Kuo, helped him to escape out of the Lin-chin Gate. Kuo then made his way to T'ai-yuan (in Shansi), and whenever he left a place he told his host where he was going (so as not to implicate the latter). The officials traced his movements to Chi Shao-kung, who committed suicide rather than give any information. After a long time, Kuo was finally arrested, but exhaustive investigation showed that all his crimes had been committed before a recent amnesty. However, events took a new turn. A Confucian scholar from Kuo's native district, when he heard someone praising Kuo, remarked, 'Kuo Hsieh makes it his business to break the law; how can he be called worthy!' When one of Kuo's retainers heard this, he killed the scholar and cut off his tongue. The officials blamed Kuo for the murder, but he really did not know who did it. The murderer was never found, and the officials reported to the throne that Kuo was innocent. However, the Imperial Censor Kung-sun Hung said, 'Kuo Hsieh is a commoner who indulges in knight-errantry and wields great power. He would kill for a slight offence. Though he does not know about this murder, his crimes are greater than the murderer's, and he deserves the penalty for high treason.' Thereupon Kuo Hsieh and his whole family were executed.

*

In addition to the above accounts, many more references to knights-errant can be found in the *Records of the Historiographer* and the *History of the Han Dynasty*. However, I hope enough examples have been given to show how the knights-errant of the Warring States and early Han periods behaved, and how influential they were.

SUPPRESSION OF KNIGHTS-ERRANT BY THE HAN EMPERORS

(*c*. 180–20 B.C.)

Although it was in the Han dynasty that Confucianism became the established orthodox ideology, the Han emperors actually ruled largely by Legalist methods, while paying lip service to Confucianism. It is therefore not surprising that they took strong measures to suppress the knights-errant, who formed a serious threat to government authority. We have already seen that Kuo

Hsieh's father was executed by order of Emperor Wen (reigned 179–157 B.C.). In the next reign, Emperor Ching (reigned 156–141 B.C.) ordered the execution of many more knights. And Emperor Wu (reigned 140–86 B.C.), as we have seen, ordered the execution of Kuo Hsieh and his family. This policy of suppression continued under subsequent emperors of the Han dynasty. The following is an account of a knight-errant who fell victim to this suppression.

Chü Chang (*ob. c.* 28 B.C.)

Chü Chang, whose courtesy name was Tzŭ-hsia, was a native of the capital Ch'ang-an. At that time, each of the bustling districts of the capital had its own powerful knight-errant. Chü lived in the western district and was known as 'Chu Tzŭ-hsia of the Western City'. He was an officer under the Metropolitan Prefect, and whenever he went to the palace with the Prefect, all the courtiers and nobles rushed forward to talk to him, while no one bothered to talk to the Prefect. Chü was afraid (this might lead to trouble), and eventually the Prefect stopped bringing Chü with him to the palace.

Chü Chang was a great friend of Shih Hsien, who was Prime Minister under Emperor Yuan (reigned 48–33 B.C.). At the beginning of Emperor Ch'eng's reign (32 B.C.), Shih was found guilty of having usurped too much power, deprived of his post, and ordered to return to his native district. He was very rich and wished to leave Chü Chang household effects worth several million cash. Chü refused to accept the gift. When someone asked him why, Chü replied, 'I am a mere commoner, yet Lord Shih befriended me. Now his family is ruined, but I can do nothing to save him. How can I accept his property? What happened is a misfortune to the Shih family; can the Chü family turn it to a fortune for itself?'

During the Ho-p'ing period (28–24 B.C.), Wang Tsun was Metropolitan Prefect and arrested many powerful knights-errant. Among them was Chü Chang, who was executed together with Chang Hui, an arrow-maker, and Chao Chün-tu, a wine seller, who were also knights-errant.

*

Other examples of the suppression of knights-errant from the *History of the Han Dynasty* have been given by Professor Lao Kan and need not be repeated here.

KNIGHTS-ERRANT IN LATER HISTORY

In spite of such suppression, many knights-errant survived in Han times. In later periods, knights-errant continued to exist. Naturally they were not equally numerous or active in all periods, nor did they all behave in quite the same way. Some openly indulged in force, while others confined themselves largely to deeds of generosity and unconventional but legal activities. Probably it all depended on the degree of government control at the time. However, different as their actions may be, they do have certain things basically in common. Indeed, most of them are described by different writers in almost identical terms (a fact which I shall try to indicate by using certain phrases repeatedly in my translations below at the risk of being monotonous). This shows that these men, widely different in social standing and profession, all had the same chivalrous temperament. The following brief accounts of the lives of chivalrous men are from various official histories as well as unofficial historical works.

1. *Later Han* (A.D. 25–220) *and Three Kingdoms* (220–65)

Chih Yun (*first century* A.D.)

Chih Yun was a native of Ju-nan prefecture (in modern Honan). He had a friend called Tung Tzŭ-chang, whose father had been murdered by another man from the same district. Unable to avenge his father's death, Tung became sick and was about to die. On his death bed, Chih came to see him. Tung looked at Chih and sobbed, no longer able to speak. Chih Yun said, 'I know you are not sad because you are fated to end your days but because you have not brought about revenge. When you are alive, I share your grief but cannot personally carry out revenge on your behalf; when you are gone, I will personally kill your enemy and grieve no more.' Tung could but look at him. Thereupon Chih left, took some friends with him, ambushed the enemy, and killed him. He brought back the enemy's head and showed it to Tung, who on seeing it breathed his last. Chih Yun then went to the district magistrate and gave himself up. The magistrate, who knew and admired him, would not send him to jail, but he insisted on going, until the magistrate threatened suicide. Later, Chih Yun became an important official at court.

Wang P'an (first century A.D.)

Wang P'an was the son of Wang Jen, Marquis of P'ing-ê (in modern Anhwei), cousin of the usurper Wang Mang. After the fall of the usurper, Wang P'an still possessed great wealth and lived in a chivalrous manner. He valued personal integrity, esteemed brave knights, and gave liberally to the poor. Later he went to the capital, got involved in an alleged political plot, and died in prison.

Lu Su (172–217)

Lu Su was a native of Tung-ch'eng in Lin-huai prefecture (in modern Anhwei). At birth he lost his father, and he grew up with his grandmother. His family was wealthy, but instead of looking after his wealth, he distributed money among the poor and even sold land to raise funds for this purpose. Therefore he made friends with many chivalrous men and was popular in the neighbourhood.

When Chou Yü, who was then garrison commander of Chü-ch'ao (also in Anhwei), came with several hundred soldiers to borrow food from Lu Su, the latter, who had two granaries each filled with three thousand bushels of rice, pointed to one granary and said, 'You can have it.' Thereupon Chou Yü and Lu Su became great friends.

Yuan Shu (a general who later styled himself Emperor for a brief period) heard of Lu Su's name and appointed him garrison commander of Tung-ch'eng. However, Lu realized that Yuan Shu was lawless in his action and not worth serving. So he left his native place with more than a hundred young knights-errant as well as old people and children, and went south to join Chou Yü at Chü-ch'ao.

Eventually Chou Yü became Commander-in-chief under Sun Ch'üan, who was fond of knights-errant and who later became the first Emperor of Wu. After Chou's death, Lu Su succeeded him.

Tien Wei (ob. 197)

Tien Wei, a native of Ch'en-liu district (in modern Honan), was a man of huge stature and immense strength. He cultivated personal integrity and indulged in chivalrous deeds. A family named Liu had an enemy called Li Yung. Tien Wei agreed to avenge the wrongs of the former on the latter. Li Yung, who had been an official, guarded his house closely. Tien Wei went to his house in a carriage, carrying chicken and wine and pretending to be paying a courtesy call. As soon as the door opened, Tien went in with his dagger and killed Li and his wife. Then he leisurely came out and calmly walked away. Li's house being near the market-place, all the people there were astonished, and several hundred men chased Tien, but none dared come near him. After walking a few miles, Tien met some friends and got away. Later he became one of the most feared warriors under Ts'ao Ts'ao (father of the first Emperor of Wei), and died in battle.

Hsi K'ang (223–262)

Hsi K'ang, poet, philosopher, musician, and amateur blacksmith, was a native of Ch'iao (in modern Anhwei). He was a Taoist, and indulged in chivalry. As a result of political and personal intrigues, he was involved in a fabricated crime and executed. He remained calm before his execution and asked for his zither (*ch'in*).[1] Having played for the last time, he sighed and said, 'Classical music will be heard no more!'[2]

2. *Chin (or Tsin) Dynasty* (265–419)

Li Yang (third century)

Li Yang, who was a famous knight-errant, won the admiration of both gentry and commoners. One hot summer's day, when he was due to take up his post as prefect of Yu-chou (in modern Hopei), he visited several hundred families to say farewell. His friends who came to his house to bid him farewell so crowded the place that some of them died of suffocation under the tables: such was his popularity.

Li Yang's prestige was so great that even a notorious shrew feared him. This was Wang Yen's wife, who was avaricious and often meddled in other people's affairs for gain. Wang was worried but could not stop her, so he said, 'It is not only I who say you

[1] A seven-stringed instrument, sometimes translated as 'lute'. I have translated it as 'zither', though I have used the same word for the *chu*, because both instruments have more in common with the zither than the lute.

[2] For more information about Hsi K'ang, see R. H. van Gulik, *Hsi K'ang and His Poetical Essay on the Lute* (Tokyo, 1941).

cannot do this; Li Yang also says you cannot.' Thereupon she curbed her activities.

Tai Jo-ssŭ (third century)

Tai was a native of Kuang-ling (in modern Kiangsu). He was handsome in appearance and free and easy by nature. In his youth he was a knight-errant and behaved in a lawless way. Once, when the famous poet Lu Chi (261–303) was travelling to Lo-yang by boat with plenty of luggage, Tai led a gang and robbed the boat. He then went ashore and gave orders to his followers to distribute the loot. Lu Chi, who watched from a distance, saw that Tai directed the whole operation with remarkable skill, so he called out, 'With your abilities, are you content to be a robber?' Tai was moved to tears, so he threw down his sword and came to talk to Lu Chi. Thereupon they became friends. Eventually Tai Jo-ssŭ rose to high rank in official life.

Tsu Ti (266–321)

Tsu Ti, a native of Fan-yang (in modern Hopei), was free and easy by nature and did not care about outward manners. In his youth, he belittled wealth and indulged in chivalry, and was known as a man of generous spirit and high integrity. Whenever he went to visit the tenants of his family, he would, in his elder brother's name, distribute food and clothing among the poor ones. Thus he gained the esteem of the local people as well as his kinsmen.

After he became an official, he remained careless about petty conventions of behaviour. Many of his retainers were fierce and brave knights, all of whom he treated as his own sons or brothers. During a time of famine, some of his retainers robbed people, but he protected them. His critics blamed him for this; consequently he received no promotion for a long time. However, later he was able to defeat the Turks and restore much territory to the Chin.

3. *Sui* (589–618) *and T'ang* (618–907) *Dynasties*

Tou Chien-tê (*ob.* 621)

Tou Chien-tê, a native of Pei-chou prefecture (in modern Hopei) was a man of outstanding ability and great physical strength. In his youth, he was known as a man of his word, and was fond of chivalry. A man from the same district lost his parent, but had no money to pay for the funeral. Tou Chien-tê, who was ploughing the fields when he heard this, at once stopped working and gave his ox to this man to pay the funeral expenses.

One night, some robbers came to his house. He waited for them to come in, and killed three of them. The rest were afraid to come in and begged for the bodies of their comrades. Tou said, 'All right, throw in a rope to haul them out!' When the robbers did so, he tied himself to the rope and let them haul him out. He then jumped up, seized a sword, and killed a few more.

Later he rebelled against the Sui and styled himself King of Hsia. However, not long afterwards he was captured by Li Shih-min (later Emperor T'ai-tsung of the T'ang dynasty) and executed.

Kuo Yuan-chen (656–713)

Kuo Yuan-chen was a native of Wei-chou prefecture (in modern Hopei). He was very tall and had a handsome beard. As a young man he already had great ambitions. While he was studying at the Imperial University, his family sent him four hundred thousand cash for his expenses. Just then, a stranger in mourning came, saying that five generations of his ancestors had remained unburied[1] and that he wished to borrow money for their proper burial. Kuo immediately gave this man the whole sum he had received from his family, without even asking the stranger's name. Kuo's fellow students were astonished and sighed with admiration.

After passing the Metropolitan Examination in his eighteenth year and becoming a magistrate, Kuo remained impulsive and acted in a chivalrous way, disregarding petty conventions of behaviour. Eventually he became a famous general under several reigns and was enfeoffed Duke of Tai.

Li Po (701–762)

The poet Li Po was a knight-errant in his younger days. His biography in official history says that 'he was interested in strategy and swordsmanship; behaved as a knight-errant; belittled wealth and gave liberally'. Li Po himself says that once he spent a fortune within a year in helping people in distress. From his friend Wei Hao we learn that the poet killed several men by his own hand.[2]

[1] It was quite common to keep the coffins of one's ancestors for years (usually in a monastery) until they could be transported to one's native district for proper burial.

[2] This has been mentioned by Arthur Waley in *The Poetry and Career of Li Po* (London, 1950), p. 6.

This aspect of Li Po's character found expression in some of his poems.[1]

4. *Five Dynasties* (907–59)

Huang Tzŭ-yeh

Huang Tzŭ-yeh was a native of Hou-kuan (in modern Fukien province) and the son of a merchant. When he was in his thirteenth year, he went with his father to Hangchow (in Chekiang province). Then his father left for another place on business and told him to guard the house. One day, a man named Wang P'i, who was travelling by boat, was shipwrecked on the river. When Huang Tzŭ-yeh saw the accident, he waved his arms and shouted, 'If any one can save this man, I'll give him a hundred pieces of gold!' Thereupon a fisherman saved Wang, and Huang took a hundred pieces of gold from his father's house and gave them to the fisherman. When the father returned, he was amazed on hearing the story. However, Huang Tzŭ-yeh said, 'It is not right for the son to get a good name while the father suffers a loss.' So he left to work as a servant. The employer, having heard about the incident, quietly paid him twice as much as his wages should have been. With the money he thus earned, Huang started a small business. After a long time, he saved quite a lot of money, half of which he used to look after his parents, the other half he distributed among his poor friends. Then, with great modesty, he began to study in earnest. Someone tried to persuade him to enter official life, to which he made no reply. Actually he regretted having allowed himself to become known, so he changed his name, burned his writing materials, and went back to his native province to farm.

Later, Wang P'i, the man whose life Huang had saved, became a high official and sent a messenger to invite Huang to join him, but the latter ran away. Wang persisted in his efforts and told the local official at Foochow to continue the search. Finally a messenger saw a man on a boat chanting some verse, who proved to be Huang. The messenger followed Huang to his home, which consisted of hardly anything more than four bare walls, except for a table with a copy of the *Book of Changes* on it. Huang pretended to be glad to see the messenger, offered him some food, and

[1] See below, pp. 64–7.

promised to meet him next day at the post-house. Next day, the messenger waited there with a carriage till evening, but Huang did not come. When the messenger rushed to Huang's home, he had already fled.

5. *Sung dynasty* (960–1279)

Chiao Chi-hsün (tenth century)

Chiao Chi-hsün, a native of Hsü-chou prefecture (in modern Honan), had great ambitions even in his youth. He grew tired of studying and said, 'A real man should accomplish great deeds in foreign lands and earn high honours. How can one be content to work diligently with the writing brush and the ink-slab?' So he gave up his studies and wandered around as a knight-errant, indulging in drinking and gambling.

He then entered military life and served several successive dynasties before he became a general under the Sung. When he replaced another official as Resident Superintendent of the Western Capital (Lo-yang),[1] where conditions had been so bad that bandits roamed the streets in broad daylight, order was restored after a month. He ended his days as a Military Governor.

Kuo Chin (tenth century)

Kuo Chin, a native of Shen-chou prefecture (in modern Hopei), was born in poverty and in his youth worked as a hired labourer in a rich man's house. He was very strong, and free and easy by nature. He acted temperamentally, associated with chivalrous men, and was fond of drinking and gambling. The young master of the house thought him undesirable and plotted to kill him. However, the rich man's wife told Kuo of the plot and he ran away.[2] Later, he became a general and served three successive dynasties.

After he had distinguished himself, Kuo sought the woman who

[1] Lo-yang was the Western Capital in Sung times, though it had been the Eastern Capital in the Han dynasty.

[2] The official history of the Sung dynasty says it was Kuo's own wife who warned him of the plot to kill him, but another historical work, the *Tung-tu Shih-lüeh* ('Brief Accounts of Events in the Eastern Capital') by Wang Ch'eng of the Sung dynasty, gives the credit to 'a rich man's wife named Chu'. It seems reasonable to identify this woman with the wife of the same rich man who was Kuo's employer, as she would be in a position to hear of the plot, while Kuo's own wife or another rich man's wife would not be.

had saved his life. He found out that she had died and her daughter was living in poverty. Thereupon he took the girl and brought her up as his own daughter, and when she married he gave her a handsome dowry.

Liu K'ai (tenth century)

Liu K'ai, a well-known official and writer of early Sung, was a native of Ta-ming (in modern Hopei). He was intelligent and brave as a child. When he was in his thirteenth year, a robber came to his father's house one night. The rest of the family were all too frightened to move, but Liu K'ai took a sword and chased the robber. When the robber tried to escape by climbing over the wall, the boy struck at him with the sword and cut off two of his toes.

After he grew up, Liu still behaved temperamentally. He cared little for petty conventions of behaviour and associated only with heroic-minded men. Once, in a tavern, he saw a scholar who looked ill at ease. Liu asked him questions and found out that he came from the capital and was too poor to pay for his parent's funeral. 'How much do you need?' Liu asked. 'Two hundred thousand cash would be enough.' Thereupon Liu gave him all the silver he had, which amounted to over a hundred taels, as well as several tens of thousands of cash.[1]

There is another anecdote about Liu K'ai, which, though not mentioned in official history and probably exaggerated, is not inconsistent with his character:

When he was on his way to the capital to take part in the Metropolitan Examination, he stayed at a post-house. At night he heard a girl crying bitterly. Next morning he made enquiries, and found out that the girl was the daughter of a certain retired district magistrate. During his tenure of office, the magistrate had been corrupt and entrusted a servant with the reception of bribes. Now the servant demanded to marry the daughter of the magistrate, who, out of fear, agreed. That was why the girl was crying. After hearing this, Liu K'ai went to see the retired magistrate, questioned him, and was satisfied that he told the truth. Liu then asked to 'borrow' the servant for one day. As soon as

[1] In Sung times one tael of silver was worth between 600 and 2000 cash. If we take each tael as roughly over 1000 cash, then 'over 100 taels' plus the 'several tens of thousands of cash' would be almost as much as 200,000 cash.

the servant arrived, Liu sent him to the market to buy food and wine. When night came, Liu called the servant and scolded him, 'So you are the one who is threatening his master and trying to marry his daughter by force!' He then took out a dagger and killed the servant. Next day, he invited the retired magistrate to dinner, and served a dish which he said was donkey meat. After the dinner, the magistrate asked where the servant was. 'It was his flesh you have just dined on,' was the reply.

Ts'ao Hsieh (eleventh century)

Ts'ao Hsieh was a descendant of Ts'ao Pin, one of the leading generals at the beginning of the Sung dynasty, and a native of Ling-shou (in modern Hopei). As a young man, he was fond of studying, had a strong sense of justice, and prided himself on being a knight-errant of integrity.

When he was commander at Hsü-chou (in Honan), one of his retainers behaved in a lawless manner and intimidated everyone. Ts'ao heard about this and invited some friends to a banquet, to which he summoned this offending retainer. He then listed the latter's crimes and was about to kill him. The offender begged for mercy, which Ts'ao granted, while warning him never to repeat his offence again.

Ts'ao Hsieh rose to be Commander-in-Chief of the Ho-yang Army (stationed in Honan). Apart from being a military man, he also wrote poetry. He studied poetry under the famous poet Mei Yao-ch'en, who praised his works.

Wang K'ê-ming (1069–1135)

Wang K'ê-ming, who originally came from Jao-chou (in Kiangsi) and later moved to Hu-chou (in Chekiang), was a famous physician. He was well read, fond of chivalry, and full of altruistic spirit. He often travelled thousands of miles to save people in distress. Once he saved the lives of several thousand soldiers during an epidemic.

6. *Yuan dynasty* (1280–1368)

Hsü Shih-yen (*fl.* 1348)

Hsü Shih-yen was a native of Hsin-ting (in Chekiang). He was generous by nature and often rushed to the aid of others. In 1348 there was a serious epidemic south of the Yangtze river. Hsü distributed food and hired men to bury the dead. Those victims who still could be cured and fed he looked after personally to save their lives. One day he saw a girl who was barely breathing. On enquiry Hsü found out she was the daughter of a scholar from Ch'ü-chou (in Chekiang). He took her back in a carriage and had her cured. Later he married her to a scholar.

7. *Ming dynasty* (1368–1644)

Sung K'ê (1327–87)

Sung K'ê was a native of Ch'ang-chou (in Kiangsu). As a young man he indulged in chivalry, yet he read widely in history and literature. He was tall in stature, fond of fencing and riding, and particularly skilful in using the cross-bow, being able to shoot down any bird in flight. His family was rich, but he spent all his fortune on entertaining his friends and drinking and gambling in the company of unruly young men.

When he reached his prime of life, he saw the empire was in disorder and wished to achieve great deeds. So he declined the company of his former drinking friends and went to study military strategy. Having mastered a book entitled *Feng Hou's Methods of Surprise-phalanxes*,[1] he was about to go north and join other heroic-minded men to discuss plans for action (i.e. revolt against the Mongols). However, he was frustrated and did not meet anyone with whom he could cooperate. Therefore he travelled around Kiangsu and Chekiang and finally returned home to lead a quiet life. There he became well known for his integrity, and many gentlemen vied with one another to make his acquaintance. Every day several dozens of carriages could be seen outside his house. Sung, on his part, made friends wholeheartedly with all who came to him, irrespective of their social status.

There were two generals who, relying on their power, behaved as bullies and assaulted scholars several times. One of them asked Sung K'ê to a drinking party. Someone advised Sung not to go, saying, 'He gets violent after drinking; you must not go near him.' Sung smiled and said, 'How can a man who needs drinking for his courage be truly brave? I will soften him.' So he went to the party, took the seat of honour, and told this man how worthy

[1] *Feng Hou Wo-ch'i Chen-fa*, also called *Wo-ch'i Ching*, a book that purports to have been written by Feng Hou, a minister of the mythical Yellow Emperor, but is in fact probably a forgery of the Sung period.

generals of ancient times behaved. The man listened in awe, put down his cup, bowed to Sung, then toasted him. To the end of the party he did not misbehave once.

The other of the two bullies once met Sung in a tavern. When he saw that Sung showed no deference to him, he gave Sung an angry look and left. Another day, he saw Sung riding alone, so he followed closely behind with armed soldiers, making a show of force. Sung deliberately rode slowly in the middle of the road, making it quite clear he had not the slightest intention of making way for the bully. The latter, realizing that Sung was no cowardly scholar, went away. Early next morning, he asked a mutual acquaintance to take him to Sung's house, apologized, and begged to become a friend.

Sung K'ê was frank and argumentative by nature and often admonished his friends for their shortcomings. If anyone offended him, he would scold the offender to his face, but would not hold a grudge against the man afterwards. In discussions, he always expected to win, but since he was so good at presenting facts and analysing reasons, no one could defeat him in argument.

When Chang Shih-ch'eng rebelled against the Mongols and called himself King of Wu, Sung K'ê privately predicted whether Chang's military operations would succeed or fail, and most of his predictions came true. Someone mentioned Sung's name to Chang, who wished to recruit him to his own staff, but Sung declined. Chang was annoyed and tried to frame Sung, but the latter saved himself with clever manoeuvring.

Although he was now poor, whenever he was presented with food and wine on festive occasions, he would summon his friends and share his feast with them. When wandering scholars came to Kiangsu, he would always find out whether they were worthy men. If they were, he would always entertain them and sing their praise to all, high and low. If anyone he knew could not afford to pay funeral or medical expenses, Sung would raise the necessary funds from the local gentry.

Later he grew tired of social activities and received few visitors. Instead, he shut himself in a room full of antiques and books and amused himself with writing verse and calligraphy. Eventually he became one of the foremost calligraphers of his day.

At the beginning of the Ming dynasty, he served as Deputy Prefect of Feng-hsiang (in Shensi province). According to the official history of the Ming dynasty, he died in his post, but another historical work says he gave up his post before he died.

Sung K'ê was a great friend of the celebrated poet Kao Ch'i (1336–74), who wrote a biography of him entitled 'The Life of Nan-kung Sheng' (this being Sung's pseudonym since he lived in a street called Nan-kung Li or 'South Palace Lane'), on which the above account is largely based.

DECLINE AND TRANSFORMATION OF KNIGHTS-ERRANT

During the Ch'ing or Manchu dynasty (1644–1911), knight-errantry declined, though it never died out completely. For instance, two of the leaders of the T'ai-p'ing revolution (1851–66), Hu Yi-huang and Lin Feng-hsiang, are described by the recent compilers of the *History of the Ch'ing Dynasty* (1961) as knights-errant. But on the whole we find few knights-errant of the traditional type in Ch'ing history.

The decline of knight-errantry may have had some connection with the rise of a system of insurance and armed escort of goods in transit, known as *pao-piao*, or 'armed protection'.[1] Under this system, an insurance company, called *piao-chü*, would undertake to guard goods in transit and make good the loss if anything was lost on the way. The armed escorts were called *piao-k'ê* or 'armed travellers', who were usually men of fine swordsmanship and chivalrous temperament. In popular chivalric tales and plays of the Ch'ing period, the heroes are often such armed escorts, who also act as bodyguards of upright officials. Though this is fiction, it probably reflects what actually happened. The earliest reference to the *piao-k'ê* that I know occurs in Kao Shih-ch'i's *T'ien-lu Chih-yü* or *Miscellaneous Notes of a Court Librarian*[2] (1690). It seems possible that about this time many knights-errant became professional armed escorts, and thus, ironically enough, became guardians of the law instead of law-breakers. However, the ideals of knight-errantry were not totally lost: no chivalrous-minded armed escort would consent to be the bodyguard of a corrupt official or oppress the poor.

[1] See Additional Note 6.

[2] *T'ien-lu* alludes to the T'ien-lu Pavilion of the Han dynasty, where Liu Hsiang and Yang Hsiung collated books. Cf. below, p. 65.

CONCLUSION

The examples of knights-errant given above show clearly that they included men from all walks of life and all social classes: professional soldiers and officials as well as poets, musicians, physicians, merchants, butchers, and vagabonds. This should be sufficient evidence that they were not a particular social class or professional group.

It is interesting to note the geographical distribution of the knights-errant. Most of them came from North China, especially what are now the provinces of Hopei and Honan. About two-thirds of the knights-errant described above came from these two provinces. This may have something to do with their proximity to northern nomadic tribes, whose way of life stressed freedom of movement and military virtues.

Although knight-errantry as such has ceased to exist, its spirit has not vanished completely. Even now, though we no longer encounter anyone actually called a knight-errant, we may still hear of men being described as having the spirit of knight-errantry or behaving in a chivalrous fashion.

2

THE KNIGHT-ERRANT IN POETRY

In spite of the absence of epic and the scarcity of long narrative poems in Chinese, reasons for which I have discussed elsewhere,[1] there is a considerable amount of Chinese chivalric poetry. The theme of chivalry first appeared in the poetry of the Han dynasty (206 B.C.–A.D. 220), became popular during the Six Dynasties (222–589), and remained a favourite theme with the T'ang poets (618–907). In the *Yueh-fu Shih-chi*, an anthology of songs in the *yueh-fu* style[2] ranging in date from earliest times to about A.D. 1100, there are many chivalric songs bearing such titles as 'Song of the Knight-errant', 'Song of Unruly Youths', 'The Unruly Youth of Ch'ang-an', 'The Unruly Youth of Han-tan', and 'Making Friends Among the Young Bloods'. The earlier ones among them were actual songs, the later ones were imitations and probably not set to music. Chivalric poetry passed out of fashion in the Sung (960–1279) and Yuan (1280–1368) periods, but enjoyed a revival during the Ming dynasty (1368–1644) before its final decline.

GENERAL CHARACTERISTICS OF CHINESE CHIVALRIC POETRY

Chinese chivalric poems include descriptions of knights-errant as well as comments on historical knights. They vary in tone from slight disapproval to enthusiastic eulogy, the majority being sympathetic. The descriptions are more or less realistic, sometimes a little exaggerated but seldom fantastic or incredible. Some poets

[1] *The Art of Chinese Poetry* (London and Chicago, 1962), pp. 152–4.

[2] The *yueh-fu* refers to folk songs collected and edited by the Yueh-fu ('Music Department') under Emperor Wu of Han (reigned 140–87 B.C.), as well as later imitations.

stress the bravery and altruism of the knights-errant; others mainly depict their free and gay way of life. Thus, in poetry, it is not always easy to distinguish knights-errant from patriotic warriors on the one hand, and from mere dandies on the other. Some poems show a genuine congeniality to the spirit of knight-errantry; others are merely conventional literary exercises. As for poems on historical knights, some poets use these as an indirect means to express their own ideals and sentiments or to comment on current events, while others only versify passages from historical works. Consequently, many poems on chivalry read rather similar, using the same kind of vocabulary and the same stock allusions. However, in order to make a representative selection and to show what the common run of these poems are like, I shall translate not only poems of real merit but also some purely conventional ones. In this chapter I shall confine my selection to poems in classical forms; popular ballads in doggerel and dramatic poetry will be dealt with later.

DESCRIPTIONS OF KNIGHTS-ERRANT

Let us begin with a few lines from *The Western Capital* by Chang Heng (A.D. 78–139):

The knights-errant of the capital city,
Men such as Chang and Chao,
Equal the Prince of Wei for ambition,
Rival the deeds of the Lord of Ch'i.
They take death lightly, but esteem
The spirit, and form cliques and gangs.
Numerous indeed are their followers,
Their attendants as thick as clouds.
Yuan of Mao-ling, Chu of Yang-ling:
Ferocious, fearless, fierce, and free,
Like roaring tigers and wild cats.
An angry glance, a 'bone in the throat',
And a body falls by the corner of the road.

This is a fairly straightforward description of contemporary or recent knights. In the second line, Chang and Chao refer to Chang Hui and Chao Chün-tu, two knights-errant executed together with Chü Chang.[1] In the next two lines, the author refers to two

[1] See above, p. 41.

of the four feudal princes famous for retaining knights.[1] In line 9, 'Yuan of Mao-ling' is Yuan Shê, a knight-errant who was killed in A.D. 23, and 'Chu of Yang-ling' is Chu An-shih, another powerful knight, who caused the death of a prime minister and his son. In line 12, the 'bone in the throat' means a trivial offence. The general tone of these lines is somewhat disapproving, especially in the last two lines, where the poet deplores the readiness with which the knights-errant wreak vengeance for slight offences.

A much more flattering portrait of a knight-errant is painted by Ts'ao Chih (192–232):

The White Steed

A white steed decked with a golden halter
Galloped past towards the north-west.
'May I enquire who the rider is?'
'A knight-errant from Yu or Ping[2] in the north.
He left his native district in his youth
And spread his fame across the distant desert.
He always carries a fine sturdy bow
With jagged arrows made of bramble wood.
Pulling the string, he hits the target on the left;
Shooting from the right, he hits it again.
Looking up, he shoots an ape in flight;[3]
Bending down, he hits the bull's-eye once more.
He is more agile than a monkey
And as fierce as a leopard or dragon.
When alarms came from the frontier
That barbarian troops had made repeated raids,
And when a call to arms came from the north,
He mounted his steed and reached the frontier fort.
He rode on right into the land of the Huns,[4]
Holding the Tartar[4] tribes in high disdain.
He threw himself before the pointed swords
Without giving a thought to his own life.

[1] See above, p. 16. The original mentions their personal names, Wu-chi and T'ien Wen, which I have changed for the sake of rhythm.

[2] Two of the nine prefectures into which ancient China was divided.

[3] It has been suggested that in the original poem *jou* ('ape') is a misprint for *hung* ('wild swan').

[4] These are used loosely for the tribal names Hsiung-nu and Hsien-pei.

He did not even worry about his parents,
Let alone his children and his wife.
His name entered the register of heroes;
His heart had no room for personal feelings.
He risked his life at a time of national disaster,
And regarded death merely as returning home.'

This description is rather idealized, and the poet may be using the theme as an excuse to give vent to his own feelings. Ts'ao Chih was the younger brother of Ts'ao P'i, who usurped the throne of Han and became the first Emperor of Wei. Being highly talented and ambitious, Ts'ao Chih incurred the jealousy and suspicion of his elder brother. It is therefore possible that in this poem he is expressing his frustrated patriotic wishes and military ambitions which his brother prevented him from fulfilling. Be that as it may, the poem remains a good illustration of some of the ideals of knight-errantry. Notice, in particular, that the knight-errant does not allow filial devotion to deter him from his heroic task.

The next two poems by Chang Hua (232–300) also strike a sympathetic note:

Two Songs of Knights-errant

I

The knight-errant loves a secluded place:
He built a chamber behind a desolated hill.
He went hunting but found few animals,
He spread a net but caught no birds.
The year is ending, bringing hunger and cold;
Heroically he sings, beating time with his foot.
Poverty stirs up a brave knight's spirit:
How can he cherish bitterness in his heart?
Sitting alone, he strokes his precious sword,[1]
Now fast, now gently, as if playing a lute.
He ploughs the fields on the slope of a dry ravine,
But his real seeds are sown at the tip of the sword.
He reaps his harvest among narrow paths:
One blow is worth a thousand pieces of gold.
He takes his rest among bears' dens,
And roams in a forest full of tigers and leopards.

[1] In the original text one word is missing from this line. I have tentatively filled the gap with 'strokes'.

His person lies beyond law and order,
He lives freely without any restraint.

II

The brave lads indulge in heady chivalry,
Their fame overwhelms unruly youths.
They wreak vengeance on behalf of friends
And kill people by the market-place.
Curved knives clang in their hands,
Or swords with edges sharp as autumn frost.
From their waists jut white halberds,
In their hands, white-headed spears.
These they wield as fast as lightning flashes,
Or whirl around as fleeting beams of light.
A hand-to-hand fight decides the issue;
One across another, corpses lie.
They'd rather die and become heroic ghosts
Than enter prison with its encircling walls.
In life, they make friends with noble men;
In death, their chivalrous bones smell sweet.[1]
Their bodies perish, their hearts do not repent;
Their brave spirit spreads everywhere.

A quieter mood is introduced by Pao Chao (*c.* 420–460) in the following poem, in which a knight-errant comes home and feels wistful on seeing others living in prosperity while he himself is a refugee from the law:

'*Making Friends Among the Young Bloods*'[2]

A fine piebald horse with a golden halter,
A curved knife worn on a brocade belt.
Displeasure incurred over a cup of wine
Led to a feud fought with glittering blades.
When suddenly soldiers came in hot pursuit,
He left for a distant land, carrying his sword.
Having left his home for thirty years,
He now once more returns to the old hills.
He ascends a peak overlooking the fortresses,

[1] Compare James Shirley's 'Only the actions of the just/ Smell sweet and blossom in the dust.'

[2] This title is taken from a poem by Ts'ao Chih, of which only a few lines are extant.

And gazes at the imperial city, in and out.
The nine roads lie as smooth as water,[1]
The double palace gates rise like clouds.
The palace is full of generals and ministers,
Lining the road stand princes and lords.
At noon the market-place is crowded and busy,
Carriages and horses pass like a running stream.
As bells strike, men dine from rows of vessels;
Driving out, they seek the company of friends.
'What is this that I alone am doing,
Frustrated and beset with a hundred cares?'

The next poem by Yü Hsin (513–81) has a strong visual appeal. Indeed, it is sometimes given as one of a series of poems on paintings on a screen. Moreover, in another poem in the same series, there is also a reference to a knight-errant. This shows that knights-errant must have formed a common subject for painters.

Song of Knights-errant

The wandering knights join their horses together,
Their golden saddles covered with willow twigs.
Fine dust rises, blocking the road;
Surprised flowers float, dazzling the eye.
Gay with wine, the men are half drunk;
Wet with sweat, the horses are still proud.
On their return, for fear they should be late,
They fight their way to the bridge over the stream.

The poems we have just seen present considerable variety in mood as well as originality in thought and expression. Not so the next three poems, which are largely derivative and conventional. The first one is by Wang Pao (*ob. c.* 571):

Song of Knights-errant

Famous songs come from the two capitals,
Powerful knights compete in making friends.
They visit the four princes south of the River,
And call on the five marquises west of the Gate.
They watch cockfighting by the highway,
Or ride on the road lined with tall catalpas.

[1] There were nine main roads in the city of Ch'ang-an.

As the mulberry-trees' shadows shift at sunset,
They linger about under the locust-trees.

This poem is full of conventional allusions. In line 3, the poet alludes to the four feudal princes famous for retaining knights,[1] and in line 4, to the five Wang brothers, clansmen of the Empress, who were made marquises on the same day in 29 B.C. and who were also fond of keeping knights. In these two lines, the 'River' refers to the Yellow River, and the 'Gate' refers to the Han-ku Gate. Lines 5 and 6 are adapted from Ts'ao Chih's *The Famous Capital*:

They watch cockfighting in the eastern suburb,
Or ride among the tall catalpa-trees.

Thus, what was an original observation now becomes a perfunctory description. Indeed, the writer here seems so poor in imagination that he has to resort to mentioning two other kinds of trees to complete the picture!

The second poem is by Yang Chin (sixth century):

'The Knight-errant Controls the Fleeting Shadow'

In the little park beside the Green Gate the view is fresh:
Flowers bloom and birds play together in the fragrant spring.
The tiered terrace with the Immortal's Hand stands in the bright sun,
On the wide road lined with tall catalpas, red dust is raised.
Those in the park follow paths under peach- and plum-trees,
Those on the highway are busy welcoming a wandering knight.
The wandering knight's heroic name is known over the empire;
Man and horse suit each other in temper and spirit.
A white jade handle decks his sword, cold as autumn water;
Black silk reins softly hold a bridle of gold.
He also has the steeds 'Fish Eyes' and 'Dragon Patterns',
And gallops as fast as if following a shadow or chasing the wind.
His shadow dashes into the Gate of Wu like a strand of silk,
His form moves to the north-west like a floating cloud.
'Send my word to the riding and shooting knights of Yu and Ping:
I'm not willing to share my fame or let them have it on loan!'

The title of this poem is taken from a poem by Lu Chi (261–303), and the poem itself is full of allusions. In line 1, the 'Green Gate' (Ch'ing-men) refers to one of the city gates of Ch'ang-an; in

[1] See above, p. 16.

line 3, the 'Immortal's Hand' alludes to the story that Emperor Wu of Han erected an image of an immortal with his hands holding a tray to receive heavenly dew; and the road lined with catalpa trees in line 4, as we have seen, is derived from Ts'ao Chih. Line 11 contains an allusion to two famous horses mentioned in the *History of the Han Dynasty*; line 13 refers to Wu-men ('Gate of Wu', modern Soochow); and line 15 mentions the two ancient prefectures particularly famed for knights-errant. All these allusions hardly add up to a very realistic or imaginative picture of a knight-errant.

The third poem is by Ch'en Liang (early seventh century):

Song of Knights-errant

The city of Lo-yang is bright with spring,
Wandering knights drive lightly by.
Their fast carriage wheels splash up water,
Their horses' hooves raise flying dust.
Clouds' shadows cover their canopies,
Flowers' fragrance permeates their clothes.
They watched cockfighting in the eastern suburb,
And went pheasant-shooting at Nan-p'i.
Returning over the bridge when day is ending,
They raise their whips and regret the sun is set.

This poem is less riddled with allusions than the preceding one, except for line 7, which is taken from Ts'ao Chih,[1] and line 8, which alludes to the fact that Ts'ao P'i once shot pheasants at Nan-p'i. The total effect of this poem is relatively light and lively compared with the other two.

The poems translated above represent chivalric poetry of the Han and the Six Dynasties. We now come to the T'ang poets. First of all, three short poems that describe knights-errant in a realistic and light-hearted way, by Wang Wei (699–759), Li Yi (*fl.* 727), and Tu Fu (712–70) respectively:

Song of Unruly Youths

At New Town,[2] good wine costs ten thousand cash a gallon;

[1] See above, p. 61.

[2] Hsin Feng, or New Feng, a town built by the first Emperor of Han near the capital Ch'ang-an to resemble his native town of Feng, for which his father had grown homesick.

From the old capital[1] come many young wandering knights.
When congenial spirits meet, they drink to each other,
Tying their horses to the drooping willows by the tall tavern's side.

Song of the Unruly Youth

A jade-handled sword across his knees,
A golden goblet drained on horseback.
At morn he wanders on the Mao-ling road,
At night he sleeps in the phoenix-city.[2]
Since the powerful officials are full of suspicion,
'Please don't bother to ask my name!'

Song of the Unruly Youth

Who is that fair-complexioned young man on horseback?
He dismounts beneath the steps and comes in to sit on the couch.
Very rude and overbearing, he does not tell his name,
But points at the silver jugs and demands to taste the wine therein.

A more serious treatment of the theme of knight-errantry is given by Kao Shih (700?–65), who was a man of heroic temperament and held high military posts. He deplores the decline of true chivalry and wistfully recalls the ancient knights and their patrons:

Song of the Unruly Youth of Han-tan

South of the city of Han-tan there is a wandering knight,
Who is proud of having been born and bred in Han-tan.
After a thousand games with huge stakes, he's still rich;
Having wreaked vengeance in several places, he has not died.
Everyday his home is full of noisy song and laughter,
Outside his door carriages and horses gather as thick as clouds.
Yet he does not know whom he can trust with all his heart,
Which makes him recall and wish for the Prince of P'ing-yuan.[3]
Don't you see
Nowadays men are shallow in friendship:
When gold is all spent, then friends grow scarce.
Sighing over this, he declined to see his old friends,

[1] The original has Hsien-yang, the former capital of Ch'in. I have changed it to 'old capital' to contrast with 'New Town'.

[2] The capital.

[3] One of the four feudal princes who kept many knights. See above, p. 16. Note the particular appropriateness of mentioning this prince, since he came from the state of Chao, of which Han-tan was the capital.

And now he asks for nothing more from the world of today.
He just drinks good wine in the company of unruly youths,
And goes shooting and hunting with them over the western hills.

It is significant that Kao Shih chose to write on a youth of Han-tan, capital of the ancient kingdom of Chao, instead of a youth of the contemporary capital Ch'ang-an. Since Chao is especially famous for its brave and blunt knights-errant, Han-tan represents the old tradition of chivalry, in contrast to the dandyism of Ch'ang-an. Moreover, Han-tan is not far from Kao's native prefecture of Po-hai (both being in the modern province of Hopei), so that even if it may be going too far to regard this poem as a self-portrait, it is certainly not too fanciful to see in it an expression of the poet's own personality.

Among all T'ang poets, Li Po, once a knight-errant himself,[1] is the one who has written most enthusiastically about chivalry, as may be expected. This is how Li Po describes a knight-errant:

Song of the Knight-errant

The man from Chao wears a tasselled hat,
And a curved knife as bright as frost or snow.
His silver saddle shines on his white steed
On which he rides as fast as a shooting star.
He would kill a man every ten paces
And go on for a thousand miles without stop.
After the event, he dusts his clothes and leaves,
To hide in secret his person and his name.

The first line is derived from the philosophical work, the *Chuang Tzŭ*: 'The Crown Prince of Chao said, "All the swordsmen that the King has seen have dishevelled hair and wear hats with rough tassels."' So are lines 5 and 6, which are taken almost verbatim from the *Chuang Tzŭ*. However, in the original passage the speaker is boasting that his sword is so sharp and strong that even if one killed a man every ten paces with it, after travelling a thousand miles it would still be as good as new, while in the present poem Li Po means that the knight-errant would kill a man every ten paces during a thousand-mile journey without bothering to stop. Thus, the emphasis in the original passage is on the durability of the sword, and in the poem, on the daring and ruthlessness of the man.

[1] See above, p. 46.

After briefly recounting the deeds of Hou Ying and Chu Hai, the two knights who helped the Prince of Hsin-ling,[1] the poet concludes:

> Though they're dead, their chivalrous bones smell sweet,[2]
> They can compare with any heroes in the world.
> Who can spend his life collating books
> And writing on metaphysics till his hair grows white?

Here the poet alludes with contempt to Yang Hsiung (53 B.C.–A.D. 18), who collated books at the T'ien Lu Pavilion and wrote the *Classic of Metaphysics* (*T'ai-hsüan Ching*).

In another poem called *Let Us Go Hunting*, Li Po again says:

> It is better to be a knight-errant than a scholar;
> What is the good of teaching the Classics till your hair grows white?

The last line literally says, 'What is the good of letting down the curtain till your hair grows white?', alluding to the scholar Tung Chung-shu (*c.* 175–105 B.C.), who lectured on the Confucian Classics with a curtain hanging before him so that many of his students never saw his face. Li Po's contempt for Confucian scholars and even sages is also shown in the following poem:

Song of the Unruly Youth

> A young man whose ambitions reach the clouds
> Carries a cross-bow beside the Chang Terrace.[3]
> While horsemen make way for him on all sides,
> He rides off, as fast as a shooting star.
> His golden pellets bring down flying birds,
> At night he enters a rich mansion to sleep.
> —What kind of men were Yi and Ch'i
> That they starved themselves on the Western Hill?

The last two lines allude to Po-yi and Shu-ch'i, two brothers who remained loyal to the fallen Shang dynasty after the establishment of the Chou (1111 B.C.) and starved themselves to death on the Shou-yang Hill (Western Hill). They are usually held up as shining examples of moral integrity, but Li Po thinks them merely silly.

Similar sentiments are expressed in another of Li Po's poems:

[1] See above, pp. 18–22.
[2] Compare Chang Hua's poem on p. 59.
[3] Either the palace or the gate so called, both in Ch'ang-an.

Song of the Unruly Youth

Don't you see
The young wandering knight from south of the river Huai
Plays polo[1] and hunts by day, and gambles by night?
He loses millions at dice without regret,
And thinks nothing of going a thousand miles to avenge a wrong.
The young wandering knight passes in triumph:
Dressed from head to foot in rich silk and gauze,
Followed by noisy singing girls as beautiful as orchids.
Everywhere he goes, music and songs are heard.
He tells himself not to grow arrogant and proud;
Many another knight he has kept within his hall.
Fine saddles, fine horses, he gave to any who begged;
Ten thousand, five thousand, he squandered in a moment on wine.
He spent his loving thoughts on those who appreciated him,
And did not grudge to use his gold to plant peaches and plums.
Several springs have passed since the peaches and plums were planted,
Each time the blossoms fall, each time they are renewed.
Prefects and mayors come to pay him respects;
Princes and lords are all his social equals.
A man should enjoy himself during his lifetime;
Why stick to books and suffer want and sickness?
A man should seek honours during his lifetime;
Why stick to principles and suffer wind and dust?
Half the richly clad officials are fighting men,
While poor scholars live among woods and springs.
You may have a family tree with roots a thousand feet deep,
But it's not as good as having many friends now.
You may have relatives all over the imperial city,
But it's not as good as being rich and noble yourself.
Let us take the wealth and honours that lie before our eyes!
What's the use of eternal fame after death?

This poem, written in a colloquial style with a loose rhythm, is not among Li Po's better works. Indeed, it has been suspected that the last twelve lines are not by him. However, the sentiments expressed here are similar to those in Li Po's other poems, and this one may be regarded as another illustration of his attitude towards knight-errantry.

[1] Polo was extremely popular among the aristocracy in T'ang times.

The last poem by Li Po I shall translate is in a lighter vein:

Song of Unruly Youths

The young men from the Five Mounds roam by the Gold Exchange,
Their silver-saddled white horses gallop in the spring breeze.
Having trod the fallen flowers, where should they go?
Amid laughter they enter a tavern with a pretty serving maid.

In the opening line, the 'Five Mounds' (Wu-ling) refer to five imperial mausoleums near Ch'ang-an, conventionally associated with wandering knights, and the 'Gold Exchange' refers to a section of the capital where many foreigners resided. In the last line, the original has '*hu chi*' or 'barbarian maid', a term applied to Central Asian girls who sold wine in China. But I doubt if Li Po means specifically a foreign girl: perhaps he is using the phrase merely as a conventional description of a pretty serving maid in a tavern. The term already occurs, for instance, in a song by Hsin Yen-nien of the Han dynasty.

In Li Po's collected works, there are other poems on knight-errantry, but they are so allusive as to be hardly translatable. On the whole, his chivalric poems reflect more his own haughty and care-free nature than the true spirit of chivalry, the more altruistic aspects of which are conspicuously absent in his verse. Some of Li Po's chivalric poems (in the original, of course) have a fine lilt and a powerful drive, while others, such as the last but one poem given above, are carelessly written and almost crude. Seldom does the poet exhibit in these poems the inspired loftiness and divine madness that mark his best works.

In the hands of some later T'ang poets whose style shows certain resemblances to that of the Metaphysical Poets in English, the theme of knight-errantry is developed with subtlety and originality. For instance, here is one by Meng Chiao (751–814):

Song of the Knight-errant

The brave knight is hard and resolved by nature,
Like fire that cracks a stone within its flames.
Fain would he kill without looking back,
And part from life as if just for a while.
How could he know eyes have tears to flow,
Or let his hair grow white upon his head?
All his life there's no one to repay:
His sword lies idle for a hundred months.

This poem is remarkable not only for its striking conceits but also for its irony: the knight would willingly give his life for someone who appreciates him, but all his life no one has ever shown him such appreciation and kindness as to call for self-sacrifice. This irony is brought home in the last line, where the phrase 'a hundred months' is used, I believe, not just for its novelty but to suggest that the knight has been impatiently counting the months go by, whereas if the poet had written 'for years', it would not have created the same effect. It is possible that the poem reveals Meng Chiao's own feeling of lack of appreciation. In any case, it can be taken as a fine illustration of the fate of those people, the tragedy with whom is, as Mr. E. M. Forster remarked somewhere, not that they are taken unprepared but that they are prepared but never taken.

In contrast to the sense of waste and frustration in the above poem, the next one by Chia Tao (777–841) expresses eagerness for action:

The Swordsman

For ten years I have been polishing this sword;
Its frosty edge has never been put to the test.
Now I am holding it and showing it to you, sir:
Is there anyone suffering from injustice?

This seems to me to sum up the spirit of knight-errantry in four lines. At the same time, one can also take it as a reflection of the desire of all those who have prepared themselves for years to put their abilities to the test for some just cause.

While poets of the T'ang period wrote enthusiastically about knight-errantry, those of the Sung period rarely touched the subject. The works of such major Sung poets as Ou-yang Hsiu, Su Shih, Wang An-shih, and Huang T'ing-chien contain hardly any chivalric poems.[1] The only Sung poet of importance who seems to have been attracted by this theme is the patriotic Lu Yu (1125–1210), whose life-ambition, destined never to be fulfilled, was to help to drive out the Tartars and restore north China to the Sung. Here is one of his chivalric poems:

[1] Su Shih wrote a poem on the tomb of the knight-errant Chu Hai, but it deals with the vicissitudes of posthumous fame rather than with chivalry.

Song of the Swordsman

No one in the world understands swords now,
The T'ai-o lies among common steel.
The rare treasure is discarded in the mud,
Yet its brilliance will never fade away.
One day it will kill a big whale
And turn the sea red for three months.
Who can tell what changes may come to it,
Hidden or revealed between heaven and earth?
Our country has not yet defeated the barbarians,
All subjects share this common duty.
Travelling unknown over mountains and seas,
Late in the year one obtains a swordsman.
High-spirited with wine, he takes out a dagger,
Whose white blade is bright as frost or snow.
At midnight he returns, having wrought revenge,
His dagger stained and smelling of blood.
How can a petty feud be worth bothering about?
We should all be angry about the great shame.
Though a subject's position is low and humble,
A subject will yield his person to be slaughtered.
I swear to cut off the barbarians' heads
And offer them to the imperial palace, bowing twice,
Then run away and change my name
To eat jade shreds among the hills.

The poet compares himself to the precious sword T'ai-o lying hidden, and hopes for the day when he will be able to avenge national wrongs. The first three lines lament his fate; line 4 shows his resolution not to give up; lines 5 and 6, with their almost Shakespearean imagery, express his wishful thinking; and lines 7 and 8 reveal the poet's attempt to console himself: one never knows what may happen. He then directly announces his ambition to defeat the Tartars and restore Chinese glory. Further, he contrasts private feuds with national struggles, and makes the personal loyalty and bravery of knights-errant appear insignificant beside patriotism. In the last two lines, he imagines himself adopting the conventional behaviour of a knight-errant 'after the event': to run away, disguise his name, and try to cultivate immortality as a Taoist recluse.

In another poem Lu Yu again tells himself not to complain of lack of opportunity but to wait for the time when he will be able to fulfil his ambitions:

Song of the Precious Sword

A recluse lies pillowed on his precious sword,
Which makes a cracking noise during the night.
They say a sword can turn into a dragon;
He almost fears it will raise wind and thunder,
Or else, indignant at the barbarians roaming unchecked,
It wishes to go on a long expedition.
He takes some wine and pours a libation to the sword:
'A rare treasure should hide its light and form.
It is not that no one appreciates you;
When the time comes, you will be free.
There is more than enough room in the sheath,
Why do you cry and complain of injustice?'

Alas, Lu Yu's dreams never came true. In a poem entitled *Drinking in a Village*, he writes,

In my youth I loved chivalry,
At the sight of wine, my spirits rose higher,

and then contrasts his chivalrous youth with his disappointed old age. Alone among Sung poets, Lu Yu found knight-errantry congenial, although he transformed it to high-minded patriotism.

Apart from Lu Yu, one other Sung poet, Ch'ao Ch'ung-chih (early twelfth century) also wrote on chivalry:

Song of the Eastern Gate
Presented to Ch'in Yi-chung

Don't you see
The man from the Eastern Gate has the spirit of Hou Ying;
He killed someone in broad daylight in the dusty market-place.
The Metropolitan Prefect knew his name but dared not arrest him,
While he leant his sword against the sky on Mount K'ung-t'ung.
He made friends with three or four like-minded men,
Together they rode freely on their piebald horses.
Looking up to heaven, he laughed and made light of all things,
Then went into his house and received guests no more.
Yet his line prospered and his descendants became officials at court.
Ah!

A man's name is weighty as a mountain, his life light as a leaf!
Let us touch the dragon's reverse scale and have no fear!
Even Hsiang-ju, who loved beauty all his life,
Heroically offended his king with blunt advice against hunting.

In the title and the opening lines the poet refers to Hou Ying, who was keeper of the Eastern Gate.[1] In line 5, the expression 'leant his sword against the sky' is derived from a piece called *Hyperboles* (*Ta-yen Fu*) attributed to Sung Yü (*c.* 290–223 B.C.), containing the line, 'The long sword lies straight and leans against the sky.' The same line also alludes to a passage in the *Chuang Tzŭ* describing how the mythical Yellow Emperor went to Mount K'ung-t'ung to enquire about the *Tao.* Line 10 literally runs, 'His family rose and his descendants wore official insignia at the Bright Light Palace', alluding to the palace so named (Ming Kuang Kung), built by Emperor Wu of Han. Line 13 alludes to Han Fei Tzŭ's comparison of the King to the dragon that will kill when the reverse scale under its chin is touched.[2] The last two lines refer to the poet Ssŭ-ma Hsiang-ju (179–117 B.C.), who eloped with the rich widow Chuo Wen-chün and who wrote a memorial to the throne against hunting. The moral drawn by the poet, that one should not be afraid to offend one's sovereign, is somewhat irrelevant to the theme of chivalry.

The scarcity of chivalric poetry in Sung times is not surprising in view of the prevalent influence of Neo-Confucianism, with its puritanic moral outlook and its tendency towards metaphysical and epistemological speculations. On the whole, Sung poets were more prone to introspection and intellectualization than their T'ang predecessors, many of whom were extroverts and men of action.

In the poetry of the Yuan period, again we find little attention paid to chivalry. This may have been due to the oppression of the Mongol rulers. The following quatrain by Ku Ying (1310–69), who led a chivalrous life at the end of the period, is a rare specimen:

I wear a Confucian gown, a Buddhist hat, a Taoist's shoes;
Anywhere in the world, under a green hill, my bones may be buried.
If you ask where heroes formerly used to gather,
They rode by the Five Mounds[3] and in the streets of Lo-yang.

[1] See above, p. 18.
[2] See above, p. 26, footnote.
[3] See above, p. 67.

The lack of interest in knight-errantry in classical Sung and Yuan poetry does not mean no chivalric literature was produced during these periods. On the contrary, a chivalric tradition flourished in popular literature—in fiction and drama, as we shall see later.

In the Ming period, the theme of knight-errantry was revived in classical poetry. This revival does not necessarily reflect a resurgence of chivalry in contemporary society, but is largely the result of the conscious efforts of most Ming poets to imitate earlier poets and to 'restore the ancient style' (*fu ku*). They wrote songs in the style of the ancient *yueh-fu*,[1] and in so doing revived such titles as 'Song of the Knight-errant' and 'Song of Unruly Youths'. While some of these poets may have felt a genuine affinity for chivalry, the majority were inspired by the purely literary motive of imitating the ancient poets. Their poems are often stylistically hard to distinguish from earlier works, but there is often a lack of personal emotion.

The first example of Ming chivalric poetry is by Kao Ch'i (1336–74), a friend of the knight-errant Sung K'ê[2] and himself a man of spirit, who incurred the anger of the first Ming Emperor and was executed.[3] In this poem he emphasizes the true friendship among knights-errant in contrast to the insincerity and ingratitude of other men:

'Making Friends Among the Young Bloods'

If you want to make friends, make friends with a knight-errant,
He would lend his life for revenge without hesitation.
For a thousand pieces of gold he bought a sharp dagger
Which he caresses and swears to use for one who appreciates him.
    On a white horse, wearing a tasselled hat,
    He rides on and on, all by himself.
    At morn he roams by the northern gate of Lo,
    At eve he drinks at the eastern market of Ch'in.
    'I am moved by one word that you have said,
    And I'll not regret dying for you.'
Chu Chia once saved the life of General Chi;
T'ien Kuang at last repaid Prince Tan of Yen.
    Don't you see

[1] See above, p. 55, footnote.
[2] See above, p. 51.
[3] See F. W. Mote, *The Poet Kao Ch'i* (Princeton, 1962).

When the Marquis of Wei-ch'i was powerful he had many friends,
Everyone of whom received kindness from him,
But when he fell, who was there to be seen?
The guest house was covered all over with cobwebs.
  Now you see it's hard to make friends,
'The spirit of friendship that moves mountains' is but an empty phrase!
Some will not repay their king to whom they owe their livelihood,
Let alone a trivial favour done among wine cups!
To make friends, one need not always choose among the gentry;
When you're in need and knock on the door, who can be relied on to answer?
Among butchers and wine-sellers are often outstanding men:
Be careful not to look down on the man in the street!

This poem is written in a rather rambling style, with a loose structure. The title, as we have seen before, is a conventional one among *yueh-fu* songs and originated from a poem by Ts'ao Chih.[1] The description of the knight-errant as wearing a tasselled hat in line 5 is derived from the *Chuang Tzŭ*, possibly via Li Po;[2] the allusions to Chu Chia and T'ien Kuang are well known.[3] In line 14, the poet refers to Tou Ying, Marquis of Wei-ch'i (*ob.* 131 B.C.), who was a cousin of the Empress during the reign of Emperor Wen of Han. In line 23, he alludes to Yuan Yang's remark that in an emergency only the knights-errant Chü Meng and Chi Hsin could be relied on to answer the door.[4] These allusions give the whole poem a tone of conventionality.

The next example, by Li Meng-yang (1472–1529), is even more conventional:

Song of the Knight-errant

Yu and Ping are the lands of heroic knights,
Yen and Chao are known for tragic songs.
For a thousand pieces of gold he bought a steed;
Over ten thousand miles he travelled to Chiao-ho.
Ministers of state presented him with a precious sword,
The King bestowed on him a jade spear.
He gave his life to save the country from disaster,
And often caused the sea to calm its waves.

[1] See above, p. 55 and p. 59.
[2] See above, p. 64.
[3] See above, pp. 35, 27–8.
[4] See above, p. 37.

In the opening lines, the poet refers to the traditional homes of knights-errant—the ancient prefectures of Yu and Ping, or the kingdoms of Yen and Chao. The second line contains a specific allusion to Han Yü's well-known valediction to a friend beginning with the sentence, 'Yen and Chao were known in ancient times for their knights who sang heroic, tragic songs.' In line 4, Li Meng-yang refers to Chiao-ho, a place in Chinese Turkestan often mentioned in poetry signifying a remote frontier. The last line contains an idiomatic expression meaning to make peace prevail.

A more interesting poem is the following one by Ho Ching-ming (1483–1521), describing a knight's desire to repay his patron's kindness and his contempt for wealth:

Song of the Knight-errant

Every morning he enters his patron's door,
Every evening he enters his patron's door.
He wishes to kill his patron's enemy to repay his patron's favour.
His patron hangs up lanterns and holds a big banquet at night,
Toasts him with a thousand pieces of gold, bids him farewell with a hundred.
Over the autumn hall dew is falling while the moon is high;
He rises and looks around, sees the steed in the stable,
And the precious sword in its sheath.
Pulling out the sword and mounting the steed, he gallops forth;
Discarding his patron's gold, he leaves without looking back.

The original is written in a language deliberately simple and awkward, so as to achieve an effect of archaic quaintness. This effect is enhanced by the conscious repetition of certain words and the rugged rhythm produced by the irregular length of the lines. The poem is also remarkable for its total freedom from allusions, which makes a refreshing change.

Finally, a poem by Hsü Wei (1521–93), better known as Hsü Wen-ch'ang, an eccentric poet, dramatist, and painter, who was accused of having murdered his third wife and said to have gone mad and attempted suicide:

The Knight-errant

Making friends among the young bloods,
How proud and high-spirited is he!

Like swallows' tails are his jagged arrows;[1]
A willow leaf is his pear-blossom spear.[2]
To lament over the tomb of Master Hou,
He rides a donkey and enters Ta-liang.

This poem is chiefly interesting because of the original descriptions in the two middle lines: the arrows like swallows' tails and the spear as light and lively as a willow leaf. The 'pear-blossom spear' refers to a special way of using this weapon, not a particular kind of spear.[2] The allusion to Hou Ying in the last two lines is merely conventional. The poem is casual but has a personal style.

During the Ch'ing dynasty (1644–1911) chivalric poetry declined again. This not only coincided with the decline of knight-errantry in real life, but was probably also due to the literary persecutions of the Manchu emperors. Poets had good reasons to avoid such an obviously risky theme as knight-errantry, which could easily be regarded as seditious. When they did touch on this subject, they only produced literary exercises, such as the *In Imitation of 'The White Steed'* by Wang Shih-chen (1634–1711) and the poems on the Prince of Hsin-ling and on Ching K'o by Yuan Mei (1716–98).

POEMS ON HISTORICAL KNIGHTS

The four feudal lords who retained knights, especially the Prince of Hsin-ling, together with the two knights who helped him, Hou Ying and Chu Hai, often drew comments from poets. Chang Hua, whose two other songs on knights-errant we have seen,[3] wrote on the four princes thus:

The Knights-errant

The four elegant young noble princes
Are praised by this dusty world for their worth.
Like dragons and tigers engaged in mortal strife,
The Seven Kingdoms fought one another for power.
Each prince kept three thousand guests
Among whom were many heroic men.

[1] In the original, this line also contains the word *tz'ŭ-ku*, a kind of water plant with leaves like swallows' tails. Since there is no English word for it and since the point is redundant, I have omitted it in the translation.

[2] See Additional Note 7.

[3] See above, pp. 58–9.

After giving a brief summary of each prince's deeds, the poet goes on to say:

> Excellent indeed are the knights-errant!
> Hard to surpass the four noble lords!

But he ends rather smugly:

> But I have a taste different from all this:
> I love the ancients and follow Old P'eng.

Here he is quoting Confucius and implying that he, like the Master, also follows the ancients and has no use for knights-errant, excellent men as they are in their own way.

Wang Wei, whose *Song of Unruly Youths* we have seen,[1] also wrote on the Prince of Hsin-ling and the two knights who aided him. Although Wang Wei is generally known for his Nature poems which reveal a Buddhist attitude to life, in this poem he shows he is capable of sympathetic understanding of knight-errantry:

Song of the Eastern Gate

> The Seven Kingdoms had not yet proved their strength or weakness;
> One after another, cities were sacked and generals killed.
> The troops of Ch'in besieged Han-tan harder and harder;
> The King of Wei refused to rescue the Prince of P'ing-yuan.
> 'His Highness stopped his four-horsed coach for my sake;
> Holding the reins respectfully, he looked ever humbler.
> My friend Chu Hai is one who wields the butcher's knife,
> And I, Hou Ying, am merely a keeper of the Eastern Gate.'
> Not only did he generously offer an amazing plan,
> But, moved by feelings, he even repaid the Prince with his life.
> Looking windward he cut his throat to bid His Highness adieu,
> For what should an old man of seventy seek to gain?

Several lines of this poem are taken straight from the biography of the Prince in the *Records of the Historiographer*,[2] but the poet has turned them skilfully into fine verse. His use of his historical source is comparable to Shakespeare's use of North's translation of Plutarch in *Antony and Cleopatra*. The last line is taken from the *History of the Chin Dynasty*, but again Wang Wei has skilfully woven the quotation into the poetic texture of his song, so that one is hardly aware that it is a quotation.

[1] See above, pp. 62–3.
[2] See above, p. 19.

Another poem on the subject is by Li Meng-yang, one of whose poems has been given above.[1] This is a farewell poem to an unnamed friend:

Sending off Someone to Nan-chün

Chu Hai, who wielded a knife, was of humble origin,
And a gate-keeper was the white-haired Hou Ying.
Their spirit did not rise because of a thousand pieces of gold,
But because to them a promise was weighty as a mountain.

Presumably the friend that the poet was seeing off was a man of humble origin and chivalric temperament; otherwise there would have been little point in writing such a poem.

Poems on the knight-errant Ching K'o[2] are even more numerous than those on Hou Ying. This one by Juan Yü (*ob.* A.D. 212) confines itself to description:

On History

Prince Tan retained brave knights,
Ching K'o was treated as an honoured guest.
Carrying the map that concealed the fatal dagger,
He drove westward to the land of Ch'in.
In a plain carriage drawn by white horses[3]
The Prince came to send him off on River Yi.
Chien-li sang while playing the zither,
Whose mournful notes moved the passers-by.
All those present joined together in lament;
Their sighs rose like clouds in the azure sky.

Another poet, Tso Ssŭ (250?–305?), emphasizes the knight's contempt for wealth and rank:

On History

Ching K'o drank at the market-place in Yen;
His spirit rose even higher with wine.
Echoing Chien-li, he sang a sad song,
As if no one else had been around.
Though he lacks a true knight's virtue,
Few can compare with him in this world.
He gazed afar over the Four Seas;

[1] See above, pp. 73–4.
[2] See above, p. 25.
[3] White is the colour of mourning.

What did he care for the powerful and the rich?
Though the noble thought themselves noble,
He looked down on them like dirt or dust;
Though the lowly thought themselves lowly,
He valued them like thousands of pounds of gold.

Another poem on Ching K'o is by T'ao Ch'ien, also called T'ao Yuan-ming (365–427), who is generally known for his poems on Nature and on wine, but who reveals a different aspect of his character here:

On Ching K'o

Prince Tan excelled in retaining knights;
His aim was vengeance on the powerful Ying.[1]
He chose one man out of a hundred
And late in the year obtained Master Ching.
A gentleman dies for one who appreciates him;[2]
Holding a sword, he left the capital of Yen.
White horses neighing on the wide road,
Heroically the prince came to see him off.
Their angry hair pushed up their tall hats,
Their fierce spirit moved the long tassels.
At the farewell banquet on River Yi
The seats were filled with outstanding men.
Chien-li played the zither sadly,
Sung Yi[3] raised his voice and sang.
Whistle, whistle, the sorrowful wind blew;
Lightly, lightly, cold ripples arose.
The *Shang* mode[4] brought tears to all,
The *Yü* tune aroused the brave knight.
He knew that he would never return again,
But would leave his name behind for ever.
He boarded his coach without glancing back,

[1] The surname of the King of Ch'in.

[2] This line is paraphrased from the ancient saying, 'A knight (*shih*) dies for one who appreciates him; a woman beautifies herself for one who loves her.'

[3] Another knight retained by Prince Tan. His name is not mentioned in the *Records of the Historiographer* but occurs in the *Huai-nan Tzŭ* and the *Yen Tan Tzŭ*. Cf. below, p. 84.

[4] This differs from the *Records of the Historiographer*, where Ching K'o is said to have sung in the *Pien Chih* mode first. (See above, p. 31). The *Shang* mode has been identified with the Mixo-Lydian. (J. H. Levis, *op. cit.*, p. 73).

And drove the canopied carriage to the Court of Ch'in.
He plunged forward over ten thousand miles,
Winding his way past a thousand towns.
When the map ended, the event occurred:
The powerful King was startled and shook in fear.
Alas, his swordsmanship was not perfect,[1]
And so the great enterprise failed!
Though this man is dead and gone,
His passion will remain for a thousand years.

Although this poem is to some extent based on the one by Juan Yü given above, it develops the theme further and shows genuine emotion. Moreover, it may be regarded as a veiled expression of the poet's sorrow over the fall of the Chin dynasty and his wish for a brave knight to assassinate the usurper. Since T'ao Ch'ien remained loyal to the Chin and refused to take public office after its fall, his life as a recluse was due to circumstances as much as to personal inclination. Thus, the other-worldly feelings in many of his poems, though they no doubt reflect his genuine philosophic views, are partly the result of enforced retirement, while the more active side of his nature is revealed in the present poem. The Neo-Confucian philosopher Chu Hsi (1130–1200) displayed considerable critical insight when he commented on this poem in a colloquial note: 'People all say that T'ao Yuan-ming's poetry is calm and delicate, but it seems to me he is really heroic and free, only he is heroic and free in a way you don't notice. Where he shows his true colours is in the poem on Ching K'o: how can a calm and delicate person say such things?'

Perhaps the best known poem on Ching K'o is the quatrain by Lo Pin-wang (*fl.* 680):

Seeing Someone off on River Yi

Here he parted from Prince Tan of Yen;
The brave knight's hair pushed up his hat.
The man of that time is dead and gone,
Today, the water of the river is cold still.

The popularity of this poem is probably due to its extremely simple yet effective language, as well as its use of the well-tried method of contrasting the apparently abiding features of Nature with the vicissitudes of human history.

[1] See above, p. 34.

The Knight-Errant in Poetry

Ho Ching-ming, whose 'Song of the Knight-errant' we have already read,[1] deals with the subject of Ching K'o's adventure from a rather unusual angle: he shows little sympathy for the knight or Prince Tan, treats T'ien Kuang's suicide in a cavalier fashion, but singles out General Fan for lament:

Song of the River Yi

The cold evening wind blew over the River Yi;
Chien-li played the zither while Master Ching sang.
Dressed in white, his friends wept as he took to the road;
At sunset he boarded his coach and left without looking back.
The King of Ch'in unfolded the map in his throne hall,
And while Wu-yang changed colour and dared not cry,
Ching K'o threw the dagger which hit the bronze pillar.[2]
The attempt failed: in vain did he squat there and curse.
Alas,
Prince Tan lacked wisdom and deserved to lose his life,
T'ien Kuang's suicide is not worth talking about,
But what a pity that General Fan died all for nothing!

The poems translated above include some of the best as well as some of the most typical chivalric poems in Chinese. Many of these are variations on given themes: they are comparable to new arrangements of folk songs. Their merit often lies in the dexterity with which the poets made use of historical sources rather than in original ideas, and their effect largely depends on rhythm, rhyme, and other auditory aspects of verse, which naturally cannot be reproduced in translation. While my translations cannot hope to do justice to the original poems, they may at least call attention to the existence of chivalric poetry in Chinese.

[1] See above, p. 74.

[2] See Additional Note 5.

3

FROM FACT TO FICTION

The dramatic careers and colourful personalities of the knights-errant not unnaturally gave rise to legends, which exaggerated their exploits and sometimes credited them with supernatural powers. In this way, knight-errantry passed from the realm of fact to that of fiction. Side by side with chivalric tales based on history, those about purely fictitious heroes also came to be written, with even more fantastic incidents. Together, the two kinds of tales form an important branch of Chinese fiction.

Chivalric tales flourished for the first time towards the end of the T'ang dynasty, in the ninth century A.D., though their prototypes can be traced back many centuries earlier.[1] These tales were written by literary men, in classical prose. At the same time chivalric tales and ballads also existed in an oral tradition. The texts of these were written by men of little learning, in colloquial or semi-colloquial prose, often mixed with doggerel verse. Some ballads were entirely in verse. During the Sung dynasty (960–1279) chivalry was one of the main subjects of oral story-telling. The texts used by the story-tellers were in the colloquial language of the day, interspersed with verse. Some of these formed the nuclei of long prose romances of the Yuan (1280–1368) and Ming (1368–1644) periods. Since the seventeenth century, new types of chivalric fiction have developed and continued to be popular to the present day.

Tales of chivalry are not to be confused with popularizations of history such as the famous *Romance of the Three Kingdoms* (*San-kuo-chih Yen-yi*). Although the two kinds of fiction may overlap in subject matter, certain differences between them exist. In chivalric tales the knights-errant act as individuals and usually

[1] See below, p. 82.

fight single-handed; in historical romances the heroes are professional warriors who lead armies in battle. In the former our attention is focused on the personal courage and loyalty of the knights; in the latter the main interest lies in battles and stratagems. Of course, a knight may also fight in an army occasionally, while a general may also exhibit great personal bravery, but the basic difference in emphasis remains.

Chivalric tales also differ from tales of purely supernatural events such as *Pilgrimage to the West* (*Hsi-yu Chi*, known to English-speaking readers as *Monkey*) and *Investiture of the Gods* (*Feng-shen Yen-yi*). The former may contain an element of the supernatural, but most of them do not strain credulousness too far; the latter make no pretence at credibility. Also, the former are concerned with justice or revenge, the latter generally not.

In short, chivalric tales occupy an intermediate position between popularizations of history on the one hand and tales of the miraculous on the other. They dwell in a twilight region where fact mingles with fancy and the commonplace with the marvellous. A writer may describe the superhuman powers of a knight in the same matter-of-fact way that he describes, say, the interior of a house, without any apparent feeling of incongruity. This naïvety, genuine or assumed, often has a disarming effect on the reader and induces a 'willing suspension of disbelief'.

CHIVALRIC TALES IN CLASSICAL PROSE

1. *Prototypes*

Prince Tan of Yen

The earliest fictionalized account of a historical event involving knights-errant is probably the *Yen Tan Tzŭ*, or *Prince Tan of Yen*,[1] a short book believed by some to be a genuine work of the third century B.C. compiled by Prince Tan's followers, and by others to be a forgery of the sixth century A.D. Even if we accept the latter (and later) date, it would still be earlier than most other chivalric tales.

The book deals with the life of Prince Tan of Yen, together with the deeds of the knights-errant T'ien Kuang and Ching K'o. The story agrees in outline with the account given in the *Records*

[1] There is an English version by Cheng Lin entitled *Prince Dan of Yann* (*sic.*, Shanghai, 1946) which I have not seen.

of the Historiographer,[1] but there are certain differences and additions, which I will describe below.

The tale begins by telling how the King of Ch'in refused to allow Prince Tan to go home, saying that permission would only be given if a crow should have a white head and a horse should grow horns. Prince Tan looked up to heaven and sighed, whereupon a crow's head did turn white and a horse did grow horns, and the King was obliged to let him go. Then the King set a trap for Prince Tan under a bridge, but when the latter arrived at the spot, the trap did not work. When the Prince reached the frontier gate, it was still night, too early for the gate to open. So he imitated a cock's crow, and all the cocks in the neighbourhood began to crow, which led the gate-keeper into thinking it was dawn so that he opened the gate.

The story goes on to tell how the Prince sought revenge on the King of Ch'in. He wrote a letter to his tutor Chü Wu (instead of asking the latter's advice personally, as in the *Records of the Historiographer*), expressing his desire for a brave knight to go and assassinate the King of Ch'in. In his reply, Chü Wu advised the Prince against this. The Prince was displeased and summoned Chü to his presence for further discussion. This led to Chü's recommendation of the old knight T'ien Kuang.

The description of the Prince's meeting with T'ien Kuang is similar to that in the historical work, but in greater detail. Moreover, in the tale, after the meeting T'ien was housed as an honoured guest, and it was only three months later that he said he was too old for the mission and recommended Ching K'o (an unnecessary delay not found in the historical work). In doing so, he made some interesting observations on various knights: 'I have been observing the knights Your Highness retains; none of them is suitable for this mission. Hsia Fu is one who has "courage in the blood": his face turns red when he is angry. Sung Yi is one who has "courage in the veins": his face turns blue when he is angry. [Ch'in] Wu-yang is one who has "courage in the bones": his face turns white when he is angry. Among all those I know, only Ching K'o has "courage of the spirit": he does not change colour when he is angry.' After the Prince warned T'ien Kuang not to reveal the secret, the latter committed suicide by swallowing his tongue (presumably after having cut or bitten it off first, a lurid

[1] See above, pp. 25–33.

detail not found in the *Records of the Historiographer*, where he simply cut his throat).

Prince Tan's efforts to please Ching K'o arc much elaborated upon in the tale. One day, Ching casually picked up a tile to throw at a tortoise, whereupon the Prince ordered an attendant to offer the knight a plate full of pieces of gold with which to hit the tortoise. Another day, when Prince Tan and Ching K'o were riding together, the latter remarked, 'I have heard that the liver of a fine horse tastes good.' The Prince at once killed his fine steed and offered its liver to Ching. On yet another occasion, Ching K'o praised the beautiful hands of a girl playing the zither (*ch'in*), and the Prince offered her to him. 'It is only her hands that I admire,' said Ching. Thereupon the Prince ordered the unfortunate girl's hands to be cut off, and presented them to the knight on a jade plate!

The tale continues along similar lines to the biography of Ching K'o in the *Records of the Historiographer*, till it comes to the farewell party on the river Yi. Here it mentions the name of Sung Yi as one who echoed Ching K'o with a song. It further relates an incident on the way—Ching K'o quarrelled with a butcher while buying meat, but stopped Ch'in Wu-yang from attacking the butcher.

The climax of the story, Ching K'o's attempt to assassinate the King of Ch'in, also contains additional details. First, the knight held the King by the sleeve and reproached him for his tyranny. Then the King said, 'As things stand today, I can only let you do what you will. But allow me to listen to the zither before I die.' So he summoned a lady to play the zither, and the words of the tune she played ran as follows:

> A singlet of thin silk can be broken;
> A screen eight feet high can be jumped over;
> A long sword with a handle can be unsheathed from the back.

Now Ching K'o did not understand music and failed to see the significance, but the King took the hint and unsheathed his sword by pushing it to his back. Thereupon he rose and ran around the screen, while Ching K'o threw his dagger at the King. It hurt the King's ear and then embedded itself in a bronze pillar, striking fire. The King then broke Ching K'o's hands and the knight squatted on the floor and cursed. (The incident about the zither, which does not occur in the historical work, is far-fetched, and the remark that Ching K'o did not understand music rather contradicts earlier references to his singing.)

At this point the tale ends, somewhat abruptly. It is possible that there were further parts of the tale now lost.

Compared with the biography of Ching K'o in the *Records of the Historiographer* translated earlier in this volume, the tale *Prince Tan of Yen* is inferior. Most of the additional incidents in the tale are either incredible or trivial, if not downright absurd. However, the prose style is not totally unlike that of the historical work—concise, plain, and straightforward. Compared with later chivalric tales in classical prose, this one is less elaborate and shows less conscious artistry.

The Maiden of Yueh

This story occurs in the *Annals of the Kingdoms of Wu and Yueh* (*Wu Yueh Ch'un-ch'iu*) by Chao Yeh (first century A.D.), a book which, despite its title, contains more fiction than history. It runs as follows:

The King of Yueh, Kou-chien, asked his minister Fan Li about the art of war. Fan replied that there was a maiden in Yueh famous for her swordsmanship and advised the King to consult her. The King therefore sent for the maiden. On her way to see the King, she met an old man who said his name was Yuan (which in Chinese puns on the word for 'ape'). He said to her, 'I hear you excel in swordsmanship. I would like to see it.' She replied. 'I dare not conceal anything from you. You may test me in any way you like.' So the old man plucked some bamboo twigs and threw them at her, but she caught them all before they touched the ground. Thereupon the old man flew up a tree and became a white ape (*yuan*).

When the maiden saw the King, the latter asked her about swordsmanship. She replied, 'I grew up in a deep forest, in the wilderness away from men. I have not studied properly and I am unknown to the feudal lords. However, I am fond of swordsmanship and I have practised incessantly. I did not receive it from anyone; I just suddenly got it.'[1] When the King pressed her further, she replied that the way of swordsmanship was very subtle

[1] It is interesting to note that this last remark was quoted by a literary critic as an analogy to poetic inspiration. See *The Art of Chinese Poetry*, p. 85.

yet easy, its meaning very obscure and profound; that it involved the principles of *yin* and *yang* (the passive or feminine and the active or masculine principles of all life); and that a good swordsman should appear perfectly calm like a fine lady, but capable of quick action like a surprised tiger. The King then gave her the title, 'The Maiden of Yueh', and asked her to instruct his troops. No one could surpass her in swordsmanship at that time.

This story, with its heroine and its supernatural element, may be regarded as a forerunner of the tales about chivalrous ladies with supernatural powers of the T'ang period.

2. *Chivalric tales of the T'ang period*

Chivalric tales in classical prose attained the height of their literary excellence during the last decades of the T'ang period (*c.* 850–900). Together with other kinds of tales written in a similar style, they are known as *ch'uan-ch'i*, 'conveying the extraordinary', a term which has several other meanings.[1] Various factors contributed to the making and the popularity of these chivalric tales. First, the political situation of China at that time was such as to encourage wishful thinking on the part of writers and readers for knights-errant to redress wrongs. The empire was then dominated by military governors who fought and intrigued against each other while oppressing the common people. Sometimes they attempted to assassinate their rivals, while retaining swordsmen to guard their own lives. Thus, their activities not only gave an impetus to writers of chivalric tales but also provided the background of some of the stories, such as the story of Hung-hsien.[2] Secondly, current Buddhist tales, with their emphasis on the supernatural, stimulated the imagination of writers and provided them with material for stories with an exotic background. Thirdly, the revival of 'Ancient Prose' (*ku-wen*, the straightforward and vigorous prose used by writers of the Han and earlier periods, in contradistinction to the ornate and artificial 'Parallel Prose' or *p'ien-wen* that had been fashionable for several centuries by then) enabled writers to tell stories in a language elegant and concise, yet sufficiently natural and flexible to allow realistic descriptions, lively narrative, and convincing dialogue.

Apart from their refined literary style, the chivalric tales of the

[1] For other meanings of the term, see Additional Note 8.

[2] See below, pp. 90–1.

T'ang period are also remarkable for their narrative skill and vivid characterization. Though generally very short, these tales contain sufficient dramatic interest as well as many picturesque and memorable characters. The protagonists of some of the stories are chivalrous ladies or 'swordswomen' instead of knights, a fact which adds to their interest, though, as we have seen, this was not an entirely new feature.

The following are some examples of chivalric tales of the T'ang period. The first four have been translated into English by the late Professor E. D. Edwards and by Professor C. C. Wang. Of these tales I shall only give synopses. The other stories given below are, to my knowledge, translated here for the first time.

The Curly-bearded Stranger[1]

This tale has been attributed to Chang Yueh (667–730) but is now generally believed to be by Tu Kuang-t'ing (850–933). The scene is set in the last days of the Sui dynasty (early seventh century), before the founding of the T'ang.

Li Ching, a great strategist, paid a visit to the Prime Minister of Sui, Yang Su, who was unable to make use of Li's talents. During the interview, a maid holding a red whisk recognized Li as a hero. She came to his lodgings at night and persuaded him to elope with her. While they were fleeing, they stopped at an inn, where they met a curly-bearded man. He was rude at first, but soon made friends with them, giving his name as Chang. Since the surname of Hung-fu ('Red Whisk') was also Chang, she and the stranger became sworn sister and brother. Curly Beard questioned Li Ching about contemporary heroes, and the latter hinted that the only man who had the making of a king in him was a young man also surnamed Li, meaning Li Shih-min, the future Emperor T'ai-tsung of T'ang. Eventually Curly Beard met Li Shih-min and realized this was the man of destiny. He himself had cherished hopes of winning the throne, but now decided to give up. So he left his mansion, servants, and riches to Li Ching and Hung-fu and disappeared. Years later, Li Ching, now a high official under the T'ang, heard that the king of a country overseas had been killed and a new king had ascended the throne. He

[1] See E. D. Edwards, *Chinese Prose Literature of the T'ang Period*, Vol. II (London, 1938), pp. 33–44.

knew this was Curly Beard who had fulfilled his ambition in another land.

The Curly-bearded Stranger is one of the finest chivalric tales of the period. The character of Curly Beard, with his rough exterior and heart of gold, his great ambitions and equally great generosity, is well portrayed. The character of Hung-fu is also skilfully drawn: beautiful, intelligent, brave, and resolute, she is a worthy addition to the gallery of chivalrous ladies in fiction. By contrast, Li Ching himself appears less colourful, though he forms a heroic trio with the other two.

The story has a possible political slant: by emphasizing the futility of striving against the true 'Son of Heaven', the author may have wished to curry favour with the reigning Emperor and warn would-be rebels against taking a dangerous course.

The K'un-lun Slave[1]

This story is probably by P'ei Hsing (*fl.* 880). It tells how, during the Ta-li period (766–80) of the T'ang dynasty, a young man named Ts'ui fell in love with a member of the seraglio of a powerful official. He became lovesick and did not know what to do, till he confided to his Negrito slave called Mo-lê.[2] The latter turned out to be a man of extraordinary ability. He first killed the watchdogs in the official's residence; then at midnight he carried the young man on his back, jumped over roofs and walls, and delivered him safely to the arms of his beloved. She revealed that she had been forced to join the official's harem and begged the young man to save her. So Mo-lê carried both lovers on his back and fled, jumping over more than ten high walls. When the young lady's disappearance was discovered next morning, the official said, 'This must be the doing of a knight-errant; better say nothing about it lest more trouble should come.' Thus the lovers were able to live together in secret. Two years later the young lady was seen by a servant of the official, who summoned the young man Ts'ui to his presence and found out the truth. The official then sent fifty soldiers to surround Ts'ui's house and arrest Mo-lê.

[1] See E. D. Edwards, *op. cit.*, pp. 101–6; C. C. Wang, *Traditional Chinese Tales* (New York, 1944), pp. 93–7. The name K'un-lun is generally believed to mean 'Negrito'.

[2] This is the modern pronunciation. The T'ang pronunciation was something like 'Mua-lak' and is said to have been taken from Arabic.

With a dagger in his hand, Mo-lê flew over the walls and vanished. More than ten years later, he was seen selling medicine in the city, looking not a day older.

The Negrito slave adds an exotic touch to the story and also provides an interesting contrast to knights in shining armour in Western chivalric literature, by rescuing a lady in distress who is not the object of his own love but another man's. The whole story is told with comparable skill to that of *The Curly-bearded Stranger.*

Nieh Yin-niang[1]

This story is also believed to be by P'ei Hsing. During the Chen-yuan period (785–804), Nieh Yin-niang, the daughter of a general, was kidnapped at the age of ten by a nun. Five years later, the nun sent her back to her parents. The girl described how, having been given a magic pill, she felt weightless and was taught by the nun to fly and to fence, after which she was twice sent to assassinate men who had done wrong. The parents did not dare question her further and lost much of their affection for her. Yin-niang then chose for her husband a young man who made his living by polishing bronze mirrors. After her father's death, both she and her husband entered the service of the military governor of Wei and Po.[2] A few years later, the governor sent Yin-niang to assassinate a hostile governor named Liu. Being an expert diviner, Liu knew that Yin-niang and her husband were coming and ordered an officer to wait for them outside the city. Next morning, the officer saw a man and a woman coming, one on a black donkey and the other a white one. When they reached the gate, a magpie cried. The man tried to shoot it with a cross-bow but missed; the woman took the cross-bow from her husband and killed the bird at one shot. Then the officer greeted them in the name of governor Liu, and they were so astonished by Liu's power of divination that they capitulated to him. Liu noticed that the two donkeys had disappeared and sent men to search for them, but without success. Later he found in a bag belonging to Yin-niang two donkeys cut out of paper, one white and one black.

A month or so later, Yin-niang told Liu that the governor of Wei and Po would send an assassin to come and kill both him and

[1] See C. C. Wang, *op. cit.*, pp. 98–103.

[2] At that time, the governor of Wei and Po ruled over five prefectures including Wei and Po, with his headquarters in Wei.

herself, and asked him not to be afraid. That night, Liu lay waiting in bed, and after midnight he saw two banners, one red and one white, floating in the air as if fighting each other. After a long while, a decapitated body fell. Yin-niang then appeared and dissolved the body with some chemical. She told Liu that two days later another assassin, with even greater magical powers than the first, would come, and she gave the following instructions: Liu should protect his neck with a piece of jade, while she would transform herself into a small fly and enter his belly. This was duly done, and while Liu was lying with his eyes closed, he heard a loud noise on the jade. Then Yin-niang jumped out of his mouth and said that the assassin had failed and fled. When Liu looked at the jade, it bore the mark of a dagger.

Later, Liu went to the capital. Yin-niang declined to follow him but left to roam the countryside. When he died, she came to the capital and cried bitterly before his coffin, before she disappeared again. Some years later, Liu's son encountered Yin-niang, still riding on her white donkey and looking as young as ever. She warned him of impending disaster and gave him a pill, saying that this would protect him for a year, but after a year he must resign from his official post, otherwise he would die. She refused to accept any gifts but drank heartily with him before she left. After a year, young Liu did not relinquish his post and really died. Since then no one ever saw Yin-niang again.

The supernatural element in this story is much more pronounced than in the previous two. Together with other stories of a similar nature, it paved the way for long romances about flying swordsmen, which we shall discuss later.

Hung-hsien[1]

This tale is attributed by some scholars to Yang Chü-yuan (late eighth century) and by others to Yuan Chiao (late ninth century). Judging by its advanced technical skill, it is more likely to be a later work and written by Yuan.

The heroine, Hung-hsien ('Red Thread'), was a maid in the household of Hsüeh Sung, military governor of Lu-chou. She was a skilful player of the lute (*p'i-pa*),[2] and was well-versed in

[1] See E. D. Edwards, *op. cit.*, pp. 123–7.

[2] A four-stringed instrument held upright and played by plucking the strings.

history and literature. So Hsüeh made her his private secretary. At that time, another governor, T'ien Ch'eng-ssŭ of Wei and Po, was increasing his forces and planning to annex Lu-chou. Seeing that Hsüeh was worried about this, Hung-hsien offered to go to T'ien's headquarters at Wei one night to investigate. Brushing aside Hsüeh's misgivings, she pushed her hair back to form a bun, put on a short jacket and black silk shoes, carried a dagger, and wrote a magic spell on her forehead. In a moment she was gone. Hsüeh stayed up alone to wait for her, and after drinking a dozen cups of wine he realized it was dawn. Suddenly he heard something falling lightly like a leaf on the ground outside. It was Hung-hsien returning. She had travelled several hundred miles and gone to T'ien's headquarters, and, without disturbing the armed guards or waking up T'ien himself, had taken from his bedside a gold case containing his horoscope. Next morning, Hsüeh sent the case back to T'ien, with a letter saying, 'Last night, a visitor came and brought this from your bedside. I dare not keep it and am returning it herewith.' On receiving this, T'ien was petrified. He sent Hsüeh rich gifts and a humble letter of apology, saying he had no aggressive intentions and was reducing his forces. All was peace and quiet.

Two months later, Hung-hsien asked permission to leave. Hsüeh was naturally reluctant to let her go, whereupon she said, 'In my previous incarnation, I was a man and a physician who, by mistake, caused the death of a pregnant woman conceiving twins. As a punishment, I was born as a girl and became a serving maid. Now that I have repaid your kindness, I must go.' Hsüeh could not stop her, so he gave a great farewell banquet in her honour. Amid sorrowful songs and tears, she quietly slipped away.

The story of Hung-hsien bears some resemblance to that of Nieh Yin-niang, but is more credible. The character of the heroine, too, is more sympathetic and convincing.

*

The next two short tales are from the *Yu-yang Tsa-tsu*, or *Miscellaneous Fare From Yu-yang*,[1] a collection of stories and notes by Tuan Ch'eng-shih (*ob.* 863).

[1] Yu-yang is the name of a mountain in Hunan province, where some ancients were said to have studied and concealed their books. Hence the title implies 'secret sources.'

The Old Man at the Inn

Wei Hsing-kuei related the following incident which he said happened to him when he was young. While travelling to the west of the capital, he stopped at an inn one evening. He was about to proceed on his journey when an old man working at the inn said to him, 'Don't travel by night; there are many bandits around here.' Wei replied, 'I have paid some attention to archery and I have nothing to fear.' So he continued his journey. After he had travelled several miles, darkness fell. Someone rose from the grass and tailed after Wei. He scolded the invisible stranger, who made no reply. Wei then shot arrow after arrow at him, and thought he had hit the man, but the latter did not retreat. When Wei had exhausted his arrows, he became afraid and galloped forth. In a moment, a thunder storm arose. Wei dismounted and stood by a big tree. Then he saw lightning flashes in the air chasing one another, like polo sticks being wielded. They came closer and closer to the tree top, and he felt objects falling helter-skelter before him. When he looked at them, he found they were chips of wood. They accumulated so fast that the heap soon reached his knees. Astonished and frightened, Wei threw away his bow and quiver, and, turning his face up towards heaven, cried for mercy. After he had bowed dozens of times, the lightning flashes rose higher and higher until they vanished altogether. At the same time, the thunder storm also ceased. When Wei looked at the big tree, all its branches were gone. His saddle and baggage were lost, so he returned to the inn. The old man was just putting a hoop on a cask. Wei sensed he must have been an extraordinary man (who had something to do with what happened), so he bowed to the old man and apologized. The old man laughed and said, 'Don't rely on archery; one must understand swordsmanship.' He then led Wei to the back yard, and, pointing at Wei's saddle and baggage, said, 'I took these just to test you.' Further, he showed Wei a stave on which were all the arrows the latter had shot the night before. Wei begged to serve the old man, who refused. But he revealed slightly the art of swordsmanship, and Wei learnt something from him.

The Old Man of Lan-ling

It is said that when Li Kan was Metropolitan Prefect, one day it was his duty to pray for rain to the Dragon King, on the bank of the Meandering Stream (Ch'ü-chiang). Thousands of spectators gathered there to watch. When Li arrived, all made way for him except an old man leaning on a staff. Incensed, Li ordered him to be punished with twenty strokes of the cane on the back, but the blows fell on him as if on hard leather. The old man paid no attention to the caning and walked away indifferently. Li suspected this was a man of extraordinary powers, so he ordered an old soldier to follow him. The soldier traced the old man to the south of Lan-ling Lane, where the latter entered a small door and said aloud, 'I am very tired and I have been disgraced. Bring me some hot water.' Thereupon the soldier returned and reported what he had seen and heard to Li. Full of fear, Li put on some shabby clothes and went with the soldier to the old man's house. It was already dark by then. The soldier went in and announced Li by his official title. Li hastened forward and prostrated himself before the old man, saying, 'It was stupid of me not to have realized what kind of man you were, old father, and I deserve ten deaths!' The old man asked in surprise, 'Who led you here, sir?' and led Li up the steps. Li knew the old man could be reasoned with, so he said slowly, 'I am the Metropolitan Prefect, and if my prestige is damaged to the slightest degree, it will harm the administration. You, old father, hide your light among the riff-raff, and only a man with the "Wisdom Eye"[1] could recognize you for what you are. If you blame people for failing to do so, then you are setting a bait to induce others to do wrong, which is not the way an upright knight's mind works.' The old man laughed and said, 'It was my fault!' Thereupon he produced some food and wine which he placed on the ground, and called the soldier to come and sit with them. The party went on till the depth of night, when the old man started to talk about the art of preserving life.[2] His words were concise and his arguments clear, so that Li felt more and more awe-struck.

[1] *Hui-yen*, a Buddhist term denoting the power to see things as they really are, not what they appear to be.

[2] *Yang-sheng*, a Taoist term often associated with the quest for the elixir of life.

The old man then said, 'I know a trick. Allow me to show it to you, Prefect!' So he went into the house, and, after a long time, returned wearing a purple robe and a vermilion scarf over his forehead and holding seven swords of different lengths. With these he performed a sword dance in the middle of the courtyard, leaping repeatedly and waving the swords as fast as lightning. Sometimes he swished the swords horizontally as if pulling silk; then he whisked them round like the two legs of a pair of compasses. One of the swords, measuring two feet long, came close to the lapel of Li's gown from time to time. Li knocked his head on the ground and trembled in fear. After a while, the old man threw down the swords, planting them in the ground in the position of the seven stars of the Northern Dipper. Looking at Li, he said, 'This was just to test your courage, Mr. Li!' Li bowed and said, 'From now on, I owe my life to you. May I beg to serve you?' The old man replied, 'Judging by your physiognomy, you have not the spirit of the *Tao* in you, and I cannot teach you at once. Come back some other day.' So saying, he saluted Li and went into the house.

When Li went home, he looked like a sick man, and it was only when he looked into the mirror that he realized that more than an inch of his beard had been cut off. Next day he went back to the old man's house, but it was empty.

*

The following two tales are from an anonymous collection entitled *Yuan Hua Chi*, which may be freely rendered *Metamorphoses*.

The Just Swordsman

An official serving in the Metropolitan constabulary was often in charge of cases of burglary. Once, a man charged with burglary was thrown into prison, though his crime had not yet been proven. While the official was sitting alone in court, the prisoner suddenly said to him, 'I am no burglar, but a man quite different from the common crowd. If you, sir, could free me, one day I would repay your kindness.' Noticing his distinguished appearance and eloquent speech, the official consented at heart, though he pretended not to. At night, he secretly called the jailor and told him to let the prisoner escape, at the same time allowing the jailor himself to flee. Next morning it was discovered that a prisoner had escaped and the jailor too had fled. The official's superiors reprimanded him. That was all.

When the official completed his term of office, he travelled around for several years and felt like a homeless wanderer, till one day he came to a district and learnt that the local magistrate's name was the same as that of the man he had let escape. So he went to call on the magistrate. When his name was announced, the district magistrate was astonished and scared, but came out to welcome him. The magistrate proved the same man that the former official had set free. Thereupon the magistrate invited his benefactor to stay with him in his official quarters. They slept on two couches facing each other, and passed the time in a friendly and pleasant atmosphere.

More than ten days went by like this, and the magistrate did not return to his private quarters. When he finally did so, the guest went to the privy which was separated from the magistrate's private quarters only by a wall. There the guest overheard the magistrate's wife ask him, 'What guest have you got that you haven't been in for more than ten days?' The other replied, 'This man did me a great kindness, for my life hung in his hands. Now I don't know how to repay him.' The wife said, 'Have you not heard, "If a great kindness has not been repaid, why not watch out for an opportunity?"'[1] The magistrate was silent for a long while. At last he said, 'You are right.'

When the guest overheard this (and realized that they meant to harm him), he ordered his servants to mount their horses and leave at once, abandoning all his luggage in the magistrate's official quarters. By night they had travelled about twenty miles and had gone beyond the boundary of the district under the jurisdiction of that magistrate. Then they stopped at a village inn. The servants had been wondering why they had been in such a hurry, and now that the former official was able to rest a little, he told them about the ungrateful magistrate. When he finished talking he sighed heavily, and all his servants wept.

Suddenly a man appeared from under the bed and stood up, holding a dagger. The former official was very scared, but the

[1] This is deliberately ambiguous, but both the magistrate and his wife understood by this remark that one should get rid of a benefactor to remove an embarrassment.

swordsman said, 'I am a just man. The magistrate sent me to get your head, and I only learnt about his ingratitude from what you have just said. Otherwise I would have wrongly killed a good man. Justice does not allow me to let this man go unpunished. Don't go to sleep yet, sir, and I will bring you the scoundrel's head in a moment.' The former official, still in fear, thanked him bashfully. The swordsman, holding his dagger, went out of the door and vanished at once, as if flying. During the second watch[1] he came back and shouted, 'The scoundrel's head is here!' When torches were brought in, it was identified as the magistrate's head. The swordsman took his leave and no one knew where he went.

Ts'ui Shen-ssŭ's Wife

During the Chen-yuan period (785–804), Ts'ui Shen-ssŭ of Po-ling went to the capital (Ch'ang-an) to take part in the Metropolitan Examination. Since he had no house of his own there, he rented a spare courtyard in someone else's house, whose owner lived in another courtyard. It turned out that there was no man in the house, only a young woman of over thirty with two maid servants. When Ts'ui observed the woman secretly, he found her quite attractive. So he sent a messenger to ask for her hand in marriage. She replied, 'I do not come from an official's family and I am no match for you. Don't do something that you may regret later.' Ts'ui then asked her to be his concubine instead, to which she consented, though she would not reveal her name. Ts'ui took her as his concubine, and for more than two years she supplied him with whatever he needed without any grudge.

Then she gave birth to a child. One night, when the baby was several months old, Ts'ui went to bed. As was his habit, he did not close the door but only let down the curtains. At midnight he woke up and suddenly found the woman missing. He was surprised and suspected her of being unfaithful to him. Angrily he got up and walked to and fro before the hall. All of a sudden, in the dim moonlight, he saw her letting herself down from the roof with a white silk band which she had wound round her body. In her right hand she held a dagger, in her left hand a man's head. She told him, 'Formerly my father was wrongly killed by the prefect, and I sought revenge for several years. Now that I have

[1] The night was divided into five watches, and 'second watch' corresponded to about 9–11 p.m.

accomplished this, I cannot stay. Allow me to say good-bye now.' So she tidied herself up and put the human head in a sack full of quick lime. She then said to him, 'I was fortunate in having been your concubine for two years and having given birth to a child. This house and the two maids were all paid for by myself, and I now present them to you to support the child.' Having said this she left at once, jumping over the wall and the roofs of neighbouring houses.

Ts'ui could but sigh in astonishment. However, hardly had he finished doing so when she came back, saying, 'Just now I forgot to feed the baby. Let me feed him for a while.' She went into the bedroom and came out after a long time, saying, 'I have fed him. This time I am leaving for ever.' After she left, Ts'ui did not hear the baby cry for some time and wondered why. When he went in to see, he found the baby dead—she had killed her child to sever all ties with the past.

The woman's action at the end of the story may seem to us too drastic, but the story-teller adds admiringly: Even ancient knights-errant could not surpass her!

A similar story, entitled 'The Merchant's Wife', occurs in the *Chi-yi Chi* or *Collection of Wonders* by Hsüeh Yung-jo (*fl.* 827–36). It is not known which story was written first.

*

The last chivalric tale of the T'ang period I shall give here is by Huang-fu Mei (late ninth century).

Li Kuei-shou

Wang To (*ob.* 884), Duke of Chin, became Chief Minister for the second time under Emperor Hsi-tsung of T'ang. He did not care to please other powerful officials but administered the government with justice. Whenever the provincial governors made any requests which were against moral principles, Wang would fight with them and refuse to grant their requests. Thus he incurred the resentment of the military governors. He was devoted to learning, and though he lived in his official residence with *chevaux de frise* before the gate and bells in the courtyard, he never tired of studying. In his residence at Yung-ning Li ('Ever-peaceful Lane'), he had a separate study built, and when he came back from the court he would retire there and spend his time happily among his books.

One day, he was about to enter the study, followed only by his pet short-legged dog named Spotted Magpie. As soon as he opened the door, Spotted Magpie started to bark repeatedly, and, holding Wang's clothes in his mouth, tried to pull him back. Wang drove the dog away, but he came back. After Wang went into the study, Spotted Magpie looked up and barked even harder. Wang became suspicious, so he took out his precious sword, placed it on his knees, and said aloud while looking up in the air: 'If there is any strange being here, come out and meet me. I am a real man: how can I be afraid of rat-like thieves?' When he finished speaking, something fell from the beams on to the floor. It was a man wearing a vermilion scarf over his forehead and a short jacket, of dark complexion and lightly built. He bowed his head again and again and kept saying, 'I deserve to die.' Wang stopped him and asked him where he came from and what his name was. The man replied, 'I am Li Kuei-shou from Lung-sai. Someone bribed me heavily to hurt you, but I was moved by your virtue and was surprised by the dog so that I could no longer hide. If you, my lord, could pardon my crime, I wish to serve you for the rest of my life.' Wang replied, 'I will spare your life.' So he told his chief secretary to register Li as a member of his staff.

Next morning, a woman came to the gate. She was hurriedly dressed, dragging her shoes, and holding a baby in her arms. She begged the porter: 'Please call Li Kuei-shou out for me.' When Li came out, he saw it was his wife, who said, 'I was wondering why you were late and I left Chi at midnight last night to look for you.'

Later, when Wang To died, Li Kuei-shou disappeared with his whole family.

*

In addition to tales devoted to the theme of chivalry, we also find examples of chivalrous behaviour in love romances. For instance, in Hsü Yao-tso's *Madam Liu,* the heroine, the concubine of Han Yi,[1] is abducted by a general during Han's absence. Han sends her a poem to express his feelings, to which she replies in a pathetic poem.[2] Then, a chivalrous man called Hsü Chün goes to

[1] Historically his name should be Han Hung.

[2] I have translated the poems Han and Liu allegedly exchanged, in *The Art of Chinese Poetry*, p. 111.

the general's house when the latter is out, takes Madam Liu, and restores her to Han.[1] In Hsüeh T'iao's *Liu Wu-shuang*, Wang Hsien-k'ê and his female cousin Liu Wu-shuang are engaged lovers. However, since Wu-shuang's father is executed for having served a rebel, she herself is taken into the palace. Wang seeks the help of a knight-errant named Ku Hung. Ku sends a maid disguised as a court lady to give Wu-shuang a drug with which to commit suicide, when in fact the drug merely produces the appearance of death (an incident that reminds one of Juliet). Ku then bribes the attendants and brings her body to Wang, whereupon she revives. To make sure no one will betray the secret, Ku kills all the servants involved in the adventure as well as himself.[2] In Chiang Fang's *Huo Hsiao-yü*, a young man Li Yi deserts the singing girl Huo Hsiao-yü to whom he has sworn eternal love. As she is pining away in sorrow, an anonymous knight-errant forces the unfaithful young man to come to her house so that she can see him once more and reproach him bitterly before she dies.[3]

Chivalric tales in classical prose continued to be written after the T'ang period, but since the later works never surpassed their T'ang models, no examples will be given here.

COLLOQUIAL TALES AND BALLADS

1. *Popular recitals in the T'ang period* (618–907)

Chinese colloquial stories came into existence in the T'ang period, in the form of popular recitals which originated from Buddhist preaching. There were two kinds of popular Buddhist preaching (*su-chiang*). In the first kind, the preacher would chant a sutra and add explanations in colloquial speech. In the second kind, the preacher would select episodes from a sutra and elaborate on them, after having chanted the title of the sutra involved. It was the latter kind that influenced the development of popular fiction, for once the preacher began to concentrate on the episodes instead of the text of the sutra, he would naturally try to make these as

[1] The story is given in E. D. Edwards, *op. cit.*, pp. 170–3, but the incident about the chivalrous man is omitted in the translation.

[2] *Ibid.*, pp. 127–38.

[3] *Ibid.*, pp. 136–48; C. C. Wang, *op. cit.*, pp. 48–59.

interesting as possible, while the audience would naturally become more and more engrossed in the story *per se*, rather than in the moral it was meant to point. Thus, this kind of popular preaching in fact became recitals of tales of the marvellous.

Then, tales not derived from Buddhist scriptures but from Chinese history, legend, and even contemporary events also came to be recited in the same manner. Among these secular tales were some that dealt with chivalry.

Recitals of both Buddhist and secular tales were known as *chuan-pien*, or 'chanting about the unusual', while the texts used for such recitals were called *pien-wen*, or 'texts of (tales of) the unusual'.[1] Since the recitals involved chanting as well as story-telling, the texts usually consisted of a mixture of prose and verse. These texts were discovered in manuscript form at Tun-huang in Northwest China at the turn of the century,[2] and since then have attracted much attention from scholars. The literary value of these texts, I feel, has been exaggerated by some scholars on the grounds of their 'folk' origin and their influence on later colloquial literature. No one examining these texts dispassionately can fail to notice their crudity of language, their often awkward attempts at combining colloquialisms with literary expressions, the abundance of *clichés* and padding, and the naïve mentality of the story-tellers. However, their historical interest cannot be denied.

Among the seventy-eight pieces of *pien-wen* that have been published, there is one concerned with chivalry. This is *The Capture of Chi Pu*, a ballad in 320 couplets of doggerel verse. One of the ten extant manuscript copies of the text bears the date 978, but this refers to the year in which this particular copy was made, not the date of composition, and the ballad itself may have existed in oral form much earlier. The ballad contains so many grammatical errors, wrong characters, anachronisms, repetitions, and inconsistencies, that it does not seem worth-while trying to translate it in full or to put it into English verse. The following is an abridged prose rendering.

[1] For a discussion of the term *pien-wen,* see Additional Note 9.

[2] For an account of the discovery of these texts, see Ch'en Shou-yi, *Chinese Literature, A Historical Introduction* (New York, 1961), pp. 318–23.

The Capture of Chi Pu

Formerly, the Kings of Ch'u and Han, having brought about the downfall of the Ch'in dynasty, contended for the empire. Neither had yet proved himself the true Son of Heaven, and both ruled, so that one could not tell which was the dragon and which the snake.[1] For successive years they fought each other till the rivers boiled over and the sun and moon went dim. Under the King of Han were strategists as numerous as rain drops; under the King of Ch'u, brave generals as thick as clouds. They assisted their respective lords to strive for the imperial throne, but for several years the issue had not been decided.

In the third year of the King of Han's reign the two sides met again by the river Tsu. The troops of Ch'u and Han formed themselves into phalanxes and took up their positions opposite each other. Chi Pu, an eloquent minister of Ch'u, said to his king: 'I have a plan which will save the trouble of fighting. Allow me to go and curse the King of Han, and I will make him withdraw without fighting.' With some doubt the King of Ch'u consented. Having obtained the King's permission, Chi Pu went forth like a furious dragon about to emit clouds. He called General Chung-li Mo[2] to accompany him and together they rode forward, each followed by a few horsemen. They stopped in front of the arrayed troops, and, pointing at the King of Han from a distance, cursed him. They derided him for his humble origin, pointed out his former military failures, and called on him to surrender.[3] When the King of Han heard this, he was so ashamed that he ran away, like a phoenix fleeing from a tree full of noisy crows, or a dragon escaping from water muddied by common fish. When he had composed himself, he asked who the two men who cursed him were. One of his ministers, Hsiao Ho, replied that they were Chi Pu and Chung-li Mo. The King of Han said in anger, 'If I am not destined to rule, there is no more to be said; but if I ever win the empire, I will pardon all generals of Ch'u who should surrender

[1] The dragon is a symbol of imperial power, while the snake represents a pretender.

[2] Historically his name should be Chung-li Mei.

[3] Dr. Waley has translated the 'cursing' in his *Ballads and Stories from Tun-huang* (London and New York, 1960, pp. 247–8) but not the rest of the ballad. There are also two very short extracts from this ballad in Lionel Giles's *Six Centuries at Tun-huang* (London, 1944), p. 20.

except these two, whom I will torture to death. Write down their names and remember them.'

Two years later, the King of Ch'u was defeated and committed suicide. All former generals of Ch'u who surrendered to the King of Han were pardoned and even given honours. Only Chi Pu and Chung-li Mo now realized the truth of the saying, 'The mouth is the door that leads to disaster.' They did not dare show their names and went into hiding separately. At that time, the King of Han became Emperor and ruled peacefully. However, whenever he remembered that Chi Pu was still at large, he knitted his brows in displeasure. So he issued an edict: anyone who could capture Chi Pu would be rewarded with gold and the revenue from ten thousand households, while the whole family of anyone who should conceal him would be executed. In ten days the edict had reached every district and village in the empire. Chi Pu was stricken with fear and did not know where to turn. He took to the mountains and hid in a valley. At night he came out and stole food from the villages; at dawn he went back to the mountains and woods. He loathed the light of the sun and moon and only loved dim starlight. Thus he spent his days in sorrow, often sighing and blaming himself for what he had done.

Finally he could bear his hardships no longer and decided to go and seek the help of an old friend. One night he stealthily went into the garden of his friend Chou and hid among the trees. Chou and his wife were just having dinner when they suddenly felt uneasy. So Chou got up and asked, 'Is that some spirit or ghost over there? If you are a stranger, speak quickly; if a ghost, go back to the graveyard. If you don't answer, I will hurt you with my sword.' Chi Pu whispered in the dark, 'I am no spirit or ghost, but an old friend coming to give you a thousand pieces of gold.' Chou replied, 'People only give so much gold to repay a great kindness. What you said cannot be true.' Chi Pu then jumped over the wall, and said in a low voice, 'Don't talk so loud and disturb the neighbours. Since you ask me, I am the one who cursed the King the year before last.' Realizing this was Chi Pu, Chou came down the steps and welcomed him, asking him how he had been. Chi Pu replied in tears, 'Since I cursed the Emperor, I have been hiding in the mountains and suffering great hardships, like a bird trapped in a net or a fish in a cauldron. I have come to entrust my life to you, kind brother, and I rely on you as to what to do.' Moved by his words, Chou said, 'Don't worry. We have always been great friends and I will risk having my whole family executed to protect you.' They sat together and had some food and wine, and Chou warned his wife not to let the neighbours know. Chi Pu hid in a double wall and nobody knew he was there. Meanwhile, Chou went as usual to the district office where he served.

The Emperor of Han, eager for revenge, asked his ministers why Chi Pu had not yet been arrested. He issued another edict, raising the reward even higher, and ordering that Chi's portrait be circulated. Moreover, every house was to be thoroughly searched, and families had to guarantee each other as to their ignorance of his whereabouts. Those who should give information leading to his arrest would be richly rewarded, while those who should help him to escape would have their families exterminated. The Emperor further appointed Chu Hsieh as Imperial Commissioner to go to Ch'i and see that the orders were carried out.

Chu Hsieh left the capital and arrived at P'u-yang[1] after ten days. When he read out the edict, the district official and his subordinates were worried lest they should be punished for failing to capture Chi. In particular, Chou felt as if a heavy stone had sunk in his heart. When he got home, he went to the wall where Chi Pu was hiding, and said that disaster was coming. Chi Pu misunderstood him and said, 'You need not frighten me. I know that when one has stayed too long, one invites contempt. If you are tired of me and want to abandon me, I cannot easily find another place to hide; I shall simply kill myself.' Chou said, 'Now listen to me. The Emperor hates you so much that he has sent an Imperial Commissioner with a new edict to come here and search for you. Before long you and I will both be caught. I and my family will die willingly for you: I am only sorry that you will perish too.' Chi then asked in astonishment: 'Who is the Commissioner?' Chou replied, 'His name is Chu Hsieh.' When Chi heard this, he smiled and said, 'If it were someone else I would fear for my life, but Chu Hsieh is a useless person. I have a plan to set myself free.' Chou was surprised and asked him how this could be. Chi said, 'My plan is this: I will cut off my hair and put on coarse clothes to pretend to be a slave, and follow you as your

[1] This is an example of the story-teller's carelessness and ignorance. There has been no previous mention in the ballad of P'u-yang as the hiding place of Chi Pu, and besides, this place was not in Ch'i.

servant. When Chu Hsieh is due to go back, sell me to him and don't argue about the price. If he buys me and, by luck, I am able to see the Emperor, I will be able to get his pardon.' Thereupon he cut off his hair, smeared his skin with charcoal, and swallowed some charcoal to change his voice.[1] He followed Chou in and out, and everyone believed he was a domestic slave.

One day, Chu Hsieh saw a slave who was six feet tall and dark skinned. As if urged by some spirit or ghost, he suddenly wanted to buy this slave. So he asked, 'Who is this slave's master? And what is his price?' Chou came forward, saluted Chu, and replied that the slave's price was a hundred pieces of gold. Chu asked, 'What can he do that he is worth so much?' Chou replied, 'Though he is a slave, he has many talents. He has been carefully brought up, can read and write, run errands, ride, and look after a whole herd of horses.' Chu then asked the slave to write to test him, whereupon Chi Pu displayed his wonderful calligraphy. Chu Hsieh then paid the price asked for and bought the slave.

Ten days later, Chu returned to the capital and reported to the Emperor that Chi Pu was not in Ch'i. The Emperor gave Chu leave to go home and rest. Chu went home and held a banquet, at which he showed off his new slave to his friends. Later, he often talked to the slave, who showed remarkable learning in his conversation. Chu therefore said to his wife, 'This slave I bought is really very learned. Heaven has made him a slave, but he is like a piece of jade hidden in the mountains or a pearl hidden in an oyster. We should no longer treat him as a servant.' Thereupon Chu Hsieh gave the slave his own surname Chu as if he had been a member of the family, and changed his clothes. The other servants were told to address him as 'young master'. When Chu asked him to try to play polo, he showed himself a past master of the game. When he was asked to wield a spear or sword on horseback or to shoot with bow and arrow, he displayed great skill and looked like a hero. Chu became suspicious and asked him, 'When I bought you at P'u-yang, I did not have time to question you in detail about your origin. You do not look like a man of humble birth; who are you really?' Chi Pu replied, 'If you do not ask me, I am content to be thought a man of low birth; since you

[1] Some of these details are borrowed from the story of Yü Jang (fifth century B.C.), who disfigured himself so as to hide his identity and seek revenge for his lord, killed by an enemy.

ask me, I am Chi Pu, former general of Ch'u and enemy of the Emperor of Han.' When Chu Hsieh heard this he was very worried and said, 'Yesterday the Royal Astrologer reported that a star of evil omen appeared in broad daylight. Who would have thought this should augur my own misfortune! How can I explain myself? I don't mind dying myself, but my family will perish too!' Chi Pu pretended to console him: 'No need to worry! Anyone who captures me will be rewarded with high office and a hundred catties of gold. If you send me to the Court, you will be promoted.' Chu Hsieh, being simple-minded, was about to call his attendants to send Chi Pu away, when the latter said, 'You are as muddle-headed as a drunken man. The edict also says anyone who conceals me will have his whole family executed. Now you have concealed me for a month, and if you send me to the court, your own family will be killed too!' Hearing this, Chu was frightened: 'Whether I hide you or send you to the court I shall lose my life. Everyone says you are full of strategy; what can I do now?' Chi Pu replied, 'I have a way to save you and myself. Tomorrow, hold a banquet and invite all the ministers to come. At the banquet, bring up the subject of my offences, and I will come out and beg some of the ministers for mercy.'

Next day, Chu did as suggested. Among others, Hsia-hou Ying and Hsiao Ho came. During the banquet, Chi Pu came out from behind a screen and begged the two ministers to save his life. They asked how they could do so, and Chi replied, 'Please say to the Emperor that you heard from Chu Hsieh that the people of Ch'i were greatly disturbed by the search for me so that they could not go about their normal business. If the Emperor would stop the search, the people would be spared. If you say so, the Emperor will certainly stop the search.' The two ministers promised to do so.

When they did repeat Chi Pu's words to the Emperor, the latter was moved and agreed to stop the search. Hsia-hou Ying came back from the court and told Chi Pu the happy news. Chi Pu, however, was not satisfied, but said, 'I have been suffering hardships for a long time. Now, though the search for me has ended, I will not appear in public unless the Emperor summons me with a thousand pieces of gold.' Hsia-hou Ying replied in anger, 'How can the Emperor be willing to summon a rebel with such a high reward?' Chi Pu bowed and said, 'Please speak to the Emperor again and say: Chi Pu is an obstinate and ungrateful man. He knows he will be punished for his crimes, so he will probably rebel, and when he does so, he will be like another King of Ch'u. If Your Majesty will summon him with a thousand pieces of gold, he will then turn into a loyal minister.'

Hsia-hou Ying went to the Emperor and repeated what Chi Pu taught him to say. The Emperor consented to his request. When Chi Pu was summoned, he sent a memorial to the throne to express his gratitude and came to the court. When the Emperor actually saw Chi Pu and recalled the past, he became angry and ordered the guards to seize him. Chi Pu raised his voice and said, 'Your Majesty summoned me with a thousand pieces of gold, but now wants to kill me. Though I deserve to die, what will posterity think of Your Majesty?' When the Emperor heard this, his anger turned to pleasure. He pardoned Chi Pu and appointed him Prefect of Ch'i. Chi Pu bowed in gratitude and left the Court. Thus, he obtained honours by having cursed the Emperor—a unique case in history!

This ballad illustrates how historical events can be exaggerated and distorted in popular literature. In authentic history, there is no indication that Chi Pu ever 'cursed' the King of Han, only that he cornered the latter in battle several times.[1] The historical knight-errant Chu Chia who saved Chi Pu's life voluntarily out of altruism becomes in the ballad a gullible official who is blackmailed into saving Chi. Even his name has been changed from Chu Chia to 'Chu Hsieh', probably due to a confusion between Chu Chia and Kuo Hsieh, the two most famous knights-errant of early Han. Not only 'Chu Hsieh' but the other officials and the Emperor also appear rather fatuous in the ballad: their credulity and sudden changes of mood are childish and make it difficult for us to take the story seriously. At the same time, there are many conventional phrases eulogizing the Emperor. These are irrelevant to the story and out of place in a chivalric tale, and have been omitted in my paraphrase. On the whole, *The Capture of Chi Pu* cannot be considered a work of great literary merit, but is interesting as a specimen of chivalric *pien-wen* and as an example of the transformation of history into imaginative literature with regard to knight-errantry.

[1] See above, p. 35.

2. *Story-telling in the Sung period* (960–1279)

During the Sung period story-tellers were patronized by all, from the court to the man in the street, and story-telling became a highly specialized profession, members of which included women. Some story-tellers specialized in fiction proper (*hsiao-shuo*, literally 'small talk'), others in popularizations of history (*chiang-shih*, 'talking about history'), still others in explanations of Buddhist scriptures (*shuo-ching*, 'explaining the scriptures').[1] According to *The Intoxicated Old Man's Gossip* (*Tsui-weng T'an-lu*) by Lo Yeh, compiled probably at the end of the Sung period, fiction proper was subdivided into eight categories, on the basis of subject-matter: 1. *ling-kuai*, 'the miraculous and strange'; 2. *yen-fen*, an abbreviation of the phrase *yen-hua fen-tai*, 'misty flowers, powder, and eyebrow paint', usually applied to women but here referring to female ghosts; 3. *ch'uan-ch'i*, 'conveying the extraordinary', a term formerly applied to stories in general but now confined to love romances;[2] 4. *kung-an*, 'public cases', stories of crime and detection; 5. *p'u-tao*, 'swords'; 6. *kan-pang*, 'clubs' or 'cudgels'; 7. *shen-hsien*, 'gods and immortals'; 8. *yao-shu*, 'magic' or 'witchcraft'.[3]

Judging by the titles of stories given as examples under each heading in this book, the subdivision was not very strict and there was some overlapping. Thus, chivalric tales were mainly classified under 'clubs', but some stories in the 'swords' category and one in the 'public cases' category also dealt with chivalry. In addition, we find two stories derived from T'ang chivalric tales, namely the stories of Nieh Yin-niang and Hung-hsien,[4] classified under 'magic'.

The texts which formed the basis of oral performances, as well as their later printed versions, are known as *hua-pen* ('story-books') in Chinese and 'prompt-books' in English. A number of these have survived, though mostly edited by later hands, or as component parts of long prose romances. However, even from such incomplete sources we can see that knight-errantry was one of the most important subjects of oral stories told in Sung times.

[1] For the classification of story-tellers, see Additional Note 10.

[2] Cf. Additional Note 8.

[3] For the subdivision of fiction, see Additional Note 11.

[4] See above, pp. 89 and 90.

FROM ORAL STORIES TO LONG ROMANCES (*c.* 1127–1644)

Some chivalric tales told orally centred round certain groups of heroes. When these tales were joined together, they formed the bases of long prose romances.[1] The most famous instance of a chivalric romance based on oral stories is the *Shui-hu*, known in English as *Water Margin* or *All Men are Brothers*. The evolution of this work from historical facts via oral legends to full-length romance has been described in detail by R. G. Irwin.[2] Here I shall only sketch its development briefly, adding a few facts not mentioned by Dr. Irwin.

Water Margin

The historical events from which this chivalric romance is ultimately derived took place near the end of the Northern Sung period. It is recorded in history that a band of outlaws led by Sung Chiang and his thirty-six comrades[3] disturbed several prefectures and repeatedly defeated government forces, before they were induced to capitulate to the government in 1121. In the same year, Sung Chiang joined the successful campaign against another rebel, Fang La. What happened to him after that is not mentioned in historical records, but according to the tomb inscription[4] of a General Chê K'ê-ts'un, unearthed in 1939, this general, after playing a major role in the campaign against Fang La, went to the capital and there received a personal order from the Emperor to capture 'the bandit Sung Chiang', a task which he accomplished within a month. It seems, then, that after having helped to suppress the rebellion of Fang, Sung Chiang himself was liquidated,

[1] These are sometimes referred to as 'novels', but since they have more in common with mediaeval European romances than with modern novels, I prefer to call them 'romances'.

[2] *The Evolution of a Chinese Novel: Shui-hu-chuan* (Harvard, 1953). Some of the conclusions in this book have since been modified by the author in his 'Water Margin Revisited' in *T'oung Pao,* Vol. XLVIII, Livr. 4–5, 1960, but these are related to textual problems and need not concern the general reader.

[3] Some scholars have taken the phrase 'Sung Chiang and his thirty-six' literally, and apparently believe that 37 men actually defeated thousands of government troops—an impossible feat. Obviously these were the leaders of a band, though the band itself probably consisted of hundreds rather than thousands of men.

[4] *Mu-chih-ming*, an account of the deceased inscribed on stone buried in the tomb, not an inscription on a tombstone over the grave.

either because he rebelled again, or perhaps on some trumped-up charge.[1]

The exploits of Sung Chiang and his comrades soon gave rise to legends, which circulated orally among the people and were then taken up by professional story-tellers during the Southern Sung period (1127–1279). Among the stories mentioned in *The Intoxicated Old Man's Gossip*, there are several concerned with members of Sung's band.[2] The texts of these stories (if they were written down) have not survived.

The earliest known written version of legends about Sung Chiang and his comrades is found in the *Anecdotes of the Hsüan-ho Period* (*Hsüan-ho Yi-shih*), a book partly based on story-tellers' prompt-books and partly derived from other literary sources. The date of this book is uncertain, but internal evidence indicates it was compiled after the fall of the Sung dynasty, though the passages about Sung Chiang may have been based on prompt-books of the Sung period (pre-1279). It relates briefly how Sung Chiang and his comrades were forced by circumstances to become outlaws, how they defied government troops, how they capitulated to the government and were rewarded with official honours. This may be considered the prototype of *Water Margin*.

During the Yuan dynasty (1280–1368), stories about Sung Chiang and his followers remained popular, as can be witnessed by the plays about these heroes written in the period.[3] As the number of stories grew, so did the number of heroes: they now became a hundred and eight. These stories seem to have existed independently or in cycles, not in one continuous narrative.

The first version of the romance which joined together the various stories about these heroes is generally believed to have been written about the end of the Yuan period, but no copy of this first version is known to exist. Its authorship is a matter of conjecture. Two names have been associated with *Water Margin*: Shih Nai-an and Lo Kuan-chung. At one time or another, the work has been attributed to one or the other, or both. Little is known about either man. Shih Nai-an has been identified with the dramatist Shih Hui (*fl.* before 1330) on the evidence contained in an early eighteenth-century dramatic bibliography.[4] Further details of his life are not known; a so-called tomb inscription of

[1] See Additional Note 12.
[2] See Additional Note 13.
[3] See below, pp. 151–64.
[4] See Additional Note 14.

Shih Nai-an, which purports to give details of his life, has been demonstrated to be a forgery.[1] Lo Kuan-chung is the courtesy name of Lo Pen, who is known to have been alive in 1364, and is credited with the authorship of several other prose romances as well as three plays. Since Shih was an elder contemporary of Lo, the two could have collaborated in producing the first version of *Water Margin*, or Lo could have revised Shih's draft.

The romance continued to be revised and enlarged throughout the Ming period (1368–1644). Various editions were published (of which the earliest extant one dates from mid-sixteenth century), and several interpolations were made. To the exploits of the heroes as outlaws and their campaign against Fang La were added three other campaigns: one against the Liao Kingdom (Khitan Tartars) and the other two against the fictitious rebels T'ien Hu and Wang Ch'ing. The fullest version, first published in 1614, runs to 120 chapters,[2] and represents the culmination of the development of this romance.

Events took a different turn in 1641 when the critic Chin Sheng-t'an (*ob.* 1661) took the first 71 chapters of the romance, revised the text, changed the first chapter into an 'Induction',[3] renumbered subsequent chapters, altered the ending, and added a preface purporting to have been written by Shih Nai-an. This truncated edition, together with Chin's commentary, was published in 1644, the year that marked the fall of the Ming and the beginning of the Ch'ing or Manchu dynasty. Chin's action was prompted by both political and artistic motives. Politically, having witnessed the effects of rebellions which led to the downfall of the dynasty, he hated all rebels and wished to condemn them. Therefore, he expurgated all the chapters related to Sung Chiang's capitulation and subsequent campaigns. In his version, the romance ends when all the rebels have assembled at Liang-shan, their mountain stronghold surrounded by marshes, and when one of them has a dream in which they are all beheaded, whereas in previous editions the work ends with the deaths of Sung Chiang and some of his comrades caused by the treachery of wicked

[1] See Additional Note 15.

[2] I use the word 'chapters' as a matter of convenience, though actually this romance, like other traditional Chinese fictional works, is divided into 'sessions' (*hui*), as if it were still told orally.

[3] *Hsieh-tzŭ*, a term borrowed from drama. See below, p. 144.

courtiers. In this way, Chin not only denied the rebels a chance to redeem themselves, but also deprived them of the sympathy of readers for their tragic deaths. Moreover, by subtle revisions and explicit comments, he changed the character of Sung Chiang considerably and made him appear a hypocrite. Artistically, Chin's truncation of the romance is more justified. The assemblage of all the rebels at Liang-shan is the climax of the romance, after which the later chapters pursue a downhill path. Also, the later chapters fail to compare with the earlier ones in vivid description and characterization. By retaining only the first 71 chapters and ending the romance at the highest point of interest, Chin has spared the reader the monotony of the various campaigns described in the later chapters and also improved the weak structure of the whole with its diffused parts. Little wonder, then, that it is this truncated version of *Water Margin* that has enjoyed immense popularity for three hundred years and that has been rendered into English.

Since there exist two English translations of the 71-chapter version as well as a synopsis of the 120-chapter version,[1] I shall not summarize the romance or give extracts, but attempt a critical appraisal of the work.

In judging *Water Margin*, we must bear in mind that it was not conceived and written by one man, but represents the efforts of several writers based on an oral tradition. We cannot, therefore, apply to it the usual criteria with which we judge a modern novel,[2] such as plot, characterization, etc. Rather, we should approach it in the spirit in which we approach a folk epic or saga, which it resembles both in its glorification of heroism and in the manner in which it came into being. We should expect an endless succession of episodes tenuously held together rather than a closely knit plot, a host of minor characters who may play important roles in particular episodes but never appear again, catalogue passages, stock phrases, digressions, repetitions, and inconsistencies.

Nevertheless, there is an over-all design in the romance,

[1] Pearl Buck, *All Men Are Brothers* (New York, 1933); J. H. Jackson, *Water Margin* (Shanghai, 1937). For their relative merits see R. G. Irwin, *op. cit.*, pp. 95–7. The synopsis of the 120-chapter version is given in Irwin, pp. 117–201.

[2] Of course I do not mean contemporary Western novel.

especially in the first 71 chapters. The episodes depicting the individual fortunes of the heroes inevitably lead to the grand gathering of the 108 rebels at Liang-shan, which marks the climax of the tale. From then on, it was apparently the original intention of the writer or writers of the first version to follow the decline of the heroes by showing the loss of about two-thirds of them in the campaign against Fang La and the tragic deaths of Sung Chiang himself and his closest associates at the end of the story. This intention is largely lost in the 120-chapter edition due to the interpolation of three other campaigns in which not a single hero of Sung Chiang's band is lost. Consequently the structure of the whole is greatly weakened.

In contrast to its relatively weak structure, the romance shows its real strength in characterization. Although the claim sometimes made that each of the 108 heroes is an unmistakable individual is an exaggeration, it is true that the main characters and even some of the minor ones are vividly portrayed. As a rule, the physical appearance of a character is described on his first entry, but his personality is only gradually revealed through his action and words. This enables the reader to feel that his knowledge of the characters is deepening as the tale goes on, till he has come to understand them fully. Considerable play is made of similarities and contrasts between characters. An interesting example is the contrast between Wu Sung and Shih Hsiu despite their similarities. Both are brave heroes uninterested in the fair sex, and both are capable of caution though outwardly rough, yet each reacts differently to very similar circumstances. When Wu Sung's elder brother's wife fails in her attempt to seduce him, she falsely accuses him of having made advances to her. Instead of exposing her, Wu Sung simply moves out. Later, before going away on official business, Wu Sung advises his brother to stay at home more. However, his precaution proves of no avail, for during his absence the woman takes a lover and murders her husband. On his return, Wu Sung discovers the murder, and having collected sufficient evidence, goes to the local magistrate to accuse his sister-in-law and her lover. The magistrate, who has been bribed by the lover, dismisses the case. Wu Sung thereupon gathers together all the neighbours, makes his sister-in-law confess before them as witnesses, and kills her. He then kills the lover too, and gives himself up to the authorities (Chapters 24–6 in the 120-

chapter version). Thus, he only resorts to violence to avenge his brother's death after having failed to obtain justice from the law, and everything he does, he does openly. The case of Shih Hsiu is different. Shih discovers the adultery between his sworn brother Yang Hsiung's wife and a Buddhist monk, and informs Yang. However, Yang believes his wife's false accusations against Shih himself. Shih then kills the monk and lays a careful trap for the woman, who is forced to confess before she is killed by her husband at Shih's instigation. Both Yang and Shih then run away Chapters 45–6). By contrast to Wu Sung, Shih Hsiu appears aggressive and unnecessarily ruthless. His action is prompted partly by his desire to prove himself innocent, though partly also by his over-zealous regard for his sworn brother's honour. He is therefore not completely altruistic in his motives. Consequently, while Wu Sung engages our sympathy, Shih Hsiu rather repels us.

In fact, not all the heroes in the romance exhibit the spirit of true knight-errantry, though the authors are at pains to show that most of them are forced to turn rebels by gross injustice. Moreover, the band as a whole behave on principles consistent with knight-errantry. Their slogan is, 'Practise the Way on behalf of Heaven', and they habitually rob the rich and help the poor. Among them, the most outstanding example of chivalry is Lu Ta. A fiery-tempered military officer with a heart of gold, he overhears a young woman crying in a tavern and finds out that she has been forcibly taken as concubine by a rich butcher. Lu gives her some money to get away, and goes to beat up the butcher. So strong is Lu Ta that he kills the bully with three fist blows. Thereupon he runs away and becomes a monk (Chapters 3–4). But his chivalrous temperament remains unchanged. On discovering an old man's only daughter being forced to marry a bandit chief, Lu offers to dissuade the unwelcome bridegroom-to-be, but actually gives him a sound thrashing and drives him away (Chapter 5). Later, Lu meets Lin Ch'ung, an instructor in the Imperial Guards, and the two become great friends. Lin's wife is coveted by the adopted son of the Grand Marshal, who frames Lin and sends him into exile. On the way, the two guards, who have been bribed, attempt to murder Lin, but are foiled by Lu, who has been following them in secret (Chapters 7–9). Such altruistic actions are typical of Lu Ta, and greatly help to justify the authors' attitude towards the rebels as chivalrous heroes and not common bandits.

Another important feature of the romance is its realistic descriptions of daily life, in spite of its main concern with heroic deeds. In this it again shows resemblance to a folk epic. Apart from details of dress which form part of the usual description of a character's personal appearance, there are numerous references to all kinds of food, to the layout and interior of houses, to games, festivals, funerals, etc. These, in addition to their sociological interest, also provide a homely setting for the extraordinary feats of the heroes and makes them seem more credible.

Linguistically, *Water Margin* is the first masterpiece written in colloquial Chinese. Earlier examples of colloquial literature are often crude and show an uneasy compromise between the classical language and colloquial speech, but in this romance the colloquial language is used with complete freedom and ease. The narrative is picturesque and the dialogues are lively, full of racy slang, idioms, and proverbs, some of which are still current today.

Water Margin has long been recognized as a masterpiece. Even in days when fiction was not considered serious literature in China, a few literary men esteemed it highly. The famous poet and essayist Yuan Hung-tao (1568–1610) mentioned Lo Kuan-chung, its alleged author, in the same breath as the great historian and acknowledged master of classical prose Ssŭ-ma Ch'ien, and the critics Li Chih (1527–1602) and Chin Sheng-t'an both placed the romance among the greatest works of genius in Chinese literature. Modern scholars and critics have been nearly unanimous in their praise of the work, though sometimes on ideological rather than artistic grounds. A notable exception is Professor C. T. Hsia, who in his paper 'Comparative Approaches to *Water Margin*'[1] criticized the work severely. While I admire his intellectual courage and honesty in raising a lone voice of censure against the general chorus of eulogy, and while some of his strictures (such as the remark that the descriptions of military campaigns lack dramatic suspense because the band always emerges victorious) are justified, I find it difficult to agree with all his criticisms against *Water Margin*. Professor Hsia attacked the work on two main grounds: first, it is pseudo-history rather than genuine fiction, and second, it exhibits a kind of 'gang morality' as well as signs of sadism and misogyny. Let us consider these charges.

[1] In *Yearbook of Comparative and General Literature*, No. 11 (Indiana, 1962), pp. 121–8.

Under the first charge, Professor Hsia asserts that the work failed to become full-bodied fiction but remained pseudo-history because it was conditioned by the 'unquestioned supremacy of the historical mode of story-telling' and that the writer saw himself primarily as a popular historian 'in direct competition with professional reciters of dynastic history'. This assertion may be questioned in the light of contemporary evidence: two writers of the Sung period stated that the reciters of history were particularly afraid of story-tellers who specialized in fiction proper, since the latter could 'resolve in a moment the events of a whole dynasty'. Therefore, whatever the failings of *Water Margin*, the blame can hardly be laid at the door of popular reciters of history. Moreover, as we have seen,[1] stories about *Water Margin* heroes were clearly classified as 'fiction proper' (*hsiao-shuo*) and not 'popularization of history' (*chiang-shih*) in Sung times, and throughout its evolution the work was never labelled *yen-yi* ('paraphrase'), a term which was, as Professor Hsia himself says, 'invariably affixed to historical novels'. It is as fiction, then, that *Water Margin* must stand or fall.

Professor Hsia's second charge is certainly not without some justification. However, it seems to me we need not approve of the morality implicit in *Water Margin* in order to appreciate it as literature, any more than we need accept Dante's Thomism or Milton's puritanism to appreciate their works. Otherwise we might as well condemn Aeschylus for believing in fate and revenge, and Shakespeare (especially in *The Taming of the Shrew*) and Molière (especially in *Le Misanthrope*) for misogyny. After all, no writer is entirely free from current ideas, assumptions, and prejudices, and we cannot condemn a work *as literature* for containing views which we do not happen to share. Professor Hsia's moral indignation against the *Water Margin* heroes has led to such surprising conclusions as that no character in this work can approach Hsi-men Ch'ing, the sadistic and lecherous villain-hero of *Chin P'ing Mei* ('The Golden Lotus'), for the 'depth and range of his humanity'. Against this we may cite the example of Lin Ch'ung. As mentioned before,[2] Lin Ch'ung was wrongfully exiled because the adopted son of the Grand Marshal coveted his wife. Before leaving, Lin insisted on giving his wife a bill of divorce so that she would be free to remarry, since in all probability he would not be able to return. Though this may seem

[1] See above, p. 109 and Additional Note 13. [2] See above, p. 113.

hard-hearted on his part, it was really prompted by a deep love and unselfish concern for her. Moreover, he did not forget her after joining the band at Liang-shan. When he had made Ch'ao Kai the leader of the band, he confided in the latter: 'Ever since I joined the band, I have wished to fetch my wife here, but because Wang Lun [the previous leader] was unreliable, I have postponed it till now. She should still be in the Eastern Capital, though I don't even know if she is alive or dead.' Ch'ao Kai then advised Lin Ch'ung to send messengers to fetch her, whereupon Lin sent two of his closest followers to fetch her. They returned two months later to report that she had committed suicide when forced to marry the Grand Marshal's adopted son. On hearing this, Lin Ch'ung shed tears and gave up hope (Chapter 20). Is this the behaviour of a sadistic misogynist?

With all deference to Professor Hsia, for whose scholarship and critical acumen in general I have the highest esteem, I still think that *Water Margin* is one of the best works of fiction, and the most outstanding piece of chivalric literature, in Chinese.

LATER CHIVALRIC FICTION (*c.* 1644–THE PRESENT)

As often happens with Chinese fiction, the success of *Water Margin* led to imitations in the form of sequels. Two such imitations published during the Ch'ing period (1644–1911) may be mentioned. *Later History of the Water Margin* (*Shui-hu Hou-chuan*) by Ch'en Ch'en (*c.* 1590–1670) takes up the story after Sung Chiang's death and relates how his surviving comrades fought against the invading Tartars and how one of them became King of Siam. Since the author lived at the end of the Ming period and beginning of the Ch'ing, this appears to be a veiled expression of his patriotic, anti-Manchu feelings. In contrast, the *Conclusion to 'Water Margin'* (*Chieh Shui-hu*), also called *Account of the Suppression of Bandits* (*Tang-k'ou Chih*), by Yü Wan-ch'un (*ob.* 1849), first published in 1851, continues the tale from Chapter 71 and sets out to prove that Sung Chiang and his followers were not allowed to capitulate to the government but were captured and executed. This shows how far writers had changed their attitudes towards knight-errantry.

Apart from sequels to *Water Margin*, many other chivalric tales were produced during the Ch'ing period, and have enjoyed popularity to this day. Even now, a considerable number of chivalric tales are still being written with some skill and read with great avidity. These tales may be divided into several types: chivalric tales combined with detective stories, tales combining chivalry with love, those which emphasize the supernatural and describe a kind of flying swordsmen, and those which stress physical feats and pugilistic skill.

1. *Chivalric-tales-cum-detective-stories*

These may be regarded as an amalgamation of stories which earlier would have been labelled 'public cases' with those which would have been classified under 'swords' and 'clubs'.[1] In a tale of this type, we usually find a group of knights-errant who protect an upright official and help him to eliminate criminals. Thus, a significant change has taken place: instead of being rebels, the heroes are now guardians of the law. This change reflects the difference between earlier and later writers in their attitudes towards knight-errantry, which we have already noted above in the contrast between Ch'en Ch'en and Yü Wan-ch'un. On the whole, the earlier writers, such as those responsible for *Water Margin* and Ch'en, expressed the wish of the people for knights-errant to uphold justice and to repel foreign invaders, while the later writers like Yü reveal the mentality of those who had accepted the rule of the Manchus and were on the side of law and order. This change may have also been due in part to the rise of professional armed escorts in real life.[2] In spite of their changed role, the knights-errant in these tales remain true to most of the ideals of knight-errantry: they are brave, loyal, and honourable; they would only support an honest official and would always help the poor and oppressed.

The Three Knights-errant and The Five Altruists

A typical example of this kind of chivalric fiction is *The Three Knights-errant and The Five Altruists* (*San-hsia Wu-yi*), a prose romance in 120 chapters first published in 1879. It was based on the oral recitals of Shih Yü-k'un (*fl.* 1851–75), a native of Tientsin who made his living as a professional story-teller in Peking. Shih's recitals included singing, but the songs are omitted in the published version. Like *Water Margin*, this romance too grew out

[1] See above, p. 107. [2] See above, p. 53.

of a long tradition of popular legends remotely derived from historical facts. The upright official who forms a pivot around which the knights-errant move in this romance is Pao Cheng (999–1062). According to the official history of the Sung period, he was a stern and honest official, and in his own lifetime was already compared to the Judge of Hades. After his death he became the subject of many legends. In the Yuan period (1280–1368) at least a dozen plays were written about him, including the well-known *Circle of Chalk* (*Hui-lan Chi*), in which Pao settles a dispute between two women both claiming to be the mother of a child much in the same way as did Solomon. In the Ming period (1368–1644) stories about Pao were published as *The Cases of Lord Pao* (*Pao-kung An* or *Lung-t'u Kung-an*[1]) of which the earliest known edition dates from 1594. These were largely concerned with crime and detection rather than chivalry. But in Shih Yü-k'un's recitals the main interest shifted from the cases solved by Lord Pao to the deeds of his chivalrous friends and subordinates. In 1889 the scholar Yü Yüeh (1821–1906) revised the romance and published it under a new title, *The Seven Knights-errant and The Five Altruists* (*Ch'i-hsia Wu-yi*), since in fact there are seven knights who play considerable parts in the tale, in addition to the five altruists. This edition has been current side by side with the earlier one under the old title. In the same year two sequels were also published: *The Junior Five Altruists* (*Hsiao Wu-yi*) and *Continuation of 'The Junior Five Altruists'* (*Hsü Hsiao Wu-yi*), of 124 chapters each. These mainly deal with the exploits of the sons of the original heroes, and though they claim to have been based on Shih's own drafts, they are inferior to the principal tale.

Since *The Three Knights-errant and The Five Altruists* consists of a great number of episodes often unconnected with each other, it is hardly possible to summarize it. I shall therefore simply describe some of the main characters and their deeds.

The most important knight-errant in the tale is Chan Chao, known as 'The Knight-errant of the South'. He comes from a wealthly family and spends his days roaming around. Whenever he sees people in distress, he will help them. He gives liberally to the poor, but is not above helping himself equally liberally to the ill-gained riches of corrupt officials and local bullies. One day he

[1] Pao Cheng is also known as Pao Lung-t'u because he received the official title, 'Scholar of the Lung-t'u Pavilion'.

encounters Pao Cheng, as yet a young scholar on his way to the capital to take part in the Metropolitan Examination. The two strike up a friendship, but each goes his own way. That night, Pao and his page put up at a Buddhist monastery. The monks in charge turn out to be villains who plot to murder Pao and his page for their luggage. Chan Chao arrives in the nick of time, saves their lives, and disappears.

After Pao has passed the examination and become a high official, he incurs the enmity of a wicked minister, whose attempts to murder him are twice foiled by Chan Chao. When Lord Pao reports this to the throne, the Emperor expresses the wish to see the knight. So, reluctantly, Chan allows himself to be presented to the Emperor, who asks him to demonstrate his swordsmanship and his skill in climbing and jumping. So agile is he that His Majesty claims, 'But this is no man: this is just like my cat!' Thus Chan Chao acquires the nickname, 'Imperial Cat', and is made an officer of the Guards serving under Lord Pao.

Chan's accidental acquisition of this nickname has unforeseen consequences. It offends another knight-errant, Pai Yü-t'ang, who is the youngest of five sworn brothers (the 'Five Altruists' of the title): Lu Fang, the 'Heaven-piercing Rat', so called because of his ability to climb tall masts; Han Chang, the 'Earth-penetrating Rat', an expert in tunnels and mines; Hsü Ch'ing, the 'Mountain-boring Rat', who can find his way through mountain caves; Chiang P'ing, the 'River-churning Rat', an adept swimmer and diver; and Pai Yü-t'ang, the 'Beautiful-furred Rat', so called because of his handsome appearance. Despite their somewhat misleading nicknames, all five are altruistic knights-errant. Now Pai takes Chan Chao's nickname as an insult to himself and his sworn brothers, and, out of youthful pride, vows to humiliate Chan, although the two men have previously met and admire each other. Pai goes to the capital, kills a wicked eunuch in the palace, and steals Lord Pao's 'Three Treasures' (an ancient mirror, a bowl, and a pillow, all supposed to possess magic powers). It falls on Chan to capture Pai and recover the stolen treasures. He goes to the island where Pai lives, and is trapped and imprisoned by the latter. With the help of Lu Fang and Chiang P'ing, who disapprove of Pai's actions, Chan is freed and Pai captured. The latter's offences are forgiven by Lord Pao, and he becomes reconciled with Chan Chao. Eventually all the five sworn brothers join

Lord Pao's entourage, and, together with Chan and other knights, plan to eliminate a Prince harbouring plots of rebellion. Pai goes alone to the stronghold of the rebel Prince, gets caught by a mechanical trap and dies a painful death. His sworn brothers manage to recover his bones, but his revenge and the capture of the rebel Prince only take place in the *Continuation of 'The Five Junior Altruists'*.

The Three Knights-errant and the Five Altruists keeps to the main tradition of chivalry in spirit. It emphasizes the altruism of the heroes, their sympathy for the poor and oppressed, and their hatred for corrupt and cruel officials. On the whole, it avoids the supernatural. Such supernatural elements as there are concern Lord Pao, but not the knights-errant, none of whom possesses magic powers.

The deeds of the knights-errant are not always closely related to the criminal cases solved by Lord Pao. In fact, the romance seeks to accommodate both without sufficiently integrating the two. As a result, our attention is focused on individual incidents rather than on a central plot. Nevertheless, the romance does hold our interest by its lively narrative and realistic portrayal of characters. The language is plain and simple but effective, retaining much of the flavour of oral story-telling. Though far from being a classic, it has enough merits to justify its continued popularity.

The Cases of Lord Shih and *The Cases of Lord P'eng*

These are similar in kind but greatly inferior in quality to *The Three Knights-errant and The Five Altruists*. Both are vaguely based on historical figures, and each uses an upright official as a convenient peg on which to hang a number of criminal cases and chivalrous episodes.

The Cases of Lord Shih (*Shih-kung An*), written by an anonymous author and first published in 1798,[1] deals with the alleged deeds of Shih Shih-lun (1659–1722),[2] an official famous for his integrity and his championing of the poor and oppressed. In the tale, his chief supporter is Huang T'ien-pa, a young knight-errant who at first attempts to assassinate Shih but is moved by the latter's

[1] For the date of this tale see Additional Note 16.

[2] See *Eminent Chinese of the Ch'ing Period* (Washington, 1944), Vol. II, pp. 653–4.

virtue to voluntary submission. With the help of other chivalrous men, Huang aids the official in his efforts to get rid of criminals and saves the latter's life time and again. The incidents follow a familiar pattern: Shih goes incognito to investigate reports about some local bully or bandit, his identity is discovered by the villain and he is imprisoned and tortured, then a friendly knight-errant or one of his own subordinates arrives just in time to save him from the sword.

The Cases of Lord P'eng (*P'eng-kung An*), written by someone who signed himself 'The Taoist Priest Greedy for Sleep' (T'an-meng Tao-jen), first appeared about 1891. The historical personage who provides an excuse for the tale is P'eng P'eng (1637–1704),[1] another incorrigible official and champion of the common people. In the story one of his aides is Huang San-t'ai, the father of Huang T'ien-pa. P'eng's role in this tale is so similar to Shih's in the other one that if we were to substitute the name of Shih for P'eng or *vice versa*, little difference would ensue.

Neither of these works has much merit: there is no plot to speak of, the characters are stereotyped, and the language is crude. Yet both have achieved great popularity, so much so that many sequels have been published. (The first edition of each work contained about 100 chapters, but current editions run to 528 and 187 chapters respectively, though some chapters are extremely brief.) Such seems to be the insatiable demand of readers for this kind of fiction.

2. *Romances combining Chivalry with Love*

It may be recalled that some love stories of the T'ang period contain an element of chivalry. However, in those stories, the knights-errant help lovers in distress but are 'unmoved, cold, and to temptation slow' themselves. For chivalrous men and women involved in love, we have to turn to later romances.

A Tale of Chivalrous Love

This romance has two titles: *A Tale of Chivalrous Love* (*Hsia-yi Feng-yueh Chuan*) and *The Happy Union* (*Hao-ch'iu Chuan*). It is written by Ming-chiao-chung-jen, a pseudonym which may be

[1] Ibid., pp. 613–14.

paraphrased as 'A Confucian Gentleman'.[1] The work probably belongs to early Ch'ing,[2] and is published in four parts totalling eighteen chapters.

The hero of the romance is T'ieh Chung-yü,[3] a chivalrous young man of great physical strength as well as literary talent, and son of an Imperial Censor. The heroine is Shui Ping-hsin,[4] a young lady whose beauty is matched by her intelligence and character, and daughter of the exiled Vice-Minister of War. The villain of the piece is Kuo Ch'i-tsu,[5] a worthless dandy and son of the Crown Prince's Chief Secretary.[6] Most of the tale is concerned with Kuo's indefatigable efforts to trick Ping-hsin into marrying him and her clever manoeuvres which foil them. One of the tricks employed by Kuo is to send messengers to Ping-hsin's house pretending to bring an Imperial edict announcing her father's pardon. When she comes out to receive the edict, she is kidnapped and carried away in a sedan chair. In the street the party encounter T'ieh Chung-yü, who intervenes when he hears her crying for help. A scuffle ensues, in which Chung-yü easily gets the better of Kuo's underlings, and they all end up in the district magistrate's court. The magistrate, partly awed by Chung-yü's chivalrous reputation and partly out of fear of his father's position, sends Ping-hsin home. But actually he is in league with Kuo, so he sends Chung-yü to a Buddhist monastery to stay, while allowing Kuo a chance to avenge himself. Kuo bribes the monk in charge to put strong laxatives in Chung-yü's food, so that he falls ill and quickly loses strength. Ping-hsin, who has suspected something like this would happen, sends a servant to fetch Chung-yü to her house, where she has him cured by a physician and takes care of him till he recovers. The two have now fallen in love with each other, but neither would show it, and Chung-yü leaves.

1 *Ming-chiao* is another name for Confucianism, since *ming* ('name') refers to the Confucian doctrine of 'Rectification of names', while *chiao* ('teaching') means moral instruction.

2 For the date of the work, see Additional Note 17.

3 The name literally means 'Jade Inside Iron'.

4 Her surname Shui means 'Water', her personal name Ping-hsin, 'Ice Heart'. 'Ice' signifies purity, not coldness.

5 The name can be construed as meaning 'Blame His Forefathers', or it could be a pun on 'Too Rough-spirited'.

6 *Tso-ch'un-fang Ta-hsüeh-shih,* literally 'Grand Scholar of the Spring Court on the Left'. 'Spring Court' was the traditional name given to the Crown Prince's establishment.

After many more complications, Ping-hsin's father is pardoned and promoted to be Minister of War. He expresses to Chung-yü's father the desire to marry his daughter to the latter's son, to which the elder T'ieh readily agrees. However, both the hero and the heroine refuse, for they wish to show that nothing improper occurred between them during his stay in her house, and that what they did for each other was done purely out of altruism on his part and gratitude on hers. At last, under duress, they go through a wedding ceremony but agree with each other not to consummate the marriage. This self-denial proves their saving later, when an Imperial Censor, at the instigation of the elder Kuo, memorializes the throne that T'ieh Chung-yü and Shui Ping-hsin had pre-marital relations and that by allowing them to be married their parents are encouraging immorality. The Emperor orders an investigation, and everyone concerned tells his own version of the story. Finally, Ping-hsin is summoned to the palace and examined by court ladies, who find her still a virgin. Their chastity thus proved, Ping-hsin and Chung-yü are officially honoured while their enemies are punished.

This romance has some unusual situations, but the author has not fully developed their dramatic and poetic potentialities, largely because of his determination to force chivalrous and romantic sentiments to conform to the strait jacket of Neo-Confucian morality. The characterization suffers from the same weakness. For example, the hero at first acts like a knight-errant—bold, impulsive, and caring nothing for official authority or social conventions—but by the end of the tale he has become a conventional scholar-official and a model of propriety. At times the technique of story-telling is somewhat primitive. We often find a character relating to another an incident which the author has already described in detail in the third person. This involves a great deal of unnecessary repetition.

The romance is written mainly in the colloquial language, but the author introduces, at every possible opportunity, verses, official documents, letters, etc., in the classical language with obvious delight and pride. These compositions, which Sir John Davis, one of the translators of the tale, so much admired,[1] are in fact merely conventional and pedantic, adding little to the literary value of the whole.

[1] *The Fortunate Union* (London, 1829), p. ix.

This mediocre work is neither highly esteemed nor widely read in China now, though it has been translated many times into Western languages. As far back as the early eighteenth century, one James Wilkinson translated the first three parts of the romance into English and the last part into Portuguese. Then, Bishop Percy, the editor of *Reliques of Ancient English Poetry*, turned the last part from Portuguese into English, edited the whole of Wilkinson's manuscript, and had it published under the title, *Hau Kiou Choaan, or the Pleasing History*,[1] in 1761. Since then, more than a dozen versions in English, French, and German have appeared, some translated from the Chinese, others re-translated from other European languages. The latest English adaptation, *The Breeze in the Moonlight* (1926) by H. Bedford-Jones, is based on the French translation, *La brise au clair de lune*[2] (1925), by George Soulié de Morant. That this second-rate work should have achieved such popularity in the West is perhaps not really surprising when one remembers the vogue of *chinoiserie* in eighteenth-century Europe. Of course the reverse can happen too: when Western literature first began to be translated into Chinese, the works of H. R. Haggard received the same attention as those of Dickens and Scott, and many Chinese readers are familiar with the stories of Maupassant in translation, but have never heard of Racine, not to mention those who have read Wilde but not Shakespeare.

A Tale of Heroic Lovers

This romance is by Wen-k'ang[3] (*fl.* 1821–60), a Manchu official and member of the Feimo clan. Though it was first published in 1878, some years after the author's death, it seems to have been circulated in manuscript form before then. The title *A Tale of Heroic Lovers* (*Erh-nü Ying-hsiung Chuan*) is a deliberate paradox: *erh-nü*, literally 'boys and girls', is a term often used with reference to

[1] This is a mistranslation of one of the original titles. Wilkinson failed to understand the expression *hao-ch'iu*, literally 'good match', which alludes to the first poem in *The Book of Poetry*. For details of the Wilkinson–Percy version, see Ch'en Shou-yi, 'Thomas Percy and His Chinese Studies', in *Chinese Social and Political Science Review*, Vol. 20 (Peiping, 1936–7), pp. 202–30.

[2] This is a literal translation of part of the first title, *feng-yueh* ('wind-moon'), which means romantic love.

[3] A Manchu was usually known only by his personal name, not by his surname. There is a biographical note on Wen-k'ang attached to the entry on Wen-ch'ing in *ECCP*, Vol. II, p. 853.

love, while *ying-hsiung*, 'heroes', is often used as its antonym.[1] The author explains in the prologue his intention in combining the two terms:

> Most people nowadays regard 'lovers' and 'heroes' as two different kinds of people, to 'love' and to be 'heroic' as two different things. They mistakenly think that those who indulge in force and like fighting are 'heroes', while those who toy with rouge and powder or have a weakness for catamites are 'lovers'. Therefore, as soon as they open their mouths, they will say, 'So-and-so lacks heroic ambitions but has a great capacity for love,' or 'So-and-so is shallow in love but has a strong heroic spirit.' What they don't realize is that only when one has the pure nature of a hero can one fully possess a loving heart, and only when one has true love can one perform heroic deeds.

Therefore, the author's main purpose in writing the romance is to depict men and women who answer to his ideal of combining heroism with love. Some of the characters may have been modelled on actual persons, but they are no doubt idealized (according to the writer's ideals, that is, though some of them may not appear ideal persons to us).

According to the preface by a friend of the author's, the romance originally consisted of 53 chapters, but since the manuscript of the last 13 were so worm-eaten as to be illegible, only the first 40, together with the prologue, were published. A sequel by another hand was published in 1898.

The plot of the romance is quite complicated but may be summarized below.

An honest official from Peking named An Hsüeh-hai was supervising the repair of a dam in Southeast China. Through no fault of his, a flood broke the dam and his superior used him as a scapegoat, depriving him of his post and ordering him to pay the damages, which amounted to about five thousand taels of silver. At home, his young son, An Chi, having heard the news, managed to borrow about half the sum, and set out with two servants to deliver it to his father. This may not sound a heroic task to us, but considering the youth was delicately brought up and had never travelled before, this took some courage, for in those days to journey for hundreds of miles with so much silver was a pretty

[1] I have inverted the two terms in the translation of the title, since 'Loving Heroes' sounds rather comic in English.

hazardous undertaking. They had not gone far when one of the servants rushed home to attend his own mother's funeral, while the other one fell ill. Thus young An Chi had to proceed with two hired donkey drivers.

These two took advantage of the inexperienced young man and plotted to murder him and rob him of his silver. They were overheard by a beautiful girl riding by on a black donkey. She came to the inn where the young man was staying and kept looking at him. Alarmed and suspicious, An tried to make sure his door would be firmly blocked at night by asking the waiters to move a heavy stone roller into his room. While they were struggling with it, the girl came over, lifted it with one hand, and asked An with a smile, 'Where would you like it?' In utter confusion, An asked her to bring it into the room, whereupon she invited herself to sit down and questioned him about himself. Having failed to fob her off with ill-conceived lies, he finally told her the truth. She was much moved by his filial devotion and his father's misfortune, and told him to wait for her till next morning. She then disappeared, without having told him her identity.

After the mysterious girl left, the two donkey drivers came back and persuaded the young man to leave. However, their plot to murder him on the way miscarried, and they all stopped at a monastery for the night. The monks turned out to be even worse villains. The abbot, after an unsuccessful attempt to poison the young man, tied him to a post and was about to stab him. In the nick of time, a missile from a cross-bow hit and killed the abbot—it was of course the anonymous young lady. She released An Chi and killed the other monks, who had murdered the two donkey drivers. Then she heard someone crying, and found an old farmer, who said his name was Chang and that he, his wife, and his daughter Chin-feng ('Golden Phoenix'), had all been forcibly detained by the monks. Eventually the mother and daughter were also found and released by the chivalrous young lady, who was struck by the fact that Golden Phoenix bore a remarkable resemblance to herself. When Golden Phoenix asked her benefactress her name, the latter would not reveal it, but said, 'Just call me Thirteenth Sister (Shih-san Mei)' and gave this brief account of her life: her father, a general, had incurred the anger of an all-powerful minister and died in prison; she would have risked her life to avenge his death but for the fact that her mother was still alive and needed someone to look after her; now she was hiding with her mother in a secluded place and making a living by robbing corrupt officials. She then gave An Chi some gold to make up the sum needed for his father.

Now a dilemma presented itself to Thirteenth Sister: the Changs were going one way, An Chi another; she could not escort both parties at once, yet it would be dangerous to let either party go unescorted, for the district was infested with bandits. She had a bright idea—let Golden Phoenix be betrothed to An Chi, then they could all travel together without impropriety. Thereupon she set about playing the marriage broker. Having first obtained the consent of the girl herself and of her parents, Thirteenth Sister overcame young An Chi's moral scruples about acting without parental permission, and officiated at a hastily improvised ceremony. She also gave some gold to Golden Phoenix as her dowry. Then all left the monastery.

Having accompanied them a short way, Thirteenth Sister said that she had to go back to look after her mother, but lent them her cross-bow, at the sight of which, she said, any bandit in the region would turn submissive. When asked how the cross-bow could be returned to her later, she replied that it should be sent to her friend and nominal teacher, a chivalrous old man known as Grandfather Teng the Ninth (Teng Chiu-kung) living at The Twenty-eight Red Willows.

At that moment, An Chi suddenly remembered that he had left in the monastery an ink-slab, a family heirloom bearing his father's name. Thirteenth Sister agreed to go back for it and keep it till her cross-bow should be returned to her, when she would give the messenger the ink-slab in exchange.

After the party had travelled a short distance, sure enough some bandits appeared. On seeing the cross-bow, the leader not only did them no harm but also provided them with two escorts who accompanied them to their destination. Thus, An Chi was reunited with his parents, and reported what had happened. The elder Ans were happy to have Golden Phoenix as their daughter-in-law despite her humble origin. The young couple were duly married, and An Hsüeh-hai, having paid the damages, was restored to his post.

However, after his unhappy experience, An Hsüeh-hai had no more interest in an official career. Moreover, by piecing together various clues, he came to the conclusion that the mysterious Thirteenth Sister was no other than the daughter of an old friend now dead. Out of gratitude to her for having saved his son's life as well as a sense of obligation to his dead friend, An Hsüeh-hai decided to give up his post and go in search of the girl.

Together with his son, An Hsüeh-hai went to The Twenty-eight Red Willows, and there learnt that Thirteenth Sister's mother had just died and that she herself would leave soon to execute the long-delayed revenge. By winning the friendship of the simple-minded but warm-hearted Grandfather Teng the Ninth, the elder An was able to see Thirteenth Sister under false pretences. (If he had declared his true intention of trying to repay her kindness, she would certainly have refused to see him.) Then, to the great surprise of Thirteenth Sister, An Hsüeh-hai announced that he himself and her father General Ho had been great friends, that her real name was Yü-feng ('Jade Phoenix'), and that her enemy had been executed by the Emperor so that there was no longer any need for her to go to avenge her father's death. On hearing this, Jade Phoenix wished to commit suicide, as there was nothing left for her to live for, but was persuaded by An Hsüeh-hai that it was her duty to accompany her mother's coffin back to Peking to be properly entombed together with her father's. Having exacted from him the promise that he would let her become a nun after the period of mourning, Jade Phoenix agreed to go.

After the burial and a year's mourning, Jade Phoenix prepared herself for the life of a nun. Little did she dream that the An family, with the connivance of Grandfather Teng the Ninth, had other plans for her. To their way of thinking, such a beautiful young lady and daughter of a general should not end her days in a nunnery, but should get married, and to whom better than to young An Chi? (The fact that he was already married was no obstacle in those days, and the two wives could have equal status.) Golden Phoenix, too, wished to show her gratitude by doing Jade Phoenix exactly the same favour that the latter had done herself. By using various arguments, such as that it was Jade Phoenix's duty to get married so that her offsprings could continue to offer sacrifices to the spirits of her deceased parents, that her union with An Chi was predestined, as could be witnessed by their unconscious exchange of tokens of betrothal (the cross-bow and the ink-slab), and that they had been in such close proximity that it would hardly be proper unless they became husband and wife, An Hsüeh-hai and Golden Phoenix finally persuaded Jade Phoenix to become An Chi's second wife, with the same status as Golden Phoenix.

The rest of the romance, dealing with the domestic life of the An family and An Chi's successful official career, is of little interest.

A Tale of Heroic Lovers is reasonably well written, but has some serious faults. It has a carefully constructed plot, an unusual feature in this kind of fiction, and its language is lively and fluent. On the other hand, the characterization is uneven and sometimes inconsistent. The most striking example is the heroine: as Thirteenth Sister, she is a remarkable character full of the noble and stern virtues of chivalry, but as Jade Phoenix, especially after her marriage, she is hardly recognizable as the same person.[1] An Hsüeh-hai is too often merely the author's mouthpiece for expressing trite Neo-Confucian moral views. An Chi is largely the conventional young gentleman, just as Golden Phoenix is the conventional virtuous wife and daughter. One well-drawn character is Grandfather Teng the Ninth: a retired professional armed escort, he is magnanimous, boisterous, ready to help others, and childishly vain of his heroic reputation and his long white beard. The romance is marred by the author's persistent moralizing and his self-satisfied explanations of his own artistry, both of which interrupt the narrative and make very tedious reading.

3. *Tales of Flying Swordsmen*

As we have seen, in some of the early chivalric tales in classical prose there was already an element of the supernatural, but it was not until the end of the Ch'ing period that long romances in the colloquial language about flying swordsmen became popular, such as *The Seven Swordsmen and the Thirteen Knights-errant* (*Ch'i-chien Shih-san-hsia*, *c.* 1910). Since then, such tales, with ever more elaborate inventions, have become the staple reading matter of a large number of people. The heroes and heroines of these tales are

[1] Her character after marriage is obviously modelled on that of Wang Hsi-feng ('Phoenix') in the *Hung-lou Meng* (known as *Dream of the Red Chamber*), whose efficient but ruthless management of household affairs, when transplanted to the present heroine, is totally out of character.

swordsmen and swordswomen with magical powers: they can turn their swords into death rays and conceal them in their bodies when not in use, they can ride in the air on these rays or on trained birds, they often use talismans in addition to their flying swords, and some of them achieve immortality. Many of them are Buddhist monks or Taoist priests, and the rest also tend to lead a life apart from ordinary men. They perform miracles and kill monsters, and their deeds become further and further removed from chivalry and more and more fantastic. That such tales should prove so popular not only among young and naïve readers but also among highly sophisticated scholars is a matter of some interest. It seems that they fill a psychological need on the part of many readers to escape from the realities of life into a world of childish fantasies, rather in the same way as science fiction and horror films appear to do in the West. These tales are often published in serial form, in practically unlimited instalments.

Among contemporary writers of this type of fiction, Huan-chu-lou-chu ('Master of the Pavilion of the Returned Pearl'[1]) is probably the best. Although the incidents he describes are all wildly impossible, he endows them with a kind of logic of their own so that one tends to forget their absurdity.

The Chivalrous Swordsmen of the Szechwan Mountains
(Shu-shan Chien-hsia)

This is his best-known work and is written in sixty series, each consisting of several chapters. Obviously there cannot be much of a plot, but there are quite a number of cross-references between earlier and later events. The incidents, fantastic as they are, are conceived and described in great detail, so that they seem to have some kind of reality. Here, for instance, is how the writer describes the killing of a monstrous serpent by a group of young swordsmen and swordswomen. The *dramatis personae* are: Sun Nan, nick-named The White Knight; Ch'i Ling-yun, daughter of the leader of the O-mei school of swordsmanship; her younger brother Chin-ch'an; and another young lady with a flying sword, named Chu Mei.

It was nearly noon. . . . Sun Nan, standing on the cliff and holding the miraculous spear called 'As-you-wish' (*ju-yi*) with its point

[1] Rumour has it that he adopted this pseudonym after a favourite concubine named Pearl deserted him, in the hope she might return.

downward, looked intensely on the cave below, where the monster lived. As soon as it should show its head, he would strike. He was getting impatient when suddenly thick smoke and fire issued forth from the cave, and though he held in his mouth the magic herb which protected him from the poisonous fume, he smelt a stink assailing his nostrils. By now it had reached high noon, and from the cave came weird screams that grew louder and louder. Then, all of a sudden, on lifting his head, he saw, across the mountain torrent, on the slope opposite, what looked like several dozens of strands of white silk, undulating and hurtling themselves forward in rows. When he came closer, he saw they were huge pythons covered with white scales, each python measuring over a hundred feet long. Sun Nan, afraid they would see him, hurriedly jumped up the cliff again. While he was wondering what this meant, the huge pythons had crossed the mountain torrent and reduced their speed. When they had moved slowly to about a hundred paces from the cave, they stopped and coiled themselves up. Then, raising their heads high, they hissed twice towards the cave, as if reporting their arrival to the monster inside. Soon the screaming inside the cave grew even more rapid, and more and more snakes came, of all shapes and sizes. Finally came two strange serpents, one big and one small, the one on top of the other, moving as fast as wind. In a moment they reached the spot before the cave and coiled up on both sides. The big one had two heads and one body, about thirty or forty feet long, fiery red all over. On each head was a coral-like horn, which glittered in the sun. The small one was only five or six feet long, with one head and two bodies. It supported itself on its tails on the ground and stood upright like a human being. Its two bodies were covered with markings like a leopard's, and it emitted fire from its mouth. After these two serpents arrived, the other snakes all lifted their heads and hissed loudly. Strangest of all, when these weird serpents and huge pythons had crossed the mountain torrent, they all moved forward in two separate lines, leaving a path about five feet wide in the middle, as if reserving it for the monster to use when it should come out. While Sun Nan was absorbed by such strange sights, he suddenly heard a long cry from the cave, and *p'ing-p'eng*!—a stone that had sealed the opening of the cave was hurled about forty feet away. This brought him to his senses: he was so busy watching the snakes that he had almost forgotten his task. So he hurriedly adjusted the position of the spear and looked down. The smoke was growing thicker and the fire fiercer, so that he could hardly see the cave. As he began to worry that he might not be able to see clearly and thus might let the monster escape, he heard a series of loud bangs that came from inside the cave and shook the mountain. He knew this was a sign that the monster was coming out soon and concentrated his attention, holding his breath and fixing his gaze on the cave. At this critical moment, a huge ball of smoke and fire issued from the cave, and he saw vaguely a human head with long tousled hair. He was about to throw his spear when the head withdrew. Luckily he had not wasted his spear. Now Sun Nan became even more careful and waited single-mindedly for his chance.

Suddenly, all the snakes outside the cave lifted their heads and gave a loud, long hiss, which was so eerie that it made one's hair stand on end. In a moment, the sun went dim and a gloomy mist spread everywhere. Meanwhile, smoke and fire spouted out of the cave for the second time. In the light of the fire, a human-headed, serpent-bodied monster, with long hair falling over its shoulders, dashed out of the cave as fast as a whirlwind. Now, Sun Nan in his early years had been used to throwing the javelin and had never missed his target. At this crucial moment, he steadily held the miraculous spear, aimed it carefully at the monster's vulnerable point, and, shouting 'As-you-wish!', hurled it. A piercing scream, a golden ray flew: the miraculous spear hit the monster's neck squarely and pinned it on the ground, with the shaft showing above ground, still tremulous.

Those poisonous snakes, when they saw the monster pinned on the ground, raised their heads and caught sight of Sun Nan. Gnashing their teeth and sticking their tongues out, they dashed upwards to the cliff. Seeing there were so many of them, Sun Nan did not dare take any risks, but turned his sword into a ray of light and rose in the air riding on it. He flew to where Ling-yun was standing and waited to see what would happen next.

It all took less time than my words: the monstrous serpent, having been hit by the spear, had the front part of its body a few feet from the cave while the remainder was still inside. . . . Goaded by pain and anger, it shook its head and wagged its tail. After stirring with its long tail a few times, it swept away half of the cave, scattering broken stones all around. If Sun Nan had not got away earlier at an opportune moment, he might have been seriously hurt. Now the monstrous serpent, while emitting fire and smoke from its mouth, arched its body a few times, and suddenly raised its head: *whizz*!—the spear was thrown several hundred feet away, and a fountain of blood, some ten feet high, squirted from its neck.

The wounded monster dashed forward as fast as wind, and at one leap moved about a thousand feet. Then it stopped and could move no more. Actually, as it moved forward, the hundred and eight magic swords that had been planted there beforehand cut into the white line in the middle of its body, which was its only other vulnerable part, and split the monstrous serpent into two. No matter how powerful it was, having been mortally wounded twice, how could it not faint away with pain? The spot it had reached was just below the slope where Ling-yun and the others were standing. Chin-ch'an was overjoyed and wanted to go and cut off its head, but Ling-yun stopped him, telling him not to take any risks.

The monstrous serpent, after struggling for a while, uttered two weird cries. The other strange serpents and pythons had all arrived. The two that seemed to be the leaders came and held the monster's skin firmly, and with one spurt the monster freed itself from its slough. It was still human-headed and serpent-bodied, only its body was now snowy white all over and without a single scale. After crying twice, it coiled up and raised its head to look around, as if searching for its enemy. The three persons (Sun Nan, Ling-yun, and Chin-ch'an) standing above were still children at heart: they were so absorbed in watching the sight of the serpent that they had forgotten the danger they were in. While they were thus entranced, Chu Mei suddenly rushed back in distress and said, 'Sister, why don't you let out the pearl? What are you waiting for?' As soon as she finished saying this, she fell on the ground. Chin-ch'an hastened to prop her up. Chu Mei's words reminded Ling-yun what she should do: she took out the Heavenly Yellow Pearl and let it go. By now the monster had seen where the four human beings were standing, and with a long whistle, it emitted a bright red ball of fire surrounded by smoke, which thrust forth towards them. The other snakes also rushed forward. It so happened that Ling-yun had just let out the Heavenly Yellow Pearl which collided with the fire ball. Now, since ancient times, evil had never been able to overcome good. The Heavenly Yellow Pearl, as soon as it was let out, produced thousands of yellow rays and yellow clouds, and filled the mountain with a smell of flowers of sulphur, and when it collided with the fire ball, *pop*! it broke the latter and turned it into serpent's saliva which fell from the air. All at once the smoke vanished and the fire was extinguished. The other snakes and pythons, on reaching the slope, were surrounded by the yellow light of the Heavenly Yellow Pearl, and, unable to stand the smell of sulphur, they were all paralysed on the ground.

The monster was about to run away, when Chu Mei, in Chin-ch'an's arms, saw it. With an effort she pushed him and said, 'The serpent's body contains a precious thing that can save me. Go quickly and kill it.' . . . Chin-ch'an took up his Rainbow Sword and rushed off.

Sun Nan, with nothing to do, thought to himself, 'Why not kill some more snakes?' So he let out his sword-ray and pointed it at random at the snakes below. Seeing this, Ling-yun also let out her flying sword. The two sword-rays moved up and down like two dragons among the yellow clouds. After an hour or so, they saw Ling-yun's mother coming with Chin-ch'an, the latter holding at the point of his sword the human-shaped head of the monster, as big as a huge water jar. (Later, Chu Mei, who had been hit by a poisonous arrow, was saved with the help of a pearl obtained from inside the monstrous serpent's head.)

All this is no doubt childish nonsense, but one has to admit the author has shown some ingenuity and imagination.

4. *Tales emphasizing physical feats*

Another type of fiction that is still very popular consists of tales whose main interest lies in descriptions of amazing feats of strength and of various schools of swordsmanship and boxing. Some of these tales are based on the lives of actual persons, but the accounts of their feats are no doubt greatly exaggerated. This kind of fiction is usually dubbed 'military-chivalric' (*wu-hsia*), though it is often more concerned with physical culture and methods of fencing and boxing than with chivalry.

The various schools of swordsmanship and boxing described in these tales fall into two main categories: those who cultivate 'inner' or 'soft' strength, and those who cultivate 'outer' or 'hard' strength. The former make use of breath control and anatomical knowledge to defeat opponents seemingly stronger, while the latter concentrate on muscular strength and are supposed to be able to lift great weights and break stones, etc. It is believed that one school of Chinese boxing was introduced to Japan in the seventeenth century and became the origin of judo. *Karate* (empty-handed combat) may also have been influenced by Chinese boxing.[1]

In these tales, no less than in real life, Chinese physical culture is shrouded in mystery, and descriptions of fencing or pugilistic methods are often couched in pseudo-metaphysical language. For example, the most famous style of boxing and one that is still practised today (even by some Westerners) as a form of exercise, the *t'ai-chi-ch'üan*,[2] is named after the mystic symbol *t'ai-*

[1] The Japanese word *karate* is sometimes written with the characters meaning 'T'ang (i.e. China) Hand', sometimes with those meaning 'empty-hand'.

[2] Cf. Sophia Delza, *Body and Mind in Harmony*: T'ai Chi Ch'üan (New York, 1961).

chi or 'Supreme Ultimate', the origin of life. When this metaphysical element is emphasized at the expense of physical possibility, the tales then become practically indistinguishable from the previous type—those dealing with flying swordsmen.

Because most of these tales have been written since late Ch'ing times, many of them show a strong nationalistic feeling and reflect the wishful thinking of a weakened nation in the face of foreign powers with superior military strength: they portray a kind of men who possess such incredible physical strength and skill that they can dispense with modern weapons. Another expression of this popular wishful thinking was of course the Boxer Uprising of 1900, whose leaders claimed invulnerability to bullets. In spite of the disastrous consequences of this uprising, men of great physical power and pugilistic skill, real or imagined, have continued to be admired as heroes in popular fiction.

The most outstanding writer of this type of fiction is probably Hsiang K'ai-jan, who wrote under the pen-name, 'The Unworthy Man of P'ing-chiang' (P'ing-chiang Pu-hsiao-sheng). A native of P'ing-chiang in Hunan province, he was an expert boxer and advocated Chinese physical culture when he was a staff member of the governor of his native province. He is said to have become a Buddhist monk after the war. It is not known if he is still alive.

Lives of Chivalrous and Altruistic Heroes (*Hsia-yi Ying-hsiung Chuan*)

He wrote this work, which runs to sixteen series totalling eighty-four chapters, over a number of years (*c.*1926–31). It consists of a succession of anecdotes about experts in swordsmanship, boxing, and wrestling, and though the author claims these are based on facts and though many of the characters actually lived at the turn of the century, some of the incidents related are so incredible that they must be regarded as tall stories.

The most important character in the book is Huo Yuan-chia, founder of the Ching-wu Physical Culture Society. He is described as an upright, altruistic, and patriotic man, as well as the unsurpassed master of one school of boxing. As a young man, he amazed some would-be trouble-makers by kicking away two stone rollers each weighing about nine hundred pounds. Later, infuriated by the advertisement of a visiting Russian 'strong man' claiming to be the world's strongest man, Huo challenged him to a tournament, but the latter did not dare take up his challenge. Despite his nationalistic feelings, Huo refused to join the anti-foreign Boxers in 1900; on the contrary, he protected the helpless Chinese Christians in Tientsin from the wanton slaughter of the Boxers. Some time later, he went to Shanghai to challenge an English 'strong man'. This time the challenge was accepted on behalf of the 'strong man' by his financial backer, but after long negotiations and repeated delays the tournament failed to materialize, though Huo's presence in Shanghai occasioned his victory over some other Chinese boxers and led eventually to his founding of the physical culture society with the purpose of raising the standard of physical strength of the Chinese people. Since Huo belonged to a school of boxing which cultivated 'outer' strength, he supposedly damaged his internal organs by his exertions. After straining himself while overcoming some Japanese judo and *sumo* (wrestling) experts, Huo died of internal injuries. With his death the book ends.

Though most of the episodes in the book are concerned with methods of fighting and physical culture rather than chivalry, some characters do display the chivalrous spirit. For instance, Big Sword Wang the Fifth (Ta-tao Wang Wu), a professional armed escort, accompanied an outspoken Imperial Censor who had offended the Empress Dowager on his way to exile, and looked after his family, though the two were not even acquainted. Wang also tried to help T'an Ssŭ-t'ung, one of the leaders of the Reform Movement of 1898 executed by the Empress Dowager. Later, Wang was mistaken for a Boxer by the Allied forces occupying Peking and shot.

Lives of Chivalrous and Altruistic Heroes cannot be considered a long romance but can be read as a collection of entertaining yarns. The same writer's *Extraordinary Knights Roaming Over Rivers and Lakes* (*Chiang-hu Ch'i-hsia Chuan*), also known as *The Burning of the Red Lotus Monastery* (*Huo-shao Hung-lien-ssŭ*), is on the whole more fantastic, though some of the incidents are based on facts, such as the assassination of the official Ma Hsin-yi by the chivalrous Chang Wen-hsiang. This work has little literary merit but has achieved considerable popularity and has provided material for plays and films.

*

The last two types of fiction described above are indeed a far cry from historical knight-errantry, and their inclusion here may be questioned. However, since they are labelled 'chivalric fiction' in Chinese and since they represent kinds of popular Chinese literature little known in the West, I have mentioned them as a matter of interest. In fact, both kinds of fiction are still being written now, sometimes in the traditional manner and sometimes in a more 'modern' style. They can be seen not only in separate volumes but also as serials in newspapers, including Chinese-language papers published in America. There are even comic strips based on such tales, known as 'continuous pictures' (*lien-huan t'u-hua*). Some of them depict knights-errant and flying swordsmen in historical costume, others present ultra-modern 'space-knights'. These can often be rented cheaply and are devoured voraciously by children.

4

THE KNIGHT-ERRANT IN THE THEATRE

NATURE OF TRADITIONAL CHINESE DRAMA

Before discussing the role played by the knight-errant in the Chinese theatre we have to realize the nature of traditional Chinese drama and know some of the conventions of the major schools of drama. At the outset, it should be emphasized that traditional Chinese drama, though it involves singing, is not 'opera', as it is sometimes called. Chinese drama differs from Western opera in several significant ways. First, in Chinese drama the music is not specially composed for each piece as in Western opera, but taken from an existing repertoire of tunes. Plays belonging to the same school often employ practically identical tunes. It is obvious, then, that what makes one play different from another is not the music but the language and dramatic action. In other words, music is not the primary medium of expression but only one of several elements of Chinese drama. Secondly, while one does not normally read the libretto of an opera as literature, Chinese theatrical texts of the Yuan, Ming, and early Ch'ing periods were and are habitually read and enjoyed as literature, contrary to what some Western scholars think.[1] Many plays which are no longer performed because the music is lost exist purely as literature now, and even when they were performed, they were admired as much for their literary qualities as for their music. A possible indication of the relative importance of language and music in Yuan and Ming drama is the fact that generally the names of the authors of the texts are known, but those of the composers of the music are not. Moreover, whereas libretti of operas to not constitute a literary *genre*, Chinese drama of the Yuan and Ming periods repre-

[1] E.g. A. R. Davis in his introduction to *The Penguin Book of Chinese Verse* (Baltimore, 1962), p. lxix.

sent the final development of traditional literary forms prior to the impact of Western literature, and occupy a place in Chinese literary history which no one would dream of claiming for libretti of operas or lyrics of musical comedies in the history of Western literature. Therefore, we are not only justified but obliged to regard traditional Chinese theatre not as opera but as drama.[1]

Chinese drama is of course by no means unique in its use of music. Music is also used in such diverse dramas as Japanese Nō and Kabuki, Sanskrit drama, and Greek drama. But Chinese drama is less ritualistic than any of these, and of all non-Chinese dramas it is the Elizabethan that has most in common with the Chinese. Similarities between the two have often been remarked upon; for instance, A. E. Zucker pointed out resemblances between the physical and social conditions of the Chinese theatre and those of the Elizabethan,[2] and the present writer compared the Elizabethan and the Yuan theatres with regard to the use of verse, the interplay of prose and verse, the use of monologue, aside, and direct address, and the use of prologue, induction, and epilogue.[3] What is more, Chinese drama and Elizabethan drama not only resemble each other in technique but also in basic conception. To the Chinese, as to the Elizabethans, drama is not what the realists called a 'sober imitation' or 'faithful reproduction of the surfaces of life',[4] but an art of expression in language and movement (with the addition of music in the case of the Chinese). The aim of the Chinese dramatist (and of the Elizabethan) is not to create an illusion of reality on the stage but to make his audience imagine a human experience in terms of fictitious persons and events and to respond to it emotionally. This has always been taken for granted by Chinese dramatists, actors, and audiences, while in Elizabethan England the point was made explicit by defenders of the theatre: Sir Richard Baker (1568–1645) asserted that plays were acted 'not to *Deceive* others, but to make others

[1] Some of the above remarks do not apply to the Peking Theatre, which is primarily a performer's art and in which the texts used are usually of little literary merit. However, even the Peking Theatre is not the same as Western opera, as pointed out by A. C. Scott in *The Classical Theatre of China* (London, 1957), pp. 15–17.

[2] *The Chinese Theatre* (Boston, 1925), pp. 194–219.

[3] *Elizabethan and Yuan* (London, China Society Occasional Paper No. 8, 1955).

[4] William Archer, *The Old Drama and the New* (London, 1923), p. 13.

Conceive',[1] and Sir Philip Sidney asked, 'What childe is there, that comming to a Play, and seeing *Thebes* written in great Letters vpon an olde doore, doth beleeue that it is *Thebes*?'[2] Indeed, Shakespeare's injunction to his audience to exert their imagination might have been written for the Chinese theatre:

> Into a thousand parts divide one man,
> And make imaginary puissance;
> Think, when we talk of horses, that you see them,
> Printing their proud hoofs i' th' receiving earth;
> For 'tis your thoughts that now must deck our kings,
> Carry them here and there, jumping o'er times,
> Turning the accomplish of many years
> Into an hour glass;[3]

Since the Chinese dramatist, like his Elizabethan colleague, is not concerned with producing an illusion of real life on the stage, he does not try to make his audience believe that the words spoken or sung by the actors are the actual speech of the characters in the play. Just as 'the Elizabethan dramatist used language to affect his audience without attempting to disguise the fact that the language was his',[4] so did the Chinese dramatist. The main difference between the two is that the former only occasionally made use of music while the latter habitually did so. This is not as great a difference as it may seem to be, because the Elizabethan actor employed a style of acting derived from mediaeval rhetorical delivery,[5] which differed from singing only in that the rise and fall of the voice was not regulated by the musical scale.[6] Apart from this, both the Elizabethan and the Chinese dramatists used poetic means to achieve dramatic ends. Therefore, to estimate the dramatic value of a given passage or line in poetic drama, we should not ask whether this is what such a person in such a situation would actually say in real life, but whether it enables us to imagine, in the dramatist's own terms, the particular experience embodied in such a character and such a situation, and whether it

[1] *Theatrum Triumphans, or a Discourse of Plays* (London, 1670), p. 22.

[2] 'An Apologie for Poetrie', in *Elizabethan Critical Essays* (ed. Gregory Smith, Oxford, 1904), Vol. I, p. 185.

[3] *Henry V*, Prologue, 24–31.

[4] B. L. Joseph, *Elizabethan Acting* (Oxford, 1951), p. 124.

[5] *Ibid.*, pp. 1–18.

[6] See Levis, *op. cit.*, p. 40.

affects our response not only to this situation but to the play as a whole. Unless we adopt this attitude of mind, we would find many long passages in Chinese drama irrelevant or undramatic.

MAJOR SCHOOLS OF CHINESE DRAMA

Various forms of entertainment—singing, dancing, story-telling, puppetry, buffoonery, acrobatics—contributed, to a greater or lesser extent, to the formation of drama in China. But here we cannot go into the early beginnings of Chinese drama, for to do so would take up too much space and would not be strictly relevant to our present purpose—to gain enough knowledge and understanding of Chinese drama in order to appreciate the role played by the knight-errant in it. Suffice it to describe briefly the main schools of drama that have developed since full-fledged drama first came into being in China.

1. *Sung and Yuan Southern Drama* (*c.* 1150–1368)

'Southern Drama' refers to the drama that arose some time during the Southern Sung period (1127–1279) in Chekiang province (traditionally regarded as part of the South, though it would be more accurate to call it the South-east). It was then known by several different names, but since Ming times it has generally been called Southern Drama (*nan-hsi*) or Dramatic Writings (*hsi-wen*). It originated from tunes employed in Lyric Metres (*tz'ŭ*)[1] of the T'ang and Sung periods, Court music and variety shows of the Northern Sung period (960–1126), local folk songs, and a kind of story-telling combined with singing known as *chu-kung-tiao* ('in various keys and modes', so called because tunes in different keys and modes were used)[2] which first appeared under the Tartar Chin dynasty (1115–1234) in North China. These ingredients were integrated into performances that combined dramatic narrative in verse and prose with music and acting.

During the Yuan period, Southern Drama failed to compete with Northern Drama for popularity. But at the end of the period it enjoyed a revival. However, later it absorbed elements of North-

[1] I have explained this term in *The Art of Chinese Poetry*, p. 30. It refers to the same *genre* as what Levis calls 'music-poems'.

[2] For the meaning of *kung-tiao*, see Levis, *op. cit.*, pp. 70–3, and Additional Note 18.

ern Drama and developed into the Dramatic Romance of the Ming period, which will be described below.

As literature, Southern Drama is inferior to Northern Drama, though some plays are quite moving. The literary style is generally plain and natural, less poetic than Yuan Northern Drama and less sophisticated than Ming drama, but not without its own charms.

The conventions of Southern Drama will be described later, in comparison with Northern Drama.

2. *Yuan Northern Drama* (1280–1368)

Northern Drama, commonly called Mixed Plays (*tsa-chü*), developed in North China, with Peking (then called Ta-tu, 'The Grand Capital') as its centre, from sources similar to those of Southern Drama. It reached the status of genuine drama at the beginning of the Yuan dynasty and soon blossomed forth into one of the brightest flowers of Chinese literature. It flourished throughout the Yuan period but declined after the early years of the Ming. Later dramatists continued to write Northern plays, but they seldom observed all the conventions of Yuan Northern Drama, and their plays were intended for the study rather than the stage.

3. *Southern Drama and Northern Drama Compared*

The two schools of drama were similar in basic nature but differed from each other in the music used and in theatrical conventions.

In both schools, a play consisted of three elements: passages in verse to be sung called *ch'ü*,[1] spoken passages called *pai* (more precisely, monologue was called *pai* and dialogue *pin*); and acting (indicated in the texts of Southern plays by the word *chieh* and in Northern ones by the word *k'ê*). The sung passages or lyrics were in various metres, numbering several hundreds,[2] according to the tunes used. Each tune involved a separate metre, which determined how many syllables there should be in each line, what 'tone' each syllable should be, and which syllables should rhyme. Some liberty was allowed with regard to the number of syllables,

[1] Strictly speaking *ch'ü* means 'tunes', but in customary usage it often refers to the words sung as well, or even to the whole drama. Thus, Yuan Northern Drama is sometimes called 'Yuan *ch'ü*', though it should be called 'Yuan *tsa-chü*'.

[2] Cf. Additional Note 19. (The number of metres is the same as the number of tunes used.)

for additional words could be inserted, called 'Padding Words' (*ch'en-tzŭ*, without derogatory implications), but the tone pattern and rhyme scheme must be observed. The tonal movement of the words as spoken always agreed with the melodic line of the music, unlike modern Chinese songs in which little or no attention is paid to this agreement between the fixed 'tones' (or 'neumes' as J. H. Levis calls them) of the spoken words and the melody of the music, so that the words often sound unintelligible or ludicrous.[1] These sung passages could form part of a dialogue or carry forward the dramatic action, but they were mainly used to express the characters' emotions, to describe the scene, or to evoke an appropriate atmosphere for the action, in the absence of heavily built-up scenery, stage lighting, etc. They formed the chief attraction of a play, both as poetry and as singing. Of course, this is not to say that the spoken passages and the acting were not important. The spoken passages were for the most part in the colloquial language of the day, though sometimes literary prose and even formal verse were used, especially at the entry and exit of a character. Of the acting little can be said, except that there is no reason to suppose that the acting style in Yuan times differed greatly from that still used in the traditional theatre today, with its choreographic movements and symbolic gestures.

Characters in both schools of drama were classified into various types. There were four main classes of characters: (1) serious male characters (some called *sheng* and others *mo* in Southern Drama, all called *mo* in Northern Drama), including male lead (*sheng* in Southern Drama, *cheng-mo* in Northern), second male lead (*fu-mo*), juvenile lead (*hsiao-mo*), 'super' or 'extra' (*wai-mo*, usually abbreviated as *wai*); (2) female characters (*tan*), including female lead (*cheng-tan*), additional female character (*t'ieh-tan*), flirtatious females (*hua-tan*), and others; (3) choleric men (*ching*),[2] men of violent temper, often but not necessarily villains; (4) clowns (*ch'ou*).

[1] E.g. in the popular song 'Rose, Rose, I Love You', the last line, which consists of the same words as the title (*mei*^{2}-*kuei*^{4}, *mei*^{2}-*kuei*^{4}, *wo*^{3} *ai*^{4} *ni*^{3}), actually sounds like 'Beautiful ghost, younger-sister return, nest low mud' (*mei*^{3}-*kuei*^{3}, *mei*^{4}-*kuei*^{1}, *wo*^{1} *ai*^{3} *ni*^{2}), for the 'tone' of each syllable, indicated here by the raised small Arabic numeral, is distorted in singing.

[2] The exact significance of *ching*, as that of the other names, is by no means clear. In later theatre this type is called 'colourful face' (*hua-mien* or *hua-lien*), but since the latter term did not exist in Yuan times, and since the *ching* resembles the 'choleric man' in Elizabethan drama, I have translated it thus.

With regard to music, we know the names of about four hundred and fifty tunes used in Sung and Yuan Southern Drama and over two hundred and thirty used in Yuan Northern Drama.[1] These tunes are now known only in later versions which kept the basic melodic lines but changed the actual notes. Consequently, Yuan Northern plays are never performed now, while scenes from Southern plays can be acted, but only in later versions. However, the metres still exist, and one can 'fill in' the words to suit the theoretical tunes. The two repertoires of tunes overlap each other by only some fourteen tunes; moreover, a tune from the Southern repertoire may bear the same name as one from the Northern but actually differ from the latter in the number of syllables to be sung. It is clear, therefore, that the music used in each school was largely different. Furthermore, the tunes used in Southern Drama were all in the pentatonic scale, those in Northern Drama employed the heptatonic scale in addition to the pentatonic. The chief accompanying instrument in Southern Drama was probably the flute (some say the horizontal *ti*, others say the vertical *hsiao*), that in Northern Drama a string instrument (according to some, the four-stringed lute *p'i-pa*; according to others, the three-stringed *san-hsien*, the prototype of the Japanese samisen).[2]

The following different conventions may be noted.

In Southern Drama, at the beginning of a performance, an actor dressed in the costume of a servant of the Sung dynasty would appear to announce the play to be performed and give a summary of its contents. This was called 'opening the scene' (*k'ai-ch'ang*) or 'family door' (*chia-men*). Since it resembles the prologue in Western drama, I shall refer to it as 'prologue'. In Northern Drama there was no such prologue, but a short scene could be added at the beginning of a play or between two acts. This was called *hsieh-tzŭ*,[3] and since it is similar in function to the induction in Elizabethan drama I have translated it as 'induction'.[4] The prologue in Southern Drama and the induction in Northern Drama are totally different in nature: in the former, the actor remains outside the dramatic action; in the latter, dramatic impersonation of a character or characters is involved.

[1] See Additional Note 19.

[2] See Additional Note 20.

[3] This term has been interpreted in different ways. The most likely literal meaning is 'peg'.

[4] *Elizabethan and Yuan*, pp. 10–11.

Southern plays had no definite length: they could run from a few scenes to some thirty scenes. Actually in Sung and Yuan times no scene-division was made; the practice of dividing a Southern play into scenes (*ch'u*) was introduced by Ming editors. In Northern Drama, with very few exceptions, every play consisted of four acts (*chê*), with an induction or even two if desired. This division into acts was also due to Ming editors, but the fact remains that normally a Yuan Northern play did consist of four distinct units (in each of which tunes in the same key and mode were used), even though they were not called 'acts' in Yuan times.[1] This difference between the two schools of drama often resulted in more dramatic tension and greater structural unity in Northern plays.

In Northern Drama, only the male or female lead was allowed to sing (but the same actor could play different roles in successive acts), or at most the two of them could sing alternately in successive acts. This placed great restrictions on the dramatist. In Southern Drama the characters could sing in dialogue or in chorus.

In Southern Drama, every play must end happily, with the hero and heroine present. This was known as 'reunion' (*t'uan-yuan*). Northern plays occasionally ended with the death of the hero or heroine, though poetic justice was always fulfilled. In neither school of drama do we find tragedy in the Aristotelian sense.

Finally, Southern Drama was not classified in any way, while Northern plays were classified into twelve categories, according to the *T'ai-ho Cheng-yin P'u*, or *Handbook on the Orthodox Music of Supreme Harmony* (1398) by Chu Ch'üan, Prince Hsien of Ning, a son of the first Emperor of the Ming dynasty. The twelve categories are: (1) *shen-hsien tao-hua*, 'attaining immortality and becoming gods'; (2) *yin-chü lo-tao*, 'living as recluses and happily following the *tao*', also called *lin-ch'üan ch'iu-ho*, 'woods and fountains, hills and valleys'—*original note*; (3) *p'i-p'ao ping-hu*, 'wearing robes and carrying the official sceptre', i.e. *chün-ch'en tsa-chü*, plays about kings and officials—*original note*; (4) *chung-ch'en lieh-shih*, 'loyal officials and heroic martyrs'; (5) *hsiao yi lien chieh*, 'filial devotion, justice, integrity, and chastity'; (6) *ch'ih-chien ma-ch'an*,

[1] In Yuan editions of plays, the word *chê* is used to indicate a quick passing scene rather than a whole act.

'scolding wicked officials and cursing flatterers'; (7) *chu-ch'en ku-tzŭ* 'exiled officials and orphaned sons'; (8) *p'u-tao kan-pang,* 'swords and clubs', i.e. *t'o-po tsa-chü,* plays involving stripping down to the waist[1]—*original note*; (9) *feng-hua hsüeh-yueh,* 'wind and flowers, snow and moon' (romantic love stories—*present author's note*); (10) *pei-huan li-ho,* 'sadness and joy, partings and reunions'; (11) *yen-hua fen-tai,* 'misty flowers, powder, and eyebrow paint', i.e. *hua-tan tsa-chü,* plays about flirtatious females—*original note*; (12) *shen-t'ou kuei-mien,* 'gods' heads and devils' faces', i.e. *shen-fo tsa-chü,* plays about gods and Buddhas—*original note.* This system of classification is obviously unscientific and involves much overlapping,[2] but it is historically significant, for it seems to have been partially derived from the classification of oral stories of the Sung period mentioned earlier in the present volume.[3] Thus, category 1 (or perhaps 12, or both) of Yuan drama and category 7 of Sung stories correspond to each other; category 9 of Yuan drama corresponds to category 3 of Sung stories. Of particular interest to us is category 8 of Yuan drama ('swords and clubs'), which is the same as categories 5 and 6 of Sung fiction. Another book, Hsia Po-ho's *Ch'ing-lou*[4] *Chi,* or *Notes on Singing Girls* (1364), mentions 'plays about royalty' (*chia-t'ou tsa-chü*), 'plays about plaintive ladies' (*kuei-yuan tsa-chü*), 'plays about flirtatious females' (*hua-tan tsa-chü*), and 'plays about outlaws' (*lu-lin tsa-chü,* literally, 'green woods plays', the term *lu-lin* or 'green woods' being a euphemism for outlaws). However, these seem to be different names for some of the categories mentioned by Chu Ch'üan rather than additional kinds of plays. 'Plays about royalty' probably refer to the same kind as Chu's category 3; 'plays about plaintive ladies' no doubt refer to romantic love stories or category 9; 'plays about flirtatious females', as we have seen, are the same as category 11; and 'plays about outlaws' may be regarded as part of category 8. There is no strong reason to suppose, therefore, that Yuan Northern Drama had more than twelve categories of plays.

[1] See Additional Note 21.

[2] Cf. J. I. Crump, 'The Elements of Yuan Opera', in *Journal of Asian Studies,* Vol. XVII, No. 3 (1958), p. 420.

[3] See above, p. 107.

[4] The expression *ch'ing-lou,*' green mansion', means a house of singing girls.

4. *Ming and Ch'ing Dramatic Romances* (*c.* 1368–1850)

At the end of the Yuan period, Northern Drama declined and Southern Drama became the vogue. However, the latter absorbed more and more tunes from the Northern repertoire and at the same time adopted stricter rules, so that it developed into a new kind of drama known as *ch'uan-ch'i,* a term which had previously been used to designate prose tales or drama in general, but now came to be applied specifically to this new drama.[1] In this sense, it may be translated as Dramatic Romance. The transition from Yuan Southern Drama to Ming Dramatic Romance was naturally a gradual one, so that one cannot draw a clear line of demarcation between the two. Roughly speaking, plays written at the end of the Yuan and during the early years of the Ming (*c.* 1368–1400) still largely followed the conventions of Yuan Southern Drama, while those written after about 1450 may be considered more truly representative of the Dramatic Romance. This new drama remained the main type of drama throughout the Ming period (1368–1644). At first, several local styles of singing were used in performing it, but during the Chia-ching period (1522–66), a newly evolved style of singing, that of K'un-shan district in Kiangsu province, surpassed all other styles in popularity, so much so that the term *K'un-ch'ü* ('K'un-shan tunes') has become identified with the drama itself, although strictly speaking it should only refer to the singing, while the texts of the plays should be called Dramatic Romances. The *K'un-ch'ü* continued to flourish well into the Ch'ing period, till it was superseded in popularity by the Peking Theatre (*c.* 1850).[2]

Ming and Ch'ing Dramatic Romances differed from pre-Ming Southern Drama in several ways. First, the former used Southern and Northern tunes together, while the latter only occasionally used tunes from the Northern repertoire. By combining the two repertoires and adding new variations, the Dramatic Romance had over a thousand tunes at its disposal. Secondly, while pre-Ming Southern Drama had no fixed length, Ming and Ch'ing Dramatic Romances generally ran from twenty to sixty scenes. Since this obviously made it difficult to perform a play *in toto*, each scene was so designed as to be more or less independent, and could be

[1] See Additional Note 8.

[2] Cf. A. C. Scott, *op. cit.*, pp. 32–4.

performed separately. Nevertheless, each Dramatic Romance as a whole usually showed much greater sense of structure than pre-Ming Southern Drama. Thirdly, the types of characters in Dramatic Romances were more numerous than in Yuan Southern Drama, though they did not go beyond the four main classes but were only subdivisions of these. Lastly, the language of Dramatic Romances tended to be much more refined and sophisticated and less natural than that of Yuan Southern Drama. In short, Ming and Ch'ing Dramatic Romances inclined towards closet drama and became further and further removed from the popular stage.

Dramatic Romances were not strictly classified, but according to Lü T'ien-ch'eng's *Ch'ü P'in*, or *Degrees of Excellence in Drama* (1610), they fell into six main categories: (1) *chung hsiao*, 'loyalty and filial devotion'; (2) *chieh yi*, 'chastity and justice'; (3) *feng-ch'ing*, 'romantic love'; (4) *hao-hsia*, 'generous knights-errant'; (5) *kung-ming*, 'official deeds and honours'; (6) *hsien-fo*, 'immortals and Buddhist deities'. Among these, it is of course the fourth one that concerns us.

Scenes from some Ming and Ch'ing Dramatic Romances, sung in the *K'un-ch'ü* style, are still performed sometimes, but the number of actor-singers who can perform them and the number of people who can appreciate them are both limited. The music is gentle and soft, and the principle accompanying instrument is the horizontal flute (*ti*).

5. *The Peking Theatre* (*c.* 1820—*the present*)

During the last decades of the eighteenth century the Dramatic Romance, as performed in the *K'un-ch'ü* style, already became too rarefied for the popular audience, although for some time it managed to hold its own against other local theatres. However, by the middle of the nineteenth century its popularity had been entirely superseded by that of the Peking Theatre.

The Peking Theatre (*Ching-hsi*) did not originate in Peking but received its name from the fact that its formation and emergence as the dominant form of theatre took place in the capital. It first appeared about 1820 and grew in popularity, till it achieved something of the status of a national theatre, a position which it still holds today.

The Peking Theatre uses mainly two types of singing which originally came from Shensi and Hupeh provinces and were brought to Peking by Anhwei troupes. These are called *hsi-p'i* and *erh-huang* (the precise meanings of which are matters of dispute) and are often referred to together by the abbreviated name *p'i-huang*.[1] The tunes used only number about twenty, with variations. This is very limited indeed compared with the vast repertoire of tunes used in *K'un-ch'ü* performances of Dramatic Romances. The chief accompanying instrument in the Peking Theatre is the two-stringed *hu-ch'in*, while percussion instruments also play important parts. The music is much louder than that of the *K'un-ch'ü*.

The Peking Theatre relies for its effect much more on the skills of the actor-singer than on the text of the play. The lyrics to be sung are for the most part in doggerel verse, and the plays are generally by anonymous writers of no great talent. Thus, in spite of its immense popularity and its undoubted artistic qualities as 'theatre', the Peking Theatre is not important from the literary point of view.

Plays in the Peking Theatre are usually short compared with Dramatic Romances. Since the plots often consist of episodes from well-known stories, attention is concentrated on the delineation of these episodes, while little regard is paid to the unfolding of the whole story, which the audience is assumed to know. A typical performance comprises scenes from different plays, rather than a complete play in itself.

The plays are broadly divided into two categories: civil and military (*wen-hsi* and *wu-hsi*). Many plays belonging to the latter are concerned with chivalry.

The characters fall into the same four main classes as in previous theatre, with further subdivisions.[2] In particular, we may note the type called 'military men' (*wu-sheng*), including 'military men in full armour' (*ch'ang-k'ao wu-sheng*) and 'military men in short dress' (*tuan-ta wu-sheng*). The former impersonate famous generals in history, while the latter often impersonate knights-errant.

*

The above digression into Chinese theatrical history (which I hope has not been entirely devoid of interest in itself) will serve as a background against which we may examine some examples of

[1] Cf. A. C. Scott, *op. cit.*, pp. 34–5.

[2] For a detailed description of the various types of characters in the Peking Theatre, see *ibid.*, pp. 66–79.

knight-errantry in drama. Since Chinese dramatists rarely invented their own plots but took their stories from history and literature as well as oral legends and current events, many of the figures mentioned earlier in these pages we shall encounter again in dramatic guise. The relation between prose fiction and drama is a particularly close one, for not only do we find dramatizations of tales or episodes from long prose romances, but also plays and tales both derived from common sources, and even episodes in prose romances based on plays, as we shall see.

KNIGHTS-ERRANT IN SOUTHERN DRAMA

Not many specimens of Southern Drama have come down to us: altogether twenty plays that can be accepted as Sung or Yuan works have survived, of which the majority belong to late Yuan. In addition, we have excerpts from a hundred and twenty other plays, and we know the titles of another thirty-two plays now lost.[1] Among the plays of which only fragments remain, three involved chivalry and are based on tales of the T'ang period. The first one, entitled *Mo-lê Tao Hung-hsiao*, or *Mo-lê Stealing Hung-hsiao*, is based on the tale *The K'un-lun Slave*.[2] Mo-lê, it will be recalled, is the name of the chivalrous slave, and Hung-hsiao, 'Red Silk', is used as if it were the young lady's name, since in the tale she is said to have worn a red silk dress when she first met her lover. Unfortunately, the seven lyrics which represent all that is left of the play are sung by the young lady or her lover and not by Mo-lê, so that we do not know how the dramatist delineated his character. The other two plays, *Wang Hsien-k'ê* and *Wu-shuang Chuan* ('The Life of Wu-shuang'), are both based on the same story, *Liu Wu-shang*,[3] in which the knight-errant Ku Hung restores the girl Wu-shuang to her lover Wang Hsien-k'ê. Again, none of the lyrics which have survived from either play is sung by the knight, but he must have played an important part in each play to bring about the desired happy reunion.

On the whole, Southern Drama was more interested in romantic love stories and domestic tales than in historical or heroic stories. So, even if there were other plays unknown to us, most of them

[1] See Additional Note 22.
[2] See above, p. 88.
[3] See above, p. 99.

probably did not deal with chivalry. As far as chivalric plays are concerned, our loss in Southern Drama is not very great.

KNIGHTS-ERRANT IN NORTHERN DRAMA

1. *Yuan period*

When we turn to Northern Drama, we find a different picture. As we have seen, chivalric plays formed one of the twelve categories of Yuan Northern Drama. In particular, plays about the chivalrous outlaws of Liang-shan[1] were very popular. More than thirty plays about them are known to have existed, of which ten are extant, including four of uncertain date (late Yuan or early Ming). Some of the plays contain episodes not found in *Water Margin*, and the characterization of the same heroes also differs at times from that in the prose romance. It appears, then, that the plays were written before the first version of the romance was made, and were probably based on oral tales, some of which also found their way into *Water Margin*. Indeed, some parts of the romance may have been based on the plays.

Among the Liang-shan heroes, Li K'uei, nicknamed 'Black Whirlwind', must have been a special favourite of Yuan audiences, judging by the number of plays written about him. We know the titles of fourteen plays by six dramatists about Li K'uei.[2] Kao Wen-hsiu (*fl.* 1264) alone wrote eight of these, of which only one, *Black Whirlwind Achieving Double Merit* (*Hei-hsüan-feng Shuang-hsien-kung*) has survived.[3] In this play, Li K'uei is sent by Sung Chiang, leader of the band of outlaws at Liang-shan, to escort a friend named Sun, who is taking his wife on a pilgrimage. It turns out that Sun's wife has been carrying on a love affair with an official and they take this opportunity to elope. When Sun goes to lodge a complaint, he is thrown into jail, for the official is no other than his wife's lover. Li K'uei saves Sun from prison, and kills the woman and her lover as punishment. One other Yuan play about Li K'uei has survived: *Li K'uei's Apology* by K'ang Chin-chih, a contemporary of Kao's. This is a much better play and deserves more detailed treatment:

[1] See above, pp. 108–110.

[2] Li K'uei also appears in several other plays, though not as the protagonist.

[3] The authenticity of this play has been questioned, but the problem is too complicated to discuss here.

Li K'uei's Apology

This is an abbreviated title of the play. In printed texts of Yuan Northern Drama, at the end of each play we find a couplet of verse, the first line being the 'subject' (*t'i-mu*), and the second line being the 'proper title' (*cheng-ming*). Sometimes four lines of verse are used instead of two. Since even one line, usually consisting of seven or eight syllables, is still too long, it is customary to shorten it to three or four syllables. The 'subject' and 'proper title' of the present play are:

In the Almond-blossom Village, old Wang Lin makes an accusation;
At Liang-shan Marsh, Black Whirlwind tenders a humble apology.

In some editions, the word 'old' is omitted in the first line, and the name 'Li K'uei' is used instead of 'Black Whirlwind' in the second line. The play is usually referred to by its shortened name *Li K'uei Fu-ching,* literally '*Li K'uei Carrying Thorns on his Back*', a conventional expression meaning to apologize humbly and alluding to General Lien Po (*fl.* 283 B.C.) who apologized in this manner to Minister Lin Hsiang-ju.

The play consists of the usual four acts. In Act I, two villains, Sung Kang and Lu Chih-en, pretend to be the Liang-shan leaders Sung Chiang and Lu Chih-shen, and forcibly take away the tavern-keeper Wang Lin's daughter, called Man-t'ang-chiao, 'Roomful of Charms'. When our hero Li K'uei comes to the tavern for a drink, he finds old Wang in sorrow and learns what has happened. Believing that his leader and one of his comrades have really done this, Li rushes back to Liang-shan.

In Act II, Li K'uei comes back to Liang-shan in righteous indignation and accuses Sung Chiang and Lu Chih-shen of having abducted the girl. Sung Chiang denies it and makes Li agree to a bet: if Sung is proved guilty, he will forfeit his life; if not, Li has to lose his.

In Act III, Li K'uei, together with Sung Chiang and Lu Chih-shen, returns to old Wang's tavern. Wang naturally denies that these are the same men who have taken his daughter, in spite of Li's desperate importunities. After the Liang-shan heroes have left, the real malefactors arrive. Old Wang plies them with wine while planning to inform the heroes.

In the final act, Li K'uei, with thorns on his back, thus carrying out to the letter the conventional manner of apology, begs Sung Chiang to forgive him, but the latter refuses. Li then decides to commit suicide, but just as he is about to do so, old Wang comes to announce the presence of the true villains in his tavern. Thereupon Sung Chiang allows Li K'uei to go and catch them to redeem himself. The play ends with Li's success and the execution of the villains.

This play is written in a delightfully lively style. In the first act, the lyrics sung by the hero, freely interspersed with spoken monologue, are justly famous. The following is a translation of the first three lyrics, together with the spoken lines. I shall try to indicate the original metres by giving as many stresses in English in each line as there are syllables in Chinese. The names of the tunes to which the lyrics are written will be omitted, and the translated 'padding words'[1] will be italicized.[2]

(*The male lead*, cheng-mo, *impersonating* Li K'uei, *enters intoxicated, and speaks*):

To be sick for wine is worse than death! I am no other than Li K'uei, nick-named Black Whirlwind, of Liang-shan Marsh. I received my elder brother Sung Kung-ming's orders, giving us three days' leave to go and enjoy the fine views of spring. Now the time is up and I should go back to the mountains, but I am already drunk. I might as well go to old Wang Lin's place and have one more drink! Let's go!

(*Sings first lyric*):

My thirst is hard to quench fully,
My drunken soul is still searching
For the village brew.
I've just asked Wang Liu:[3]

(*Speaks*): I asked him: Where can I get some wine? The rascal wouldn't say anything but started to walk away. I shouted, Where are you going? and caught up with him. I seized him and was about to hit him when he said, Don't hit me, father, there is wine, there is!

[1] See above, p. 143.

[2] The same rules will be followed in subsequent translations from dramatic works.

[3] In Yuan drama, Wang Liu and Sha San are conventional names, like 'Tom, Dick, and Harry'.

(*Sings*):

He said, Ah,
There, in that tavern, there is wine!

(*Second lyric*):

It is just
The time of the Clear and Bright Festival,[1]
When, (who would have thought?) wind and rain grieve for the flowers.
The mild wind gradually rises,
The evening rain has just stopped.

I can see
The willow trees whose shades half hide the wine shop,
The peach blossoms whose bright colour reflects the fishing boats,

As well as
The fresh green water of the Spring river with its wrinkling ripples,
The swallows flying to and fro,
And the sea gulls far away.

(*Speaks*): If anyone says our Liang-shan Marsh has no scenery, I'll hit the rascal on the mouth!

(*Sings third lyric*):

Here we have
Graceful blue mountains locked up by mist,
Green-willowy islets covered with smoke.

(*Speaks*): See how that oriole on the peach-tree there pecks and pecks at the petals and drops them on the water! How pretty! Now, who was it who said something about it? Let me think. Yes, I remember, it was my brother Scholar Wu[2] who said:

(*Sings*):

He said this is called
'The flirtatious peach blossoms chasing the water in its flow'.[3]

(*Speaks*): Let me pick up a petal and have a look. How red the petal is! (*Laughs*). And how black my fingers are!

[1] *Ch'ing-ming*, a time when people visit their ancestral graves. It falls about Easter.

[2] Wu Yung, nicknamed 'Scholar', a village schoolmaster who joined the Liang-shan band as one of its chief strategists.

[3] From a quatrain by Tu Fu.

(*Sings*):

Truly this is
A powdery lining setting off the deep rouge.

(*Speaks*): Rather than letting you go to waste, little petal, I'll let you go and chase the other petals like you. Let's chase them, let's chase them! Ah, while chasing the fallen petals,

(*Sings*):

I've already come to
This tavern by the rustic bridge over the willowy ford.

(*Speaks*): No good! I'm afraid to be late and break my brother's orders. I simply have to go back!

(*Sings*):

Yet if I don't drink,
This tavern's hanging sign is tempting me so:

See, see, how it
Dances in the eastern wind at the tip of the bending pole!

The above lyrics and spoken lines illustrate how the dramatist intermingles verse with prose, singing with speech, so as to bring to life Li K'uei's childlike personality and at the same time paint a spring landscape. Of course, the poetic language belongs to the author and not the hero: no more are we meant to suppose that the Liang-shan outlaw could speak thus and even remember a line from Tu Fu (admittedly having heard it from Scholar Wu) than we are supposed to regard the First Murderer in *Macbeth* as indulging in poetic fancy when he says, 'The west yet glimmers with some streaks of day'.[1] Nevertheless, the lines do create an impression that Li K'uei has some sensibility which forms a humorous contrast to his rough exterior and endears him to us.

In the second act, Li K'uei's outburst of anger to Sung Chiang for the latter's alleged evil deed is well portrayed, together with the hero's sympathy for the old man. In a lyric full of colourful epithets and quasi-onomatopoeic words (alliterative and rhyming syllables, some of which are meaningful and others suggestive by their sound alone), Li K'uei describes the old man's suffering. The following is a clumsy attempt to give some idea of this passage:

[1] *Macbeth*, Act III, Sc. iii.

LI K'UEI (*sings*):

That old man,
For a little while,
Cries bitterly in that thatched tavern of his.

(*Speaks*): Looking towards our mountain stronghold, Sung Chiang, how he hates you!

(*Sings*):

He thus
Stands, worried, anxious, all upset!
That old man,
For a little while,
Puffs like an angry bull outside his rustic door.

(*Speaks*): And he cries, Oh, Man-t'ang-chiao, my child!

(*Sings*):

He thus
Fumes with rage, doubled up with pain!

SUNG CHIANG (*speaks*): How does he show his sorrow?

LI K'UEI (*sings*):

That old man,
For a little while,
Sinks down depressed by the big wine jar.

(*Speaks*): He takes up a scoop, lifts the straw cover, scoops up a ladleful of cold wine,[1] and gulps it down!

(*Sings*):

He thus
Gets drunk bewildered, befuddled, bemused!
That old man,
Holding a straw mat,
Slowly, slowly, puts it on his earthen bed.[2]

(*Speaks*): He goes outside the door, takes a look, and doesn't see her.

And he cries, Oh, Man-t'ang-chiao, my child!

[1] In China, wine is usually heated before serving, and cold wine is considered undesirable.

[2] In North China, many people sleep on beds built with earth and/or bricks, called *k'ang*.

(*Sings*):

He thus

Goes to sleep, all bundled up!
Oh, how can he carry on like this!
Oh, how can he carry on like this!—

SUNG CHIANG (*speaks*): What about him?

LI K'UEI (*sings*):

He says that

At our Liang-shan Marsh,
The water is not sweet and the men are not just!

In short, various traits of Li K'uei's character—his childlike simplicity, his rashness, his sympathy for the oppressed, his strong sense of justice—are all vividly presented. This portrait of Li K'uei is somewhat different from that in *Water Margin*: in the play he has more charm and shows less violence. This difference in characterization between the play and the prose romance may be partly due to different oral traditions on which each was based, and partly due to different qualities of the two literary *genres*—poetic drama and prose fiction. In the more realistic prose romance, Li K'uei sometimes seems to us too cruel, but in the consciously artificial atmosphere of the drama his character is softened, for in Chinese drama it is the combined effects of poetic language, music, and stylized acting which create the necessary 'aesthetic distance' without which some of the action (such as the casual despatch of the villains at the end of this play) would have seemed callous and shocking. The same principle applies to other non-representational theatres: the blinding of Oedipus and of Gloucester, and even Hamlet's killing of Polonius, had they occurred in realistic plays, would have appeared no less shocking than some of the deeds carried out by Chinese knights-errant in the theatre. Another relevant consideration is the necessity of observing theatrical conventions. Since in Yuan Northern Drama only the male or female lead could sing, in this play the dramatist had to cast Li K'uei as the male lead (*cheng-mo*), a type that required certain dignity of appearance and manners. In later theatre Li K'uei is often cast as a *ching* or 'colourful face' and therefore appears both more violent and less serious.[1]

[1] See below, p. 171.

Another Yuan play in which Li K'uei appears will be described below:

The Chrysanthemum Valley (*Huang-hua Yü*)

This is an anonymous Yuan play, the 'subject' and 'proper title' of which run thus:

Li Shan-erh plays the detective at Water-south Stronghold;
Lu Chih-shen enjoys the view of the Chrysanthemum Valley.

Li Shan-erh is another name for Li K'uei, apparently his pet name, which is often mentioned in Yuan plays but not in *Water Margin*. Lu Chih-shen is the name assumed by Lu Ta after he becomes a monk.[1] The poetic title of the play, alas, is really quite irrelevant to the plot: it is taken from the short opening scene in which the Liang-shan leader Sung Chiang gives his men three days' leave to go and enjoy the fine view of chrysanthemums in autumn.

In the next scene of the first act, a young scholar Liu Ch'ing-fu and his wife stop at a village inn for a drink. While Liu's wife entertains him with a song, she is overheard by Master Ts'ai, a powerful official's son and a bully. The villain demands that Liu's wife should serve him wine, and when Liu refuses, he is bound and beaten up. Yang Hsiung, one of the Liang-shan heroes, comes in and finds out what the situation is. Thereupon he beats Ts'ai and drives him away. He then releases Liu and reveals his own identity, telling the latter to come to Liang-shan if he should have any more trouble. After Yang has left, the young couple are full of apprehensions. Liu's wife gives her husband a comb as a token, in case they should be separated. Her premonition is all too soon fulfilled: the villain comes back and abducts her, taking her to his hide-out called Water-south Stronghold (Shui-nan Chai).

In the second act, Liu arrives at Liang-shan and lodges a complaint with the leader Sung Chiang. Li K'uei volunteers to go to Water-south Stronghold to investigate. Liu gives Li his wife's comb as a means of recognition, and Black Whirlwind leaves, having promised Sung Chiang that he will disguise himself and exert caution.

In the third act Li K'uei comes to Water-south Stronghold, disguised as a hawker. Finding Liu's wife alone, he shows her the comb, which she recognizes. When the villain Ts'ai comes home,

[1] See above, p. 113.

he is soundly thrashed by Li K'uei and runs away. Li then takes the woman back to her husband.

In the final act, Ts'ai seeks refuge in a Buddhist monastery supported by his family. Lu Chin-shen, the chivalrous officer turned outlaw in monk's habit, also comes to stay for the night. When he hears Ts'ai is here, he provokes the latter to a fight and chastises him. Other members of the Liang-shan band appear and capture Ts'ai.

This play is a good illustration of the chivalrous behaviour of the Liang-shan heroes, and shows in what light these heroes were regarded by Yuan dramatists and audiences. When the scholar has lost his wife, he knows better than to go and lodge a complaint with the local official, but goes to Liang-shan instead. And when the villain is caught, he is ordered by Sung Chiang to be executed. Obviously both the dramatist and his audience took all this as a matter of course—an ironic reflection on the justice and efficiency of officialdom!

One interesting feature of this play is that the male lead (*cheng-mo*) impersonates three different characters: in Act I, he plays Yang Hsiung; in Acts II and III, Li K'uei; and in Act IV, Lu Chih-shen. This was a makeshift forced on the author by the convention that only the lead could sing,[1] while the plot demanded three heroes to play major roles (naturally the same hero could not beat up the villain at first encounter and then go to spy on him and meet him again in the monastery). I believe that in such cases the same actor played and sang the different roles in successive acts, rather than that several actors of the same type shared the parts, as a contemporary Chinese scholar suggested, for the stage directions clearly state '*cheng-mo* impersonating Li K'uei', '*cheng-mo* impersonating Lu Chih-shen', etc., which suggests that it was the same *cheng-mo* actor. The same arrangement is still practised in the Peking Theatre sometimes.

The remaining extant Yuan plays about the Liang-shan heroes are less interesting and will not be discussed.

It is amusing to realize that some of the heroes must have been played by women in Yuan times, for according to *Notes on Singing Girls* at least three actresses specialized in playing heroes of the green woods (i.e. outlaws). What is more, we are told that

[1] The song sung by Liu's wife in Act I, being presented *as a song* and not as part of a monologue or dialogue, does not break this convention.

one of them had small feet (not bound feet), and another had a blind eye and tatooed arms and legs. One wonders what they looked like as heroes on the stage!

2. *Ming period*

There are nine extant Ming Northern plays concerned with chivalric subjects (apart from those which may be late Yuan or early Ming works mentioned above): three about the Liang-shan heroes, four based on chivalric tales of the T'ang period, and two based on history. Let us first consider the plays about the Liang-shan heroes.

Black Whirlwind's Altruism

The full title of this play is *Black Whirlwind, displaying altruism, lightly parts with wealth* (*Hei-hsüan-feng Chang-yi Shu-ts'ai*). It is written by Chu Yu-tun (1379–1439), Prince Hsien of Chou, a grandson of the first Emperor of the Ming dynasty.

The plays follows Yuan conventions in its structure. In Act I, scene 1, Sung Chiang sends Li K'uei and Yen Ch'ing to buy some provisions for his men. In the next scene, an old peasant Li Pieh-ku enters with his wife, his eighteen-year-old daughter, and two younger children. He reveals that because he owes the government some grain as tax in kind, he is going to town to sell the two younger children. It being nightfall, Li and his family go to a temple to stay for the night. Then the villain, Inspector General Chao, enters with his attendants. On seeing old Li's pretty daughter, he wants to take her for his wife. When the old man refuses, Chao ties him to a tree and forces the girl to serve him wine. At this juncture, Li K'uei and Yen Ch'ing enter. When they have heard the story, Li K'uei offers to pay the amount of grain owed by the old man in return for his release. The villain agrees to free the old man but insists on marrying the daughter on the spot. When Li K'uei remonstrates with him, Chao orders his men to attack. Li K'uei and Yen Ch'ing return the blows, and chase the villain and his followers away. They then give old Li the amount of grain he needs and tells him their names.

In Act II, Inspector General Chao comes to old Li's house and threatens to kill the family unless the girl is married to him soon. Old Li goes to Liang-shan and reports this to Sung Chiang, who summons Li K'uei to come and help. Li asks a female member of the band, nicknamed Yi-chang-ch'ing ('Ten-foot Black'[1]), to accompany him, for he has thought up a ruse: he will disguise himself as the bride while she will go as the marriage broker.

The ruse is duly carried out in Act III: in a highly comic scene, Li K'uei is carried in the bridal palaquin to Inspector General Chao's house, accompanied by Yi-chang-ch'ing as the marriage broker. After a mock wedding ceremony, they throw off their disguises, beat up the villain, and tie him to a post. Li then writes four lines of verse on the wall to show that he is responsible for this. After their departure, Chao has himself freed by a neighbour, and on seeing the writing on the wall (in more than one sense), runs away in fear.

In Act IV, Chao seeks refuge in a Buddhist monastery, and is found and caught by Wu Sung and Lei Heng, two other Liang-shan heroes sent by Sung Chiang to reinforce the others.

Although the plot of this play obviously owes much to earlier plays, notably *The Chrysanthemum Valley* described above, it shows some ingenuity. The ruse involving Li K'uei's disguise as the bride seems to be the author's original invention and adds to the dramatic interest. On the other hand, the final act is superfluous and has little justification except that it makes up the required number of acts. However, as with most Yuan and Ming plays, the plot is not of prime importance.

The episode described in this play does not occur in *Water Margin*, and the characterization of Li K'uei also differs considerably from that in the prose romance. Whereas in *Water Margin* he is portrayed as a rough, simple-minded, and illiterate man, though with a heart of gold, in the play he displays some patience, is capable of devising a ruse, and even writes verse.

The main interest of the play lies in its language: the dramatist has successfully combined verse with colloquial speech so as to bring out the altruistic spirit of the hero, in a manner worthy of the Yuan masters. Here, for example, is a passage from the end

[1] The word *ch'ing* sometimes means 'green' (as when applied to grass) and sometimes 'blue' (as when applied to the sky), but when applied to clothes it usually means 'black'. In this nickname, 'Ten-foot' is obviously a hyperbolic reference to her tallness, but there is no reason why she should be called either 'green' or 'blue'. Since chivalrous men and women often wore black jackets and trousers, it is likely that the nickname means 'Ten-foot Black', i.e. a tall woman in black.

of Act I, when Li K'uei, together with Yen Ch'ing, has driven away the villain and saved the old peasant Li Pieh-ku:

LI K'UEI (*sings*):

With all my heart I wish to
Save the orphaned and the poor;
Half my life I have been
Helping those in distress.
How could I
Relax in doing altruistic deeds and distributing wealth?
Look at what I, Shan-erh, have done this time:
I've made that
Cursed rascal shudder, stricken to the heart with fear!
When I return,
My elder brother
Should be pleased and smile broadly!

YEN CH'ING (*speaks*): Hey, old man! How much grain do you owe the government?

LI PIEH-KU (*speaks*): I owe fifty piculs of grain.

YEN CH'ING (*speaks*): Brother, let us give him these fifty piculs of grain to pay his tax.

LI PIEH-KU (*speaks*): I dare not take it.

LI K'UEI (*speaks*): You take it; it's all right!

LI PIEH-KU (*speaks*): Thank you so much! You two, my brothers, have saved the lives of my whole family, and now you are paying my tax for me. Brothers, you are my second parents who have given me my life anew! My whole family would repay you, even if we were reborn as horses!

YEN CH'ING (*speaks*): Brother, now that we have given him this grain, when we go back to our mountain stronghold, will brother Sung Chiang blame us?

LI K'UEI (*sings*):

What is so unusual about giving him so much grain?

LI PIEH-KU (*speaks*): Brothers, what if that Inspector General Chao comes to demand my daughter again?

LI K'UEI (*sings*):

If he again demands your daughter
To serve at table and pass the cup,

If he again
Annoys her and tries to take her by force,
I'll turn that
Inspector General's blasted office into the gate of hell!
(*Exit*).

It is remarkable that the author, an imperial prince, is aware of the existence of bullying officials and shows his sympathy for the common people. He strikes a sarcastic note in the following dialogue when the old peasant comes to Liang-shan to lodge a complaint:

SUNG CHIANG: Why doesn't he go to the magistrate's office to lodge a complaint, instead of coming to us?

SCHOLAR WU: I suppose those corrupt officials can't deal with it. Let us take care of him!

While this sympathy is much to the credit of Prince Hsien of Chou, at the same time it indicates how firmly the Liang-shan heroes had established themselves in popular imagination as champions of justice.

The same dramatist also wrote *The Leopard Monk Returning to Secular Life* (*Pao-tzŭ Ho-shang Tzŭ-huan-su*), which deals with Sung Chiang's efforts to make Lu Chih-shen return to secular life and rejoin the Liang-shan band. This is a much less successful play and need not detain us.

There remains one more Ming Northern play about the Liang-shan heroes:

Sung Chiang Disturbing the Lantern Festival[1]
(*Sung Kung-ming Nao Yuan-hsiao*)

This play by Ling Meng-ch'u (1580–1644) is partly based on the 120-chapter version of *Water Margin*[2] and partly on other literary sources. Against the background of the love triangle among the Emperor Hui-tsung, the famous courtesan Li Shih-shih, and the poet Chou Pang-yen, the play describes Sung Chiang's attempt to ask the courtesan to intercede on his behalf so that he may be allowed to capitulate to the imperial government. To this end, Sung disguises himself together with some of his followers, and visits Li Shih-shih during the Lantern Festival celebrations. His attempt miscarries when Li K'uei loses his temper, fights with

[1] The first full moon of the lunar year.
[2] Chapter 72.

Grand Marshal Yang, and announces the presence of the Liang-shan heroes, thus bringing the play to an inconclusive end.

In many ways, this play has more in common with Ming Dramatic Romances than with earlier Northern Drama. To begin with, it uses Southern tunes together with Northern ones, and follows some Southern conventions: it opens with a prologue as the first 'act', it has nine short 'acts' instead of four, and it assigns singing parts to several characters instead of one only. Moreover, it is more 'literary' than 'dramatic' in nature, being written in an elegant style but showing little dramatic power. Finally, in its attitude towards the Liang-shan heroes, it forms a marked contrast with Yuan and early Ming Northern plays, such as those mentioned above. Emphasis in this play is laid not on the band's chivalry and justice but on Sung Chiang's underlying loyalty to the Emperor and his wish to be allowed to capitulate to the imperial government.

Plays based on T'ang chivalric tales will be discussed next.

Lady Hung-hsien (*Hung-hsien Nü*)

This play in four acts is by Liang Ch'en-yü (*c.* 1522–95), better known as Liang Po-lung, one of the chief initiators of the *K'un-ch'ü*. The play follows the original T'ang story[1] closely, with additional details taken from history.

In Act I, Hung-hsien recalls the golden age of Emperor Hsüan-tsung, of his infatuation for Yang Kuei-fei, which brought about the rebellion of An Lu-shan and her tragic death. The heroine then shows concern over the disorder now prevailing in the empire, and expresses her wish to imitate ancient knights-errant like Ching K'o. To her master Governor Hsüeh Sung's invitation to some pleasant pastime, she replies that he should devote himself to more serious matters.

In Act II, Hsüeh is worried because Governor T'ien Ch'eng-ssŭ is showing every sign of aggression. Hung-hsien finds out the cause of his worries and volunteers to go to T'ien's headquarters to investigate. She laughingly declines Hsüeh's offer of armed escorts and sets out alone.

Act III is the highlight of the drama: Hung-hsien arrives at T'ien's headquarters, steals the gold case by his bedside, and playfully disarrays the dresses and jewels of the maid servants who

[1] See above, p. 90.

are fast asleep. She then leaves. T'ien wakes up, discovers the loss of the case, and orders a search. In the next scene, Hung-hsien returns to her master, reports what she has done, and advises him to send the case back to T'ien as a warning.

In Act IV, Hsüeh's messenger brings the case to T'ien, who sends back rich gifts in return. In the next scene, Hung-hsien appears wearing the dress of a Taoist nun, tells Hsüeh about her previous incarnation, and announces her intention to leave. The play ends with the farewell party in her honour, at which several famous poets recite valedictory verses and Hung-hsien advises Hsüeh to retire soon from public life.

The language of this play is refined to the point of being too erudite in places. Consequently, the heroine at times sounds almost like a pedantic moralist, such as when she lectures her master on his duties in Act I. However, there are passages of genuine poetic beauty. The following is a fairly literal translation of a selection from Act III:

HUNG-HSIEN (*speaks*): It is early autumn, and tonight happens to be the Seventh Night of the Seventh Moon.[1] I, Hung-hsien, having said goodbye to my master, flew out of the south-eastern corner of Lu-chou city, as free as a huge fish let loose in the sea, as light as a wild swan's feather borne by a strong wind. I soar among the nine heavens, and my spirit wanders beyond the eight extremities of the earth. Ah, when I attain immortality in the future and ascend to paradise, it will be no better than this!

(*Sings*):

Crooked, crooked:
The moon bends her long eyebrow;
Helter-skelter:
The clouds hang their beautiful hair;
Flowery, flowery:
A pair of silk shoes I wear;
Straight, straight:
Two golden hair-pins stand.
Rush, rush:
The sea waves roll on;
Loud, loud:
The winds from heaven blow at random;

[1] The night when the Spinning Maid and the Cowherd (two constellations) are supposed to have their annual reunion across the Heavenly River (Milky Way).

Flash, flash:
The dagger in my hand;
Float, float:
I ride on the crane's back,
Putting to shame
A light sail against the stream: *far, far*;
A galloping steed on the battlefield: *puffing, puffing.*

This of course does not do justice to the original, which evokes the picture of a chivalrous lady flying over land and sea, beautiful yet formidable, a strange combination of superhuman power and feminine grace.

There was another Northern play on the same story by Hu Ju-chia (*fl.* 1553), which several Ming writers considered superior to Liang's, but unfortunately no copy of Hu's version is known to exist.

The K'un-lun Slave (*K'un-lun Nu*)

This play was written in 1584 by Mei Ting-tso (1549–1615), based on the T'ang story of the same name,[1] with a few additional details. In the play the powerful official whose concubine Hung-hsiao ('Red Silk') elopes with the young man Ts'ui is identified with the famous Kuo Tzŭ-yi, who was mainly responsible for the suppression of the rebellion of An Lu-shan and the restoration of the T'ang dynasty. Since Kuo is generally held in great esteem and even in this play not portrayed in an unfavourable light, this tends to weaken our sympathy for the young lovers, whereas in the original tale the unnamed powerful official[2] is felt as a rather sinister presence, and consequently the young woman's elopement seems more justified.

Another point on which the play differs somewhat from the original story is that greater emphasis is put on the supernatural element here. While in the tale the Negrito slave Mo-lê simply vanishes, in the play he comes back as a Taoist immortal and advises the young lovers to leave this dusty world too. This is also a change for the worse, for it makes Mo-lê appear more like a priest than a chivalrous swordsman.

[1] See above, p. 88.

[2] In the T'ang tale the high official is referred to as '*Yi-p'in*', which is not his name but simply means 'first rank'.

Apart from these departures from the original, the play follows the tale quite closely, though with various embellishments. Like many other Ming plays, it is written in a highly sophisticated and refined literary style, which at times becomes too allusive and artificial to be dramatically effective.

There were two earlier plays about Mo-lê and Hung-hsiao. One was by Yang No (*fl.* 1400), a dramatist of Mongol origin, the other by Liang Ch'en-yü, whose play *Lady Hung-hsien* we have discussed. Both these plays are now lost, so that we do not know what relation, if any, existed among the three plays—whether they were all independent dramatizations of the same tale, or successive versions of the same drama. It was quite common for Chinese dramatists to base their plays on the same story or to revise earlier plays. Neither case was considered plagiarism, any more than were similar practices by the ancient Greek and the Elizabethan dramatists.

The Curly-bearded Old Man (*Ch'iu-jan Weng*)

This is one of a triology by Ling Meng-ch'u,[1] based on the story by Tu Kuang-t'ing.[2] The three plays had as their protagonists, respectively, Hung-fu ('Red Whisk'), Li Ching, and Curly Beard. The first play exists in a rare edition which I have not been able to see, the second one is lost, and the third one will be described below.

In the first act a Taoist priest enters and reveals that his friend, surnamed Chang and known as Curly Beard, is a great hero and a potential king. In the next scene, Li Ching and his wife Hung-fu confide to us that they are going to support Li Shih-min, who is destined to be the true Son of Heaven. Then Curly Beard himself enters, and in several lyrics expresses his heroic ambitions. He peeps at Hung-fu combing her hair, whereupon Li Ching angrily draws his sword. However, Hung-fu stops her husband, calmly finishes her toilet, and addresses Curly Beard. On discovering that they both have the same surname, they become sworn brother and sister. Curly Beard then discusses contemporary heroes with Hung-fu and Li Ching, and asks the last-named to arrange a meeting with Li Shih-min.

In the next act Curly Beard and his Taoist friend arrive at the

[1] See above, p. 163 and Additional Note 23.

[2] See above, p. 87.

place appointed for the rendezvous. When Li Ching brings Li Shih-min, Curly Beard is impressed by the future emperor's presence and leaves in a crestfallen mood.

In Act III, Li Ching and Hung-fu come to Curly Beard's house, where he entertains them royally and presents them with all his wealth. He announces his intention to sail overseas to seek his fortune, and predicts that in ten years' time he will succeed.

We see his prediction coming true in Act IV: he enters as the King of Fu-yü. On receiving an official letter from Li Ching, now Minister of War and Generalissimo of the T'ang empire, Curly Beard realizes they have both fulfilled their ambitions, and promises to help the T'ang to conquer Korea. On this triumphant note the play ends.

This is a successful dramatization of the original story. While most of the incidents in the play are taken from the story, they are presented in dramatic terms. The character of the hero is well portrayed, and the language of the play is more natural and less erudite than that of *Sung Chiang Disturbing the Lantern Festival* by the same author.

The two Ming Northern plays derived from history are connected in subject:

The Cold River Yi (*Yi Shui Han*)

This play by Yeh Hsien-tsu (1566–1641) is largely based on the biography of Ching K'o in *Records of the Historiographer,*[1] though it also incorporates a few details from *Prince Tan of Yen.*[2]

The play opens with Ching K'o drinking with his friend Kao Chien-li in a tavern and expressing heroic sentiments:

> *When joyful,*
> I sing several long or short songs;
> *When depressed,*
> I shed a few drops of heroic tears.

The old knight T'ien Kuang enters and asks Ching K'o to go and meet the Prince. Ching at first defers, but is persuaded by Kao and T'ien, who remind him that 'a woman beautifies herself for the one who loves her, a knight dies for the one who appreciates him'. At this point, T'ien says in an aside:

[1] See above, pp. 25 *ff*.   [2] See above, p. 82.

> I have heard that an honest man does not arouse other people's distrust in his action. Now, the Prince warned me not to betray the secret when he saw me to the door. If he distrusts me as much as this, how can I prove myself a knight of integrity? Now that I have completed my mission, it would be best for me to commit suicide, first to show I will not betray the secret, and secondly to spur Master Ching to speedy action.

He then commits suicide.

Some time has elapsed when Act II begins. Prince Tan of Yen holds a banquet for Ching K'o, already a high official, and also invites General Fan Wu-chi, the refugee from Ch'in. A swordsman from Chao comes and presents Ching with a precious dagger. Then a messenger arrives to announce that the Ch'in troops are approaching the frontier. Thereupon the Prince asks Ching K'o for advice, and the knight in turn asks General Fan (in an aside) for his head. The general at once cuts his throat with the dagger that Ching has just obtained.

Act III, which is devoted to the farewell party on the River Yi, is lyrical in character and contains little action, though it is this act which gives the play its title.

Act IV is set in the Court of Ch'in. Ching K'o presents the head of General Fan and the map to the King of Ch'in, and attempts to assassinate the latter. The Ch'in courtiers are thrown into helpless confusion. Eventually the King swears to return all the territories he has conquered to the other feudal rulers. His mission now accomplished, Ching K'o is led to paradise by a Taoist immortal.

This play has considerable merits but also one major weakness. By telescoping events which in the historical account spread over a fairly long period of time, the dramatist has greatly heightened the dramatic tension. Other minor changes also add to the intensity of the play: for instance, whereas in the historical work the Prince searches for a particularly strong dagger and eventually buys one from Chao, in the play a swordsman comes and presents it to Ching K'o, and what is more, General Fan commits suicide with this very dagger which is to be used on his enemy, the King of Ch'in. On the other hand, the play is marred by the happy ending which destroys the tragic atmosphere so carefully built up in the previous acts.

We may note in passing that in this play several chivalric poems we have seen before are incorporated. In Act I, the waiter who serves wine to Ching K'o and Kao Chien-li recites four lines of verse adapted from Wang Wei's quatrain on knights-errant;[1] at the beginning of Act II, when the Prince makes his first entry, he quotes the first four lines of the poem by Pao Chao;[2] and the swordsman who comes to present his dagger quotes the quatrain by Chia Tao.[3] It is of course common practice in Chinese drama to quote earlier poets, but the author of the present play has done so with particular aptness.

The Zither at the Court of Ch'in (*Ch'in T'ing Chu*)

This play by Mao Wei (*fl.* 1590) concentrates on the deeds of Kao Chien-li after Ching K'o's death. It has only three acts. In the first act, the farewell party on the Yi river is once more enacted. In Act II, Kao Chien-li appears as a labourer at Sung-tzŭ and reveals that the only reason why he did not commit suicide is that he wishes to fulfil his friend Ching K'o's unaccomplished mission. Next, he hears a guest playing the zither, criticizes the latter's playing, and is persuaded to play the instrument himself. When the listeners suspect his identity, he leaves. In Act III, Kao, having been blinded, is summoned to the Emperor's presence and told to play. He asks for some wine to stir up his courage, then plays his zither, going through a variety of moods. This affords the dramatist great scope for describing the effects of music and a number of lyrics rich in elaborate imagery and allusions are devoted to this end. Finally Kao attempts to kill the Emperor with his zither filled with lead, but only hits the latter's foot. He is seized and taken away, and the play ends with the Emperor sighing over Kao's noble altruism and courage.

By comparison with Yeh Hsien-tsu's *The Cold River Yi*, the present play is historically more accurate and artistically more satisfying in at least one way: it has not altered the facts of Ching K'o's and Kao Chien-li's failures and thus preserves the tragic ending of the story.

Apart from the plays mentioned above, there were at least three other plays on chivalric themes which have not survived.

3. *Ch'ing period*

Some Ch'ing dramatists wrote Northern plays following Yuan

[1] See above, p. 62.
[2] See above, p. 59.
[3] See above, p. 68.

conventions, while others wrote what may be called 'Southernized' Northern Drama. In both kinds may be found plays on chivalric subjects.

The Black and White Donkeys (Hei Pai Wei)

This play by Yu T'ung (1618–1704), one of the most gifted writers of early Ch'ing, is a dramatization of the story of Nieh Yin-niang, with the addition of a few minor characters from other well-known chivalric tales, such as The Maiden of Yueh (now identified with the nun who teaches Yin-niang swordsmanship) and Hung-hsien.[1] It is in four acts and observes the conventions of Yuan Northern Drama. The characterization of the heroine is to some extent an improvement on that in the original story, for the dramatist emphasizes her sense of justice and her hatred of evil-doers rather than her supernatural powers. There are passages of magnificent verse worthy of the Yuan masters, but the play as a whole is more 'literary' than 'dramatic'.

The Road to Chi-chou (Chi-chou Tao)

This is a one-act play by Chang T'ao (*fl.* 1662), based on an incident in *Water Margin*.[2] Tai Tsung, one of the Liang-shan heroes, is on his way to Chi-chou, together with Li K'uei, to fetch the Taoist priest Kung-sun Sheng, whose help is urgently needed by the leader Sung Chiang. Tai possesses magical powers which enable him and his companion to travel at a miraculous speed. Since the temperamental Li K'uei proves rather a difficult travelling companion, Tai Tsung plays a few magic tricks on him until he vows to be obedient. This simple plot has little dramatic interest, and the play is mainly intended to be comic, with the result that Li K'uei (now cast as a *ching*) acts like a fool—a sad decline from the rash but noble hero he is depicted to be in Yuan and early Ming drama.

The Slope at the Cross-roads (Shih-tzŭ P'o)

This is another one-act play based on a *Water Margin* incident.[3] Written by T'ang Ying (*fl.* 1740), it tells how Wu Sung foils the attempt of the female warrior Sun Erh-niang to drug and rob

[1] See above, pp. 89, 85, and 90.
[2] Chapter 53 in the 120-chapter version (52 in the 71-chapter version).
[3] Chapter 27 in the 120-chapter version (26 in the 71-chapter version).

him, and then makes friends with her and her husband Chang Ch'ing. The play has little plot or characterization to speak of, but could have afforded great scope for stage fighting and acrobatics.

KNIGHT-ERRANTRY IN DRAMATIC ROMANCES

Among the hundreds of Dramatic Romances of the Ming and Ch'ing periods, there are many that deal with chivalry, especially the deeds of the Liang-shan heroes. In view of the great length of Dramatic Romances, we cannot discuss them all, but have to concentrate on the more important ones. Since few works in this *genre* of the Ch'ing period can compare with their predecessors, most examples will be chosen from Ming works.

1. *Dramatic Romances about the Liang-shan heroes*

Romance of the Precious Sword (*Pao Chien Chi*)

This Dramatic Romance in fifty-two scenes by Li K'ai-hsien (1501–68) was written in 1547 and first printed in 1549. The plot is based on *Water Margin*,[1] but various additions and alterations are made.

After a short prologue, we meet the hero Lin Ch'ung as an upright military official and a dutiful son and loving husband. He is grieved that the Empire is in a sad state, for the Emperor is indulging in pleasures and entrusting the government to corrupt officials. Stroking his precious sword, a family heirloom, Lin Ch'ung regrets that he is unable to put it to proper use. His wife, Chang Chen-niang, encourages him to be fearless. Later, Lin sends a memorial to the throne to denounce the powerful eunuch T'ung Kuan and the Grand Marshal Kao Ch'iu for their wicked deeds. This naturally incurs their enmity and Kao lays a trap for Lin Ch'ung. He commands Lin to come and show his precious sword, on the pretext that the Emperor has ordered some swords made and Lin's is wanted as a model. When Lin arrives, he is ushered into the White Tiger Hall, which no one is allowed to enter without special permission, on pain of death. Lin is seized and accused of attempting to assassinate the Grand Marshal; then thrown into jail and tortured. His friend, the chivalrous monk Lu Chih-shen, brings the bad news to Lin's family, whereupon

[1] Chapters 7–12 in the 120-chapter version, or 6–11 in the 71-chapter version.

Chen-niang goes to visit her husband in prison. Lin tells her he does not expect to live, and asks her to wait till his mother's death before remarrying. She replies that she will look after his mother and will never remarry. She then goes to the court with a petition to the Emperor to save her husband's life, and attempts suicide while handing it in (a time-honoured way of desperate appeal to the throne). She is saved by an official who promises to help. Consequently Lin Ch'ung is sent to be retried by the Metropolitan Prefect, who turns out to be an honest official and finds Lin not guilty. However, though Lin's life is spared, he is sentenced to exile. After a tearful parting scene, he sets out with two guards. These two, having been bribed by Kao Ch'iu to murder him on the way, try to fulfil their wicked mission in a forest, but are foiled by Lu Chih-shen, who then escorts Lin to his destination.

While Lin Ch'ung suffers further hardships in his place of exile, at home his wife Chen-niang has her troubles too. Kao Ch'iu's son, Kao P'eng, having seen her at a temple, falls in love with her and makes persistent efforts to convince her that Lin Ch'ung is dead and she should remarry. When she sternly refuses, Kao P'eng sends his underlings to go and kill Lin Ch'ung, so as to substantiate his own lie. Lin discovers the plot against his life by accident and kills the two emissaries. Imperial troops are sent to arrest Lin Ch'ung, who is forced to flee by night and seek refuge at Liang-shan. Meanwhile, news of his 'crime' and flight reaches home, and more pressure is put on Chen-niang to marry Kao P'eng. Lin's old mother, thinking that she herself is the obstacle to her daughter-in-law's remarriage, commits suicide. But Chen-niang still refuses to marry Kao, preferring death to this disgrace. Thereupon her maid servant, Chin-erh, offers to go and marry the villain, disguised as her mistress. Chen-niang then runs away, accompanied by old Mother Wang, a chivalrous neighbour. When the maid Chin-erh arrives in Kao P'eng's house, she commits suicide before the marriage is consummated. Kao then sends an officer, Wang Chin, to go and chase Chen-niang, and gives him Lin Ch'ung's sword, saying that if Wang succeeds in bringing her back, he may keep the sword, but if she still refuses, he should kill her with it. Wang catches up with Chen-niang but, moved by a sense of justice, cannot bear to force her or kill her. Instead, he gives her back her husband's sword and seeks refuge himself.

Now Lin Ch'ung, together with Li K'uei, leads the Liang-shan outlaws to launch an attack on the capital. At the same time, Chen-niang and old Mother Wang lose each other on their way. Chen-niang makes one more unsuccessful attempt to kill herself, is saved by a nun, and becomes a nun herself. Next, the court sends a high official to announce that Lin Ch'ung is pardoned and that his enemies will be handed over to him for punishment. This is duly carried out: Kao Ch'iu and Kao P'eng are both executed and Lin Ch'ung's revenge is complete. However, he still has not been reunited with his wife, until by chance he sees his own sword hanging in a temple and finds out it belongs to the abbess. Recognition and reunion follow, and the Dramatic Romance ends with Lin and his wife offering sacrifices to his mother and the maid Chin-erh, while an Imperial envoy arrives to bestow honours on the living and the dead.

This complicated plot is slowly developed throughout the play, and there are many repetitions and superfluous scenes. After the prologue, first we see the filial Lin Ch'ung celebrating his mother's birthday, and in the next scene we see Kao Ch'iu and his family having a feast. This is probably intended as a contrast, but since the dramatist uses similar phraseology in both scenes, the impression we get is one of redundancy rather than contrast. Lin Ch'ung's sufferings in jail and in exile are described many times (scenes 12, 14, 15, 24, 27); so are his wife's constancy and virtue. Her three attempts at suicide (scenes 16, 43, 48) become almost ridiculous instead of being tragic as they are no doubt meant to be. The scenes depicting Lin Ch'ung's mother's funeral (scenes 41, 42) and the final scene in which sacrifices are offered to her soul are also somewhat repetitious. There are other unnecessary scenes such as that of Lin Ch'ung's dream of evil omens (scene 10) and those devoted largely to the tomfoolery of Kao P'eng and his underlings (scenes 5, 25, 28).

On the whole, this Dramatic Romance has a diffuse structure and is less intense in dramatic impact than the parts dealing with Lin Ch'ung in *Water Margin*. However, some of the additions and changes are interesting and justifiable. For instance, in *Water Margin*, Lin's sword is the excuse with which Kao Ch'iu traps him, and as such it already plays a significant part in the plot; in the Dramatic Romance, much greater play is made of the sword: it becomes the means by which the hero and his wife are reunited, and it runs throughout the play as a recurrent symbol of Lin's heroic and chivalrous virtues. Another interesting change is that while in *Water Margin* Lin's troubles are due simply to young Kao's desire for the former's wife, in the play Lin incurs the enmity of the Grand Marshal by his fearless denunciation of the latter's evil deeds to the throne. In this way, Lin's actions are seen to be motivated by more than personal feelings and become of wider significance.

On the other hand, some changes from the story as given in *Water Margin* have an adverse effect. For example, while in the prose romance Lin's wife commits suicide when forced to marry her husband's enemy, in the play the maid substitutes for her. This is of course a contrivance the dramatist has to resort to in order to provide the happy ending demanded by convention; nevertheless it remains a fact that the original tragedy is spoilt.

The characterization of the hero also differs considerably from that in the prose romance. In *Water Margin*, Lin Ch'ung is a simple soldier forced to turn rebel; in the play, he is described as something of a statesman, well versed in learning as well as swordsmanship, the descendant of the famous scholar and poet Lin P'u,[1] and the son of a prefect. In his effort to idealize Lin Ch'ung (which is not without a hint of snobbery), the dramatist has made the hero appear more like a Confucian gentleman than a chivalrous knight. In the prose romance Lin Ch'ung shows a straightforward nature, a great capacity for friendship, and a deeply felt though awkwardly expressed love for his wife. In the play he is more sophisticated and displays more filial devotion than affection for his wife. (We may notice in particular that instead of forcing his wife to accept a bill of divorce so that she will be free,[2] he now asks her not to remarry till his mother's death.) The result is a hero more acceptable to Confucian scholars but less interesting to modern readers.

Lin Ch'ung's wife plays a much more important role in the Dramatic Romance than in *Water Margin*. She is resolute and brave, virtuous and filial. Yet in spite of all her virtues (or perhaps because of them) she remains a stereotyped character. The other characters, too, are largely conventional types with little individuality.

[1] This attempt to elevate Lin Ch'ung's ancestry is ill-conceived, for Lin P'u was a celibate (unless the dramatist is doing this purposely as a sort of scholarly joke).

[2] See above, p. 115.

The language of *Romance of the Precious Sword* is highly refined and often excessively allusive. Even in the spoken passages, the ornate 'Parallel Prose' is frequently used instead of colloquial speech. While one admires the author's erudition and taste, one cannot help feeling that such passages, put in the mouth of minor characters such as servants, are rather out of place. However, in some scenes the author has fulfilled the chief purpose of the dramatic poet: to express the imaginary emotions of his characters in poetic language. The scene in which Lin Ch'ung flees by night (scene 37) is especially effective and is the only scene from this play that is still performed today.[1] Another moving scene is scene 20, in which the author describes Lin Ch'ung's feelings on his way to exile:

LIN CH'UNG (*sings*):

Lifting my eyes, I see numberless clouds and mountains;
Turning back my head, where can I see my home?
The mountains are steep, the rivers dangerous;
Hurried, anxious, I can't get out of
This sheep-gut-like path.
The birds cry at random,
In the deep forest there are few passers-by.
My body is completely worn out,
Any moment
I may breathe my last,
Leaving behind
My white-haired mother leaning on the door, waiting for me.
Letters, news—
Across a thousand miles
Of gates and mountains, I've not received half a word;
Sighs, moans—
In two places
Thinking of each other, we are suffering the same pain!

(*Recites*):

Since I parted from my mother and left the capital,
Day and night I've beeen thinking of her, and tears fill my eyes.

[1] This scene has been translated into English by Harold Acton in *T'ien Hsia Monthly*, Vol. IX, No. 2 (Shanghai, 1939), pp. 180–8, though the translation is based on a modern acting version which differs somewhat from Li K'ai-hsien's original text.

Turning back my head, where can I see my home?
Yet I've not awoke from the wanderer's dream of returning.
Grieved by wild fords,
Pained by mountain journeys,
I am stricken to the soul by the sad cries of wild geese.
With the white clouds, flowing water, and blue mountains,
The beautiful view invites the weary traveller to linger on.

While expressing Lin Ch'ung's weariness and thoughts of home, the dramatist at the same time depicts the scene and evokes a sad mood so that we can enter sympathetically into the character's state of mind. And of course the effect of the words would be greatly enhanced when accompanied by music and appropriate gestures miming the actions of mountain climbing, river crossing, etc.

Romance of the Precious Sword was later revised by Ch'en Yü-chiao (1546–*c.* 1612), who renamed it *The Marvellous Precious Sword* (*Ling Pao Tao*). Ch'en's version consists of thirty-five scenes and is more concise than Li's original play, but it also introduces some incidents not found in the earlier version.

There was another *Romance of the Precious Sword* by Shen Ch'u-ch'eng, but since it is no longer extant, its relation to Li's play is not known.

Romance of the Altruistic Knight-errant (*Yi Hsia Chi*)

This Dramatic Romance is by Shen Ching (1553–1610), one of the leading dramatists of the Ming period and an authority on theatrical music. The play was first printed before 1607, and a few scenes from it are still performed in the *K'un-ch'ü* style. The hero is Wu Sung, one of the most important of the Liang-shan rebels, and the plot is taken from *Water Margin.*[1]

The play consists of thirty-six scenes. After the prologue, Wu Sung enters and gives a brief account of his life: orphaned since childhood, he has only one relative, an elder brother, and though his parents engaged him to a girl of the Chia family, due to his wanderings he has not yet married her. Now he is staying with Ch'ai Chin, a member of the imperial clan of the previous dynasty and a famous patron of knights-errant, but wishes to go and visit

[1] Chapters 23–31 in the 120-chapter version (22–30 in the 71-chapter version).

Sung Chiang, celebrated for his chivalry (and not yet a rebel leader). A few days later Wu Sung sets out, and on his way encounters a tiger, which he kills with bare fists. The magistrate of the district appoints him a captain of the local militia, and on a triumphal parade through the town he is recognized by his brother, Wu the Eldest (Wu Ta-lang). Thereupon Wu Sung moves in with his brother and the latter's wife, P'an Chin-lien ('Golden Lotus'). Since Wu the Eldest is short and ugly while Wu Sung is a hero, Golden Lotus falls for her brother-in-law and attempts to seduce him. Wu Sung repels her and leaves in anger. Later, he goes away on official business, and before leaving advises her brother to stay at home.

In another place, Ch'ai Chin is arrested for having communicated with the Liang-shan rebels, and one of his guests, named Yeh Tzŭ-ying, voluntarily goes to prison with him. But soon afterwards they are rescued by Sung Chiang, now leader of the rebels, whereupon Ch'ai joins the band and Yeh goes away.

Meanwhile, Golden Lotus forms a liaison with Hsi-men Ch'ing,[1] and when their adultery is discovered by the husband, they poison him. On his return, Wu Sung finds out the murder, fails to obtain redress from the law, and kills Golden Lotus and her lover to avenge his brother's death. He gives himself up to the authorities, but the prefect, who feels sympathy for him, finds him guilty of manslaughter instead of murder and sentences him to exile. On his way to exile, Wu Sung passes Liang-shan, visits Sung Chiang and his men, but refuses to join them, insisting on serving his sentence.

Previous to this, Wu Sung's fiancée Chia Jo-chen and her mother, having been burgled and lost their possessions, went in search of Wu Sung. They stopped at the inn kept by the amazon Sun Erh-niang, who arranged for them to stay at a nunnery near by. Now Wu Sung himself also comes to stop at this inn, and Sun Erh-niang, not knowing who he is, attempts to rob him by putting a drug in the wine. Her attempt is foiled by Wu Sung, and on learning his identity she and her husband Chang Ch'ing beg his forgiveness and they become friends.[2] Though he hears that his

[1] This forms the starting point of the novel *Chin P'ing Mei*, known as *The Golden Lotus*.

[2] This is the same incident treated in the Northern play *The Slope at the Cross-roads* (see above, p. 171).

fiancée is near by, Wu Sung realizes he is in no position to get married and decides to go on his way without seeing her.

On arriving at his destination, Wu Sung is befriended by Shih En, son of the prison camp commandant. Shih formerly owned a restaurant but has been forced to hand it over to a bully known as Chiang the Door God. Wu Sung chastises the bully and makes him apologize to Shih and hand back the business. Chiang then complains to his friend, Garrison Commander Chang, who, together with another officer of the same name, Superintendent General Chang, plot Wu Sung's death. The last-mentioned pretends to befriend Wu by inviting him to a banquet and bestowing a singing girl on him as his concubine. She plants some gold and silver vessels in his luggage, and he is accused of having stolen them from the Superintendent General. Wu Sung is caned and sent into exile to an even remoter region. The guards are told to murder him on the way, but having been warned by Shih En, Wu Sung anticipates them: when they reach a river, he kicks them into the water and breaks his handcuffs. He then goes back to the town and kills the two officers and Chiang the Door God. Tired and suffering from his recent caning, Wu Sung falls asleep in a temple, and is taken by four followers of the innkeeper Chang Ch'ing and his wife Sun Erh-niang. A recognition scene follows, and Wu Sung meets his fiancée and her mother. At this moment, three members of the Liang-shan band arrive, having heard about Wu Sung's plight. All depart for Liang-shan in disguise.

Finally, the court pardons Sung Chiang, Wu Sung, and the others, and bestows honours on them. Amid general rejoicing, Wu Sung celebrates his wedding, and the play ends.

Romance of the Altruistic Knight-errant follows *Water Margin* closely in most of the incidents about Wu Sung, except for the invention of a fiancée. This is necessitated by the convention that the hero and the heroine should both be present at the end of the play, and adds little to the dramatic interest or the characterization of the hero. Another addition is the character Yeh Tzŭ-ying, who voluntarily accompanies Ch'ai Chin to jail and then leaves when the latter's troubles are over. Though his presence is not strictly necessary, it helps to emphasize the spirit of chivalry, particularly personal loyalty to an appreciative friend.

The action of the drama moves on fairly fast, and in spite of subplots, is dominated by the hero Wu Sung, who is upright, brave, and warm-hearted. The language is more natural and less refined than that of *Romance of the Precious Sword.* Consequently the play is more lifelike, but has few passages of great poetic beauty. It may be described as a competent rather than inspired work.

Romance of the Water Margin (*Shui-hu Chi*)

Written by Hsü Tzŭ-ch'ang (*fl.* 1590), this Dramatic Romance in thirty-two scenes was first published in 1590 and achieved considerable success. Scenes from it were frequently performed during the Ming and Ch'ing periods, and though they are no longer performed in their original form now, pieces in the Peking Theatre and other local theatres based on them are still very popular.

The drama deals with episodes taken from the prose romance of the same name.[1] When the scene opens, Sung Chiang is as yet only a clerk in the district office and has no thoughts of rebellion in spite of his great reputation as a chivalrous and altruistic man. He lends some money to a widow called Mother Yen, who insists that he should take her daughter P'o-hsi as his concubine. Reluctantly Sung agrees and sets her up in her mother's house, but takes little interest in her. (In the play Sung is already married, but often stays in his office instead of going home.) A colleague of his, Chang the Third (Chang San-lang), who has seen P'o-hsi before, takes advantage of Sung Chiang's indifference to her and becomes her lover. Sung hears about it and stops visiting her altogether.

Meanwhile, another plot is afoot. Sung's friend, Ch'ao Kai, a village elder famous as a chivalrous man, together with several others, succeed in robbing the rich birthday gifts which the corrupt prefect Ts'ai the Ninth is sending to his father, the minister Ts'ai Ching. When an official messenger comes with orders for Ch'ao's arrest, Sung Chiang gets the news first and warns him, so that he and his friends escape. They make their way to Liang-shan, where Ch'ao Kai becomes the new leader of the band of outlaws. He sends someone with a letter and some gold to Sung Chiang to express his gratitude. After the messenger has left, Sung comes across Mother Yen, who drags him home, hoping to reconcile

[1] Chapters 14–16, 18–21, 39–40, in the 120-chapter versions (13–15, 17–20, 38–9, in the 71-chapter version).

him with her daughter. Sung takes the first opportunity to leave, but forgets his bag, in which he has put the letter from Ch'ao Kai and the gold. When he comes back for it, P'o-hsi has found out the contents and blackmails him with it, so that he is forced to write her a bill of divorce allowing her to marry Chang the Third. However, even after this, she still withholds the incriminating evidence and dares Sung Chiang to kill her. Provoked beyond endurance, he stabs her to death. Mother Yen tries to hand him over to the authorities, but he manages to escape. Later, Sung Chiang is caught after having written a seditious poem on the wall of a restaurant and sentenced to be executed. Ch'ao Kai and the other Liang-shan heroes save him from the sword in the nick of time and bring him back to their stronghold, to which his wife has already been brought, and the play ends with their reunion.

In a previous scene, the ghost of Yen P'o-hsi, unable to stand her loneliness, snatches her lover Chang the Third bodily to the nether world.

This play really deals with two stories, the one about Sung Chiang and the love triangle which leads to his committing murder and fleeing, the other about Ch'ao Kai and his friends robbing the birthday gifts and going to Liang-shan. Though the two stories are quite skilfully interwoven, there is a constant shift of focus between them so that one does not know which is meant to be the main plot and which the subplot. The characters and incidents are mostly taken from the prose *Water Margin*; such additional ones as there are seem to be superfluous. For instance, in the prose romance Sung Chiang is not married, but in the drama he has a wife, who appears to have been introduced simply so that she may be reunited with her husband to provide the conventional happy ending, and who otherwise proves more of a nuisance than a help to the action. Another addition is the episode of P'o-hsi's ghost snatching her lover to death. This scene is also irrelevant and unnecessary, but it has won great popularity, probably because of the eerie fascination of the situation.[1]

The play is written in an extremely erudite and allusive style. While the frequent allusions to ancient knights-errant like Chu Chia and Kuo Hsieh are appropriate enough, others are merely pedantic and make the dialogue stilted and unconvincing. The

[1] For a description of this scene as performed in the Peking Theatre, see A. C. Scott, *op. cit.*, pp. 206–7.

use of 'Parallel Prose' also reaches absurd lengths, so that we find common outlaws, servants, and clowns all declaiming hundreds of meticulous antithetical lines.

This drama was later revised by one Wang Yi, who deleted Sung's wife and other superfluities, but the revised version is no longer extant. There was yet another play of the same name by an anonymous writer, which is said to have been totally different from Hsü's version, but only fragments of it remain.

The Lantern Festival Disturbance (*Yuan-hsiao Nao*)[1]

A Dramatic Romance in twenty-seven scenes by Li Su-fu (*fl.* 1640), it is based on *Water Margin*[2] and has its central character Lu Chün-yi, a wealthy and chivalrous man. Sung Chiang tries to recruit Lu to his band, but the latter refuses. Lu's wife, who has committed adultery with the butler, denounces her husband as a rebel to the authorities and he is sentenced to death. The Liang-shan heroes rescue him from the executioner's sword. The play is full of action but has no great literary merit.

The Wild-goose-feather Armour (*Yen-ling Chia*)

Another Dramatic Romance based on *Water Margin*,[3] this one is probably by Fan Hsi-chê (*fl.* 1604) and is also known as *Romance of Stealing the Armour* (*T'ou Chia Chi*). It consists of thirty-six scenes and deals with the Liang-shan rebels' fighting against the Imperial forces. The main character is Hsü Ning, Instructor of the Lancers, who owns a precious armour made of wild-goose feathers and gold, a family heirloom. Since he is the only one who knows how to defeat the Imperial cavalry, he is needed by the Liang-shan rebels. Therefore Sung Chiang sends Shih Ch'ien, a member of the band who was formerly a professional thief, to steal Hsü Ning's armour. When Hsü chases the former, he is trapped and induced to surrender. He then trains the outlaws to defeat the Imperial forces. Finally, together with the other rebels, he is pardoned by the Emperor and given honours. The play as a whole is not well known, but one scene, that in which Shih

[1] Despite the similarity of this title to *Sung Chiang Disturbing the Lantern Festival* mentioned on p. 163, the two plays deal with different episodes.

[2] Chapters 61–3 and 66 in the 120-chapter version (60–2 and 65 in the 71-chapter version).

[3] Chapters 56–7 in the 120-chapter version (55–6 in the 71-chapter version).

Ch'ien steals the armour, is still performed, though greatly modified. In modern performances the main interest lies in the actor's display of his agility and acrobatic skill, and Shih Ch'ien is one of the favourite roles for the 'military clown' (*wu-ch'ou*).

The Green-jade Screen Mountain (Ts'ui-p'ing Shan)

Of this Dramatic Romance by Shen Tzŭ-chin (*c.* 1584–1660), a noted expert on theatrical music, only several scenes remain. The action concerns Shih Hsiu's efforts to guard his sworn brother Yang Hsiung's honour and his killing of Yang's wife and her paramour.[1]

Some of the Dramatic Romances about the Liang-shan heroes were incorporated into a cycle called *A Precious Mosaic of Loyalty and Justice* (*Chung-yi Hsüan-t'u*) by literary courtiers during the early years of Emperor Ch'ien-lung's reign (1736–95). This formed one of several cycles of plays performed at court. Though quantitatively impressive, they were compiled and performed largely for spectacular rather than literary or dramatic effects.

2. *Dramatic Romances based on T'ang chivalric tales*

Romance of the Red Whisk (Hung-fu Chi)[2]

This Dramatic Romance in thirty-four scenes by Chang Feng-yi (1527–1613) is based on *The Curly-bearded Stranger*,[3] with the well-known story about Princess Lo-ch'ang as the subplot. The second story runs briefly as follows: Princess Lo-ch'ang, sister of the last ruler of the Ch'en dynasty (557–589), is married to Hsü Tê-yen. Realizing the impending fall of the dynasty and their probable separation, they break a mirror and each keeps half as a token for future recognition. After the fall of the Ch'en, the Princess enters the household of Yang Su, Prime Minister of the new Sui dynasty. Eventually she sends a servant to try to sell her half of the mirror at the market, where Hsü recognizes it and shows his half. Moved by their mutual faith, Yang Su allows them to be reunited. This story, which gave rise to the idiomatic expression 'the broken

[1] See above, p. 113.

[2] In this play, the words *hung-fu* ('red whisk') are used both as the heroine's name and in their literal sense, referring to the actual object she holds in her hand.

[3] See above, p. 87.

mirror has become round again' (*p'o ching ch'ung yuan*), is introduced into the play since the same Prime Minister Yang Su is also the master of Hung-fu, the heroine. Though this shows some ingenuity, the subplot is not really relevant to the main story. Other additions are also quite unnecessary. For example, there is a scene (scene 4) in which Li Ching prays to the God of the Western Mountain for guidance, and the God prophesies his future. This tends to detract from his heroic character. The final scenes, which deal with Li Ching's campaign against Korea and Curly Beard's support, are also less interesting than the earlier ones which follow the original story. However, in spite of these shortcomings, the play was a success in its day. Its language is generally lively and effective, but not without the common faults of Ming dramatists—pedantry and artificiality. Allusions abound in the play, and the ornate 'Parallel Prose' is frequently used. Compared with the Northern play about Curly Beard by Ling Meng-ch'u,[1] Chang's Dramatic Romance is less concise and less exciting.

There were two other Dramatic Romances on the story of Hung-fu contemporary with Chang Feng-yi's version, but these are no longer extant.[2] Later, Feng Meng-lung (1574–c. 1645) published his version entitled *A Heroic Woman* (*Nü Chang-fu*) in two parts, the first part being adapted from Chang Feng-yi's play and another play by Liu Chin-ch'ung, the second part from Chang's play and Ling Meng-ch'u's trilogy in the Northern style.[3] These different versions bear witness to the continued popularity of the story.

Romance of the Two Hung's (*Shuang Hung Chi*)

This Dramatic Romance in twenty-nine scenes, so called because it brings together the stories of Hung-hsien ('Red Thread') and Hung-hsiao ('Red Silk'), is by a Ming writer named Yü Hang(?),[4] and incorporates passages from Liang Ch'en-yü's *Lady Hung-hsien* and Mei Ting-tso's *The K'un-lun Slave*.[5]

In this play, Hung-hsien and Mo-lê are two immortals both condemned to live for a certain period of time in the human world. The former is reincarnated as a girl and becomes the

[1] See above, p. 167.
[2] See Additional Note 24.
[3] See Additional Note 24.
[4] See Additional Note 25.
[5] See above, pp. 164, 166.

private secretary of governor Hsüeh Sung, while the latter becomes the slave of young officer Ts'ui, a friend of Hsüeh's. By Hsüeh's recommendation, Ts'ui is presented to the all-powerful Kuo Tzŭ-yi, Prince of Fen-yang, one of whose concubines, Hung-hsiao, falls in love with the young man. With the help of Mo-lê, the two lovers succeed in eloping. Meanwhile, Hung-hsien repays the kindness of governor Hsüeh by going to a rival governor's headquarters at night and stealing a gold case from the latter's bedside, thereby warning him not to engage in any aggression. The dramatic action then returns to the story of Hung-hsiao. Her presence is accidentally discovered by Kuo Tzŭ-yi's servants, who report it to their lord. Soldiers are sent to arrest Mo-lê, who easily escapes. Finally, a reconciliation is arranged between Kuo and the young lovers, and both Mo-lê and Hung-hsien return to heaven, their missions accomplished.

The two stories are ingeniously interwoven, but since various passages are lifted from other plays, the work gives the impression of being a pastiche in places. The language is fluent in the lyrics but often too artificial in the spoken dialogue, being cast in the form of Parallel Prose.

In addition to Dramatic Romances concerned chiefly with chivalrous characters, knights-errant also appear in love romances. In *Romance of the Bright Pearl* (*Ming-chu Chi*) by Lu Ts'ai (*fl.* 1525), based on the story of Liu Wu-shang,[1] the knight-errant Ku brings about the reunion of Wu-shuang and her lover. In *Romance of the Purple Hair-pin* (*Tzŭ Ch'ai Chi*), written by the greatest Ming dramatist T'ang Hsien-tsu (1550–1617) and based on the story of Huo Hsiao-yü,[2] the anonymous knight-errant who in the original story forcibly brings the faithless young man to the dying heroine now brings about their reconciliation, for their former separation is all due to a misunderstanding and some wicked man's intrigue.

3. *Dramatic Romances based on history*

Romance of the Knight of Integrity (*Chieh Hsia Chi*)

This Dramatic Romance in thirty-two scenes by Hsü San-chieh (sixteenth century?) is based on the life of P'ei Chou-hsien of the T'ang dynasty (eighth century).

The play is set in the time of the notorious Empress Wu Tsê-

[1] See above, p. 99.

[2] See above, p. 99.

t'ien. The hero P'ei Chou-hsien is a chivalrous young man and nephew of Chief Minister P'ei Yen. The latter offends the Empress by objecting to her plans to set up her own nephew as the heir apparent, and is executed. P'ei Chou-hsien remonstrates with the Empress and protests against his uncle's death, with the result that he himself is caned and banished to Ling-nan (modern Kwangtung) in the far south. It so happens that his fiancée and her mother have also been exiled to this region, so that he takes this opportunity to get married. After marriage P'ei continues to associate with chivalrous men, including one called Liu Sheng. P'ei's activities attract the attention of his enemies, who seize on his attempted visit to his ancestral tombs as evidence that he is trying to escape and have him banished to the northern frontier alone, while his wife and her mother are sent back to Ling-nan. When he reaches the northern frontier, he is befriended by the Khan of the northern tribes, who marries his daughter to P'ei as second wife. With the Princess's dowry, P'ei retains many knights who report to him on the happenings at the court. Alarmed by this, his enemies persuade the Empress to issue an edict ordering the execution of all banished officials. P'ei and his second wife, together with his chivalrous friend Liu who has come to see him, try to flee to the Princess's own country, but are overtaken by the Imperial forces. In the skirmish, Liu is killed and P'ei and the Princess captured. While P'ei is awaiting execution, the Princess is fetched home by the Khan. In the meantime, the wicked Empress has been forced to abdicate and the rightful Emperor restored to the throne. The Emperor now rescinds the edict decreeing the execution of officials in exile, and the messenger arrives just in time to save P'ei's life. What is more, given new powers, P'ei is ordered to superintend the execution of the very official who has supervised his own impending execution! Finally, P'ei is reunited with his two wives.

This plot follows in the main the biography of P'ei Chou-hsien in official history, but adds some characters and incidents. For example, official history does not mention a first wife, only that P'ei married a 'barbarian girl' who brought him wealth. In the drama, he has a first wife and his second wife is a Princess. It seems the dramatist first elevated the status of P'ei's 'barbarian' wife, and then thought even a 'barbarian' princess was still not good enough to be the hero's first wife! This merely betrays the author's prejudices and adds little to the dramatic interest. Another addition is P'ei's friend Liu Sheng. This is relevant to the theme of chivalry, for Liu is a shining example of altruism and personal loyalty, though the name is anachronistic. Liu Sheng is mentioned in various chivalric songs dating from *c.* A.D. 500 but not in any historical work. Even his full name is not known: the word *sheng* simply means 'young man', and Liu Sheng corresponds to 'Master Liu', though in the play this is given as if it were his name. There are other changes from the historical account of P'ei's life. Historically, it was the Empress herself, who, realizing the wide-spread resentment caused by the edict to exterminate all banished officials, rescinded it and pretended that her order had been misunderstood. In the drama, the credit is given to the newly restored Emperor, who thus becomes the *deus ex machina*. The play is well constructed, but its language is far too learned and artificial, so much so that not even a 'barbarian' can open his mouth without using allusions and antitheses.

Romance of Stealing the Tally (*Ch'ieh Fu Chi*)

This Dramatic Romance in twenty-four scenes by Chang Feng-yi, whose *Romance of the Red Whisk* we have discussed above, is mainly based on the life of Prince Wu-chi of Wei in the *Records of the Historiographer*,[1] with additional episodes, some taken from history, others invented by the dramatist.

Many of the additions concern Lady Ju, who stole the tally that enabled Prince Wu-chi to take over the army. The historical work only mentions that her father had been killed by an enemy, that Prince Wu-chi sent one of his guests to kill the enemy, and that out of gratitude she stole the tally for him. Nothing is said as to why her father was killed. In the drama, we get something of a biography of Lady Ju. We first meet her as a Miss Wang, daughter of Old Wang. An officer under General Chin Pi, by the name of Ch'iu Jen (a pun on *ch'ou-jen*, 'enemy'), covets her beauty and wants to have her as his concubine. Old Wang refuses, whereupon he is beaten to death by Ch'iu. As the villain is about to carry the girl away, Prince Wu-chi arrives by chance, and Ch'iu escapes to Chao. When the Prince reports the affair to the King, the latter summons the girl to his presence. So overcome is he by her beauty that he offers to make her a royal concubine, promising to

[1] See above, pp. 17–25.

avenge her father's death. Out of her desire for revenge, she reluctantly agrees, and thus becomes Lady Ju. However, since the murderer is now under the protection of a general of Chao, the King of Wei is unable to apprehend him. Lady Ju then appeals to Prince Wu-chi. When Hou Ying, the old knight in retirement befriended by the Prince, hears of this, he sends his disciple Chu Hai (who in the historical work is a friend) to go and kill the murderer. Chu succeeds in his mission and brings back the enemy's head, which Lady Ju offers to her father's spirit as sacrifice. Later, when the Prince needs the tally to take over the army, Lady Ju steals it for him. This is made the climax of the drama, and the author shows her initial fear, then her resolution at the recollection of what she owes the Prince, and finally, her success. After the Prince has taken control of the army, the King is naturally angry at the loss of the tally and suspects the court ladies. While he is interrogating them under torture, Lady Ju confesses and asks for punishment. The King forgives her and all ends well.

These elaborations on the life of Lady Ju greatly enrich the drama and enable the dramatist to build up, from a mere hint in the historical work, the character of a noble, brave, and warm-hearted woman. Instead of someone engaged in a private feud, she now appears as an innocent person forced by grievous wrongs to take revenge, and it is her desire for revenge alone which makes her consent to become the King's concubine. After the Prince helped her to obtain revenge, she repays her benefactor's kindness with an act of daring, and afterwards she is not afraid to own to it, at the risk of being punished by death.

Another point on which the Dramatic Romance departs from the historical record is the death of Hou Ying. According to the *Records of the Historiographer,* Hou committed suicide on the day the Prince should have reached the army, so as to show that he would have accompanied the Prince and shared the latter's dangers had his own age allowed him to do so. Though this is very noble of him, his death seems unnecessary. In the drama, his death occurs differently. When the Prince shows hesitation when advised to kill General Chin Pi and asks Hou if he has a better plan, Hou replies, 'I have a way to compensate for the loss of his life,' and then commits suicide. Thus, his death is necessitated by his realization that his plan calls for the death of an innocent man and his sense of justice which prompts him to make up for this with his own death. This change from history also constitutes an improvement. However, it is spoilt to some extent by Hou Ying's subsequent resurrection and his bodily assumption into heaven, whence he returns to fetch his disciple Chu Hai, who likewise achieves immortality!

The action of the play moves on smoothly and fairly fast, and the language is fluent and not pedantic, unlike that of the same writer's *Romance of the Red Whisk*. Though it seldom rises to great heights of poetic beauty, neither does it sink to the banal or vulgar. It may be justly regarded as one of the best chivalric plays of the Ming period.

*

The plays mentioned above comprise the majority of extant Dramatic Romances concerned with chivalry. In addition to these, there were others now totally or partially lost. Among them were several dealing with the Liang-shan heroes, one dealing with the four feudal princes famous for retaining knights-errant,[1] two about Ching K'o and Kao Chien-li,[2] one based on the prose romance *A Tale of Chivalrous Love*,[3] and one about a swordsman who defeated Japanese pirates.

KNIGHT-ERRANTRY IN THE PEKING THEATRE

Many chivalric plays in the Peking Theatre are adapted from Dramatic Romances. Some scenes from Dramatic Romances included in the Peking Theatre repertoire are still performed with *K'un-ch'ü* tunes, but more often the *p'i-huang* tunes are used instead,[4] and simple words substituted for the original sophisticated language. Thus, we find many Peking Theatre pieces bearing the same names and dealing with the same incidents as scenes from Dramatic Romances, but differing widely from the latter in content. There are also some chivalric pieces based on Yuan drama or on tales of the T'ang and later periods. Since the Peking Theatre relies more on the performer's skill than the literary qualities of the text, and since it is beyond my power to convey in words the actual experience of witnessing theatrical performances that involve singing, declamation, acting, miming, and stage

[1] See above, p. 16.
[2] See above, pp. 25–34.
[3] See above, p. 121.
[4] See above, p. 149.

fighting, I shall not attempt to describe these plays but merely mention the more important ones as an indication of the popularity of the theme of chivalry in this theatre.

1. *Plays about the Liang-shan heroes*

Scenes taken from Dramatic Romances and still sung in the *K'un-ch'ü* style, though modified, include 'Lin Ch'ung's Flight by Night' from *Romance of the Precious Sword,* 'Wu Sung Killing the Tiger' from *Romance of the Altruistic Knight-errant*, and 'Shih Ch'ien Stealing the Armour' from *Romance of the Wild-goose-feather Armour.*[1]

Plays about the Liang-shan heroes using the *p'i-huang* style of singing include *The Green-jade Screen Mountain* (*Ts'ui-p'ing Shan*),[2] *The Black Dragon Court* (*Wu-lung Yuan*), which deals with Sung Chiang's killing of his mistress Yen P'o-hsi,[3] and *Ting-chia Mountain* (*Ting-chia Shan*), the last-named being based on the Yuan play *Li K'uei's Apology*.[4]

In addition, some plays are derived from sequels to *Water Margin*. Among these, the most famous one is *The Fisherman's Revenge* (*Ta-yü Sha-chia*), which has been translated into English.[5]

2. *Plays based on T'ang chivalric tales*

In the last few decades, several Peking Theatre plays about chivalrous ladies described in T'ang stories have been written, partly based on Dramatic Romances about the same heroines, often with the purpose of showing off the talents of celebrated players of female roles.[6] Thus, a play about Hung-hsien[7] was written for the world-famous Mei Lan-fang; one about Hung-fu[8]

[1] See above, pp. 173, 178, and 182.

[2] Derived from the Dramatic Romance of the same name mentioned on p. 183. For English translation of the Peking Theatre play, see L. C. Arlington and Harold Acton, *Famous Chinese Plays* (Peiping, 1937), pp. 364–89.

[3] See above, p. 181.

[4] See above, pp. 152–7.

[5] Yang Hsien-i and Gladys Yang (tr.), *The Fisherman's Revenge* (Peking, 1956).

[6] I am avoiding the expression 'female impersonators' because of its unfortunate connotations. A Chinese actor who plays female roles employs a special technique, which takes years of training to acquire, to express feminine qualities; he is not just a man dressed up as a woman to cater for perverted tastes. Aesthetically, a *tan*-player and a 'female impersonator' in a night club are poles apart.

[7] See above, p. 90.

[8] See above, p. 87.

and one about Nieh Yin-niang[1] were written for Ch'eng Yen-ch'iu, second only to Mei in reputation; and one about Hung-hsiao[2] for Shang Hsiao-yun. As literature, these plays cannot compare with the Dramatic Romances which preceded them; as theatre, they have remained more or less exotic pieces, and have not achieved such wide popularity as the plays about the Liang-shan heroes.

3. *Plays based on later chivalric tales*

Plays about the heroes of *The Three Knights-errant and the Five Altruists*[2] and about those of *The Cases of Lord Shih* and *The Cases of Lord P'eng*[3] already existed in 1824. Since they appeared at about the same time as, or even earlier than, the first known editions of the tales concerned, some of them may have been based on oral traditions which also formed the bases of the printed tales. Many of these pieces are still popular today, and their heroes are household names. In particular, Huang T'ien-pa, the chief supporter of Lord Shih, is one of the most popular stage heroes of the Peking Theatre.

A more recent play is *Thirteenth Sister*, based on the prose romance *A Tale of Heroic Lovers*,[4] which affords the actor or actress playing the title role ample scope for displaying physical agility as well as feminine grace.

Generally speaking, the chief interest of chivalric plays in the Peking Theatre lies in stage fighting. A typical knight-errant on the stage must possess an imposing appearance and be able to engage in sword fights with lightning speed and hair-splitting precision. He is commonly a 'military man' (*wu-sheng*) of the 'short dress' (*tuan-ta*) variety, though sometimes he may be cast as a 'colourful face' (*huan-lien*) or even 'military clown' (*wu-ch'ou*). He usually wears tight-fitting jacket and trousers, colourful or plain black (the latter kind used specially for night sorties), with low boots, a soft cap or a hat decorated with pom-poms, and sometimes a rich cloak which he throws off with great flourish before fighting. He fights on foot, with a sword, rather than on horseback, with a spear or halberd.

I have described chivalric plays in various schools of drama in some detail at the risk of being repetitious, so as to show the

[1] See above, p. 89.
[2] See above, p. 117.
[3] See above, p. 120.
[4] See above, p. 124.

continuity of the tradition of knight-errantry in popular literature, and the interrelations among history, prose fiction, and drama. No mention has been made of contemporary 'spoken drama' (*hua-chü*), because this is largely an imitation of Western realistic drama and is principally concerned with contemporary social problems, though there are a few modern plays about ancient knights-errant.

5

SOME CONCLUSIONS AND COMPARISONS

We have followed the development (and degeneration in some cases) of knight-errantry in Chinese history and literature during the course of some twenty-four centuries, and observed the changes that have taken place in its nature, both in fact and in fiction. We have seen such a varied gallery of characters, real or fictitious, to whom the term 'knight-errant' has been applied, that the reader may question the justification of its use. However, on reflection he might be convinced that there are in fact certain common denominators among those who have been graced with the appellation, such as their sense of justice, their loyalty to friends, their courage, and their impetuosity. Historically, knight-errantry is a manifestation of the spirit of revolt and nonconformity in traditional Chinese society, sometimes lying underground and sometimes erupting to the surface. Its ideals are admirable, though these have not always been realized in practice, and may have even provided excuses for mere lawlessness. It is further possible that the ideals of knight-errantry inspired the moral codes of secret societies of a subversive kind. As for chivalric literature, it is a moot point whether it has incited rebellion or, on the contrary, has had a 'cathartic' effect on the readers. The popular Chinese saying, 'The young should not read *Water Margin*; the old should not read *The Three Kingdoms*', seems to indicate that the former is generally believed to be the case, though there is of course no irrefutable proof of this.[1] Whatever its social and political effects may have been, chivalric literature has certainly added to our enjoyment.

Our survey has shown the close interrelation between history

[1] I find it hard to agree with those who seriously believe that *Water Margin* has had a profound influence on Mao Tse-tung.

and literature, for whereas historical personages and events provided material for imaginative literature, literary works in turn have thrown light on history—if not on the periods with which they are ostensibly concerned, then on those in which they were actually produced. For instance, chivalric tales written in late T'ang times, when war-lords were rampant, reflect the desire of readers and writers to be rid of these; stories and plays about the Liang-shan heroes that came into being during the Southern Sung and Yuan periods reveal the wish of a people suffering from corrupt government and foreign domination for champions of justice and patriotic warriors; tales and plays of the Ming and Ch'ing periods, in which the heroes are often on the side of the law, together with the attempt of some writers and editors to Confucianize rebellious heroes,[1] indicate a change of attitude towards knight-errantry, a change possibly due to fear of the literary inquisitions carried out by several Ming and Ch'ing emperors; tales extolling physical strength and prowess written since the decline of Chinese power in the nineteenth century are the results of wishful thinking of an enfeebled nation, while contemporary tales depicting flying swordsmen afford a means of escape from the often harsh realities of modern life. These are of course broad generalizations to which exceptions can be found, but they remain basically true.

Another fact which emerges from our survey is that the different treatments of the same characters and incidents in different literary *genres* bring out in relief the characteristics, the fortes, and limitations, of each *genre*. Thus, classical poetry, with its strict meters and concise language, excels in short pithy comments on historical knights or vivid vignettes of chivalrous life, but, due to the inherent danger of monotony of long narrative poems, has not produced a heroic epic. When popular writers tried to write long heroic poems, what they produced were merely ballads in doggerel (such as *The Capture of Chi Pu*). It was left to the prose romancers to produce something with epic qualities like *Water Margin*. Here, the relative freedom of prose, particularly colloquial prose, enabled the writers to create memorable characters in lively narrative, with the aid of convincing dialogue. However, these characters are observed as it were from the outside: they are

[1] For the attempt to Confucianize the Liang-shan heroes, see above, p. 175. and Additional Note 26.

revealed through their action and words, rather than their thoughts and feelings. By contrast, in poetic drama, the characters are seen from within, so that they are less individualized but more representative of universal experiences than those in prose fiction. For example, in *Water Margin*, the ordeals of Lin Ch'ung are those of one man, but in the Dramatic Romance *The Precious Sword*, Lin Ch'ung speaks for all those who have suffered oppression, injustice, and exile. When we read *Water Margin* and other prose romances, we know what the heroes look like, how they talk and behave, but we rarely enter into their thoughts and feelings; in poetic drama, since the characters are classified into conventional types, they cannot be highly individualized in appearance and manners, yet we feel we know them intimately because we share their innermost feelings which they reveal to us in speech or singing. In other words, 'characterization' in prose fiction and poetic drama does not mean quite the same thing; in the former, the author is intent on creating individuals in whom we can believe and for whom we can care; in the latter, characters exist only to 'give a local habitation and a name' to universal human emotions, and are only individualized in so far as the emotions to be expressed are particular and precise. Since the aim differs from one literary *genre* to another, not to mention the technique, it would be wrong to apply the same criteria to them all. While recognizing the limitations and compensations of each *genre*, we should judge a work in that *genre* in terms of its own purpose and technique.

CHINESE AND WESTERN KNIGHTS COMPARED

The reader must have been struck again and again by the similarities, and probably even more by the differences, between the Chinese knights and mediaeval European ones. Although, as I remarked in the introduction, it is beyond the scope of my knowledge and of this book to carry out thorough comparisons between Chinese and Western chivalry, we may note some interesting parallels and striking contrasts, with regard to both historical chivalry and chivalric literature. Let us consider the historical knights first.

Differences between the European and the Chinese knights are quite obvious. First of all, the former formed a definite social class, while the latter, as we have seen, came from all classes of society. This naturally influenced their respective ways of behaviour. The Western knights were the backbone of the feudal system; the Chinese ones represented a disruptive force in feudal society. The former extended courtesy only to their social equals and had a strong sense of class solidarity;[1] the latter made a point of breaking down social barriers and were entirely free from class consciousness and social snobbery, as can be witnessed by Prince Wu-chi's treatment of Hou Ying and Chu Hai,[2] or Prince Tan's of Ching K'o.[3]

Another basic difference between the European and the Chinese knights is that the former had religious sanction and the latter had no religious affiliation. Though it may be an idealistic exaggeration to claim, as Léon Gautier did, that 'chivalry is the Christian form of the military profession; the knight is the Christian soldier',[4] European knights did profess to be Christians and were supposed to defend the faith, while Chinese ones did not necessarily believe in any religion.

These two basic differences—the one regarding social status and the other religious sanction—led to further dissimilarities between the Western knights and the Chinese. Being a social class, the former naturally confined chivalry to members of their own class and applied strict rules for admission. When Christian moral standards were superimposed on these, they formed the rules of the various orders of knighthood. By contrast, the Chinese knights never organized themselves into orders and never possessed any monopoly over chivalry: anyone behaving according to the ideals of Chinese chivalry became *ipso facto* a knight. Furthermore, a Western knight owed loyalty to his king or over-lord; a Chinese knight only acknowledged personal loyalty to a *chih-chi* ('one who appreciates you'), whatever his social status may have been. A Western knight had the duty of defending the Church; a Chinese one had no special obligations to any religious or social institution. Being noblemen and Christians, the Western knights were enjoined to be moderate, temperate, and refined in manners; indeed, their whole life was governed by

[1] For an extreme instance of this, see Sidney Painter, *French Chivalry* (Great Seal Books, New York, 1961), p. 59.

[2] See above, pp. 18–9.

[3] See above, pp. 28–9.

[4] *Chivalry* (tr. Henry Frith, London, 1891), p. 2.

elaborate ritual. The Chinese knights, reacting against Confucian ritualism, had little patience with manners and often acted without restraint. Western chivalry (though not in its beginning) was associated with courtly love: the ideal knight was also the perfect lover; Chinese knights were generally either indifferent to the fair sex, regarding all amorous activities as unmanly (an attitude that may have been influenced by the popular belief that sexual abstinence would help to preserve one's vitality), or light-hearted in their attitude towards love, taking women as an object of pleasure rather than adoration.

In spite of these differences, the Chinese and the Western knights did have certain common ideals. In fact, most of the ideals of Chinese chivalry were such as a Western knight would have readily subscribed to. It will be recalled that among the chief ideals of the Chinese knights were altruism and justice, especially with regard to the poor and oppressed. The Western knights, too, were expected to uphold justice and unselfishly protect the poor and the weak. For instance, John of Salisbury mentions as one of the duties of a knight the protection of the poor from injuries;[1] William Caxton, in his *Ordre of Chyualry* translated from the French of Ramon Lull, also states, 'Thoffyce of a knyght is to mayntene and deffende wymmen wydowes and orphanes and men dyseased and not puyssaunt ne stronge'.[2] Further, the Chinese knights aimed at high courage and fame, preferring death to dishonour; so did the Western ones. The former were generous and regarded wealth with contempt; the latter also esteemed generosity, to the extent that *largesse* was considered by some the chief virtue of noble knights.[3] Finally, the Chinese knights stressed mutual faith and truthfulness; the European knights were also told that 'fals swerynge and vntrewe othe be not in them that mayntene thordre of chyualrye'.[4] All these ideals shared by the knights Chinese and European represent universal human aspirations and create a spiritual bond between them across space and time and despite their differences. Our use of the words 'knights' and 'chivalry' throughout this book is therefore not without some justification.

[1] From *Policraticus,* tr. J. Dickinson, excerpt included in *The Portable Medieval Reader* (New York, 1961), p. 90.

[2] Early English Text Society (London, 1926), p. 38.

[3] Sidney Painter, *op. cit.*, p. 32.

[4] Caxton, *op. cit.*, p. 43.

The similarities and differences between the historical Chinese and European knights are naturally reflected in literature. In addition, there are also resemblances and differences in literary purpose and technique. Since these two kinds of similarities and dissimilarities are closely related to each other, no attempt will be made to separate them rigidly in the following discussions on chivalric literature.

To begin with poetry. There are two types of Western poetry with which Chinese chivalric poetry may be compared: heroic poetry and chivalric poetry. The former, as defined by Sir Maurice Bowra, includes such works as the Homeric epics, *chansons de geste*, and *Beowulf*; under the latter may be classified chivalric romances such as the Arthurian romances of Chrétien de Troyes, and 'literary' epics concerned with chivalry such as Ariosto's *Orlando Furioso* and Spenser's *Faerie Queene*. The two types overlap to some extent: The *Chanson de Roland*, for instance, is a heroic poem which at the same time exhibits chivalric ideals.

Chinese chivalric poems (except dramatic poetry and doggerel ballads) are basically different from Western heroic poems in that the former are short descriptions of chivalrous life or comments on historical knights instead of being usually long narrative poems. Secondly, while heroic poetry is essentially concerned with depicting action undertaken in pursuit of honour, as Sir Maurice Bowra pointed out,[1] Chinese chivalric poems are more concerned with motives of chivalrous deeds than with the deeds themselves, and though honour is one of these motives, it is far from being the only or the most important one. Thirdly, heroic poetry is primarily intended for oral recital before popular audiences, while Chinese chivalric poetry (with the same exceptions as above) is mostly written by literary men for other literary men to read.

At the same time, Chinese chivalric poems also differ from Western chivalric romances and literary epics concerned with chivalry. The former contain little allegory, while the latter are imbued with Christian allegory. In particular, we may note how Chinese poets prefer to comment implicitly on current affairs by means of historical analogy, where Western poets might employ allegorical presentation. Thus, T'ao Ch'ien revealed his feelings about the change of dynasties in his time by writing a poem on the

[1] *Heroic Poetry* (London, 1952), pp. 1–3.

ancient knight Ching K'o,[1] while Spenser alluded to contemporary persons and events allegorically. Had Spenser been Chinese, he would probably have written about Boadicea to flatter Elizabeth I instead of creating such allegorical figures as Gloriana and Belphoebe. This is not to say that the use of historical analogy is unknown in Western chivalric literature (it can be found, for example, in Sir Thomas Malory's *Morte d'Arthur*[2]); only that it is far more common in Chinese poetry, so much so that 'poems on history' have long been recognized as a special class of poetry in Chinese.

Furthermore, Western chivalric poetry is as much concerned with courtly love as with heroic deeds. Ariosto sums it up by saying:

> Le donne, i cavalier, l'arme, gli amori,
> Le cortesie, l'audaci impresse io canto.[3]

Likewise, Spenser announces that he will 'sing of Knights and Ladies gentle deeds', adding, 'Fierce warres and faithfull loues shall moralize my song.'[4] By contrast, Chinese chivalric poets only occasionally mention the fair sex, and then in the spirit of 'wine, women, and song' rather than serious love. We may recall Li Po's young knights-errant who are followed 'by noisy singing girls as beautiful as orchids' or 'amid laughter . . . enter a tavern with a pretty serving maid'.[5]

In spite of such differences, we sometimes find similarities between Western poets' conceptions of chivalry and those of Chinese poets. Take, for instance, Chaucer's well-known portrait of the perfect knight:

> A Knight ther was, and that a worthy man,
> That fro the tyme that he first bigan
> To ryden out, he loved chivalrye,
> Trouthe and honour, fredom and curteisye.
> Ful worthy was he in his lordes werre,
> And therto hadde he riden (no man ferre)

[1] See above, p. 78.

[2] See *Le Morte d'Arthur,* ed. Sir Edward Strachey (London, 1906), p. 2; and W. H. Schofield, *Chivalry in English Literature* (Harvard, 1925), pp. 88–93.

[3] *Orlando Furioso,* Canto I, lines 1–2.

[4] *Faerie Queene,* Book I, Canto I, stanza i.

[5] See above, pp. 66–7.

As wel in Christendom as hethenesse,
And ever honoured for his worthinesse.[1]

This is not very different from Ts'ao Chih's knight who 'left his native district in his youth / And spread his fame across the desert' and who 'rode on right into the land of the Huns, / Holding the Tartar tribes in high disdain':[2] both knights are brave, honourable, and loyal, and both have fought for what they believe to be just causes, the only difference being that the one fights to defend the Christian faith while the other does so to protect Chinese civilization. Or take these lines from Spenser:

Nought is more honourable to a knight,
Ne better doth beseeme braue cheualry,
Then to defend the feeble in their right,
And wrong redresse in such as wend awry.[3]

The ideal expressed here is very much after the heart of Chinese knights, such as the one in Chia Tao's quatrain, who shows his sword and asks, 'Is there anyone suffering from injustice?'[4] Again, Spenser's description of the Knight of Justice Artegall's 'steedy brand' which was once used by Jove himself to fight the Titans with and which was made of 'most perfect metall'[5] reminds one of Lu Yu's precious sword which will 'kill a big whale / And turn the sea red for three months.'[6] Both poets use the sword as a symbol of the might of justice.

To be sure, these are ideals rather than facts. When we come to more realistic portraits of Chinese knights, we find them quite different from Western ones. In contrast to the Chaucerian knight who is 'as meke as is a mayde'[7] and Spenser's Sir Guyon whose countenance is 'demure and temperate',[8] Tu Fu's young knight-errant is 'very rude and over-bearing',[9] and while Chaucer's knight is not 'gay' in his dress but wears plain fustian,[10] Li Po's knight is 'dressed from head to foot in rich silk and gauze'.[11] Due to such differences, the knights in Western poetry often seem

[1] *Canterbury Tales, Prologue,* lines 43–50.
[2] See above, p. 57.
[3] Spenser, *op. cit.,* Book V, Canto II, stanza i.
[4] See above, p. 68.
[5] Spenser, *op. cit.,* Book V, Canto I, stanza x.
[6] See above, p. 69.
[7] Chaucer, *op. cit.,* line 69.
[8] Spenser, *op. cit.,* Book II, Canto I, stanza i.
[9] See above, p. 63.
[10] Chaucer, *op. cit.,* lines 75–6.
[11] See above, p. 66.

prim and a little forbidding, while those in Chinese poetry generate gaiety and conviviality.

While Chinese chivalric poetry differs largely from Western heroic poetry, Chinese chivalric romances in prose, based as many of them are on oral traditions, resemble heroic poetry in origin and technique. Various features of heroic poetry mentioned by Sir Maurice Bowra are also found in Chinese chivalric prose romances. Let us examine one of these features: the uses of 'formulae'. Sir Maurice defines a formula as 'a set of words which is used, with little or no change, whenever the situation with which it deals occurs'.[1] Such formulae are frequently met with in Chinese chivalric romances, not only those directly based on oral traditions but also those written by individual authors in the same style. For example, an uneventful journey is generally indicated by the formula, 'They ate when hungry, drank when thirsty; set out in the morning, slept at night'; to cope with events taking place simultaneously, the romancer may use the formula, 'I, the story-teller, with one mouth cannot tell what is going on in two families. While such-and-such is happening to A, B is doing the following. . . .' One particular form of the formula, that of noun-adjective combination, seems less common in Chinese romances than in Western heroic poetry. Nevertheless, the practice of affixing nicknames to heroes, such as 'Leopard-headed Lin Ch'ung', 'Timely-rain Sung Chiang', has an effect akin to that of noun-adjective combinations like 'white-armed Hera'.

We also find some resemblance between Chinese chivalric prose romances and Western chivalric poetry, in that both show an obvious delight in pageantry and pay great attention to colourful details. An interesting parallel is provided by a tournament between two heroes in *Water Margin* and the one between Palamon and Arcite in Chaucer's *The Knight's Tale*. In the Chinese romance, the tournament between the heroes Yang Chih and So Ch'ao is preceded by descriptions of the drill ground, the arrayed officers and soldiers, the colourful banners, the beating of drums and sounding of horns, and preliminary combats between Yang Chih and lesser figures.[2] In *The Knight's Tale*, Chaucer too first describes the construction of the lists (in even greater detail), the rich

[1] Bowra, *op. cit.*, p. 222.

[2] *Water Margin,* Chapters 12–13 in the 120-chapter version (11–12 in the 71-chapter version).

costumes of the knights and their attendants, the martial music, and the bustling crowd before the actual combat.[1] In *Water Margin*, the appearances of the two combatants are described with zest. First So Ch'ao:

> On his head he wears a tempered steel 'lion' helmet, with a red tassel as big as a bushel trailing behind; on his person he wears a suit of armour formed of iron leaves, with a gilt belt, decorated with a beast's face (as clasp), round his waist, and bronze breast-plate and back-plate; on top of this he wears a scarlet robe patterned with medallions, over which dangle two green velvet belts; on his feet, he has a pair of leather boots; on his left, he carries a bow; on his right, a quiver full of arrows; in his hand, he holds horizontally a battle-axe decorated with gold; his mount is Superintendent General Li's snowy white steed that is well used to battle.

Now the other combatant, Yang Chih:

> On his head he wears a steel helmet that looked as if it had been strewn with frost and shone in the sun, on which was a black tassel; on his body he wears a suit of armour forged with plum-blossom and elm-leaf patterns, fastened with a girdle of red velvet, with beast-face-shaped breast-plate and back-plate, on top of which he wears a white silk robe with flower patterns, with a purple velvet belt dangling; on his feet he has a pair of thick-soled brown leather boots; he carries a leather-backed bow, and several sharp-headed arrows; in his hand he holds a spear of tempered steel; his mount is Minister Liang's fiery-coloured steed that can run a thousand *li* a day and neighs in the wind.[2]

When we turn back to Chaucer, we find the same kind of loving care about minute details of personal appearance and costume, though not lavished on the two chief combatants, Palamon and Arcite, but on their associates, the kings of Thrace and India. The former has a black beard, glowing eyes, massive limbs, and broad shoulders; stands on a golden chariot; and wears a black bearskin over his armour and a heavy wreath of gold on his head, set full of rubies and diamonds. The latter rides a bay steed harnessed in steel and covered with cloth of gold, his coat of arms being made of cloth of Tartary and decorated with pearls, his saddle made of burnished gold, his mantle crusted with

[1] Chaucer, *op. cit.*, lines 1026–1230.

[2] *Water Margin*, Chapter 13 in the 120-chapter version (12 in the 71-chapter version).

sparkling rubies, his hair curly and yellow, his nose prominent, his eyes bright 'citryn', and his complexion 'sangwyn'.[1] Both the Chinese romancer (or romancers) and the English poet have imagined their heroes in concrete detail and conjured them up before our eyes with compelling force.

Among Western literary works, it is the ballads about Robin Hood and his merry men which show the greatest affinity in spirit with Chinese chivalric romances, especially *Water Margin*, different as they are in form. Though the Robin Hood ballads are not normally classified as 'chivalric literature', they do exhibit some of the ideals of Western chivalry, so much so that Robin has in fact been called a knight-errant.[2] Both the Liang-shan heroes and the Sherwood Forest band are chivalrous outlaws, both rob the rich and help the poor, both can be harsh and cruel but are capable of great kindness and generosity. More specifically, Robin Hood's character could be a composite portrait of several Liang-shan heroes, notably Ch'ao Kai, leader of the band till his death, and Hua Jung, the unsurpassed archer, while Robin's death caused by the treachery of the Prioress of Kirkleys nunnery reminds us of Sung Chiang's death caused by the treachery of some courtiers who poisoned the wine bestowed on him by the Emperor. Robin's treatment of the Sheriff of Nottingham is very much the same as the Liang-shan heroes' treatment of corrupt and oppressive officials, and his help to the impecunious knight can be easily paralleled by deeds of generosity carried out by the Liang-shan band. Among Robin's followers, Friar Tuck naturally challenges comparison with the chivalrous monk Lu Chih-shen, and Little John somewhat resembles Yen Ch'ing, the ever-faithful follower of Lu Chün-yi. As for Maid Marion, she has, alas, no counterpart at Liang-shan, even though the band boasts of three female warriors among their numbers.

One type of Chinese chivalric fiction—romances about flying swordsmen and swordswomen—resembles Western chivalric romances in several ways. Both are largely dissociated from contemporary reality and afford an escape into fairyland. Referring to the Arthurian romances of Chrétien de Troyes, Professor Erich Auerbach remarked, 'The landscape is the enchanted landscape of fairy tale; we are surrounded by mystery, by secret murmurings

[1] Chaucer, *op. cit.*, lines 1271–89; 1297–1310.

[2] Joseph Ritson, *Robin Hood* (London, 1887), Vol. I, p. xl.

and whispers. All the numerous castles and palaces, the battles and adventures . . . are things of fairyland.'[1] These words can be applied with equal truth to Chinese romances such as *The Chivalrous Swordsmen of the Szechwan Mountains*,[2] wherein abound knights with magical powers, monsters, enchanted temples, etc. Moreover, in both Chinese and Western romances, the knights undertake endless adventures to prove their worth: adventure is their very *raison d'être*. To quote Auerbach again, 'The world of knightly proving is a world of adventure. It not only contains a practically uninterrupted series of adventures; more specifically, it contains nothing but the requisites of adventure.'[3] This is also true of Chinese romances about knights with supernatural powers. Finally, Western chivalric romances imply a kind of class ethics which is 'absolute, raised above all earthly contingencies' and which 'gives those who submit to its dictates the feeling that they belong to a community of the elect, a circle of solidarity set apart from the common herd';[4] the knights in Chinese romances, too, form an élite set apart from ordinary people, though their exclusiveness is not based on social class but on natural ability, often combined with a kind of mystical predestined affinity.

One major difference between Western and Chinese chivalric romances concerns the treatment of love. While in the former love is often the chief inspiration of deeds of chivalry, in the latter it plays no such important part. To be sure, romantic love does appear in some Chinese chivalric tales (Hung-fu's elopement with Li Ching is an example); but more often we find illicit love depicted simply as shameless lust, such as Golden Lotus's affair with Hsi-men Ch'ing. The kind of love celebrated in Western romances, such as Lancelot's love for Guinevere and Tristram's for Iseult, would have been condemned by Chinese romancers. None the less, though the knights in Chinese romances are seldom involved in love themselves, they sometimes help young lovers to be united or reunited.[5] Moreover, in romances combining chivalry with crime detection, the heroes habitually save ladies in distress, especially when their virtue is threatened by

[1] *Mimesis* (tr. Willard R. Trask, Princeton, 1953), p. 130. I owe this reference to Dr. Elizabeth McCutcheon of the University of Hawaii.

[2] See above, p. 130. [3] Auerbach, *op. cit.*, p. 136. [4] *Ibid.*, p. 137.

[5] See above, p. 99.

unscrupulous 'flower-picking thieves' (*ts'ai-hua tsei*, villains or renegade swordsmen who ravish women). In this respect, the Chinese knights resemble their Western counterparts.

Paradoxically perhaps, though love plays no important part in Chinese chivalric romances, female *hsia* (chivalrous ladies or swordswomen) feature prominently. These ladies—Hung-fu, Hung-hsien, Thirteenth Sister, and others—are a species apart. They are well versed in swordsmanship and sometimes gifted with magical powers; they are brave, loyal, and wise; yet, though expert fighters, they are no rough Amazons, but retain their feminine charms. They are very different from the delicate beauties of Western chivalric romances, but have something in common with certain heroines of heroic poems of the 'aristocratic' kind, who may possess prophetic powers and can fight like men.[1]

Another considerable difference between Western and Chinese chivalric romances is that the former contain hardly any trace of humour while the latter is freely endowed with it. This is not surprising, for humour would be out of place in romances based on the austere ideals of mediaeval European chivalry and the artificial conventions of courtly love, but in Chinese romances, since Chinese knights-errant in real life often acted unconventionally and iconoclastically, descriptions of their deeds would not suffer from a touch of humour. One notable example of a chivalric romance written in a humorous vein is *Master Chi the Living Buddha* (*Chi-kung Huo-fo*), of which the earliest known version is dated 1569. The character of Master Chi is based on legends about a Buddhist monk called Tao-chi who lived during the Southern Sung period (1127–1279). In the romance, he behaves in a seemingly outrageous manner: he is dressed in rags, eats meat and drinks wine (contrary to monastic rules), and even visits houses of pleasure (though remaining untainted); but actually he carries out deeds of charity and altruism: he cures the sick, drives away evil spirits, and assists various knights in their efforts to eliminate villains and save those in distress. The work is basically not very different from other chivalric romances like *The Cases of Lord Shih* but for its rolicking humour, thanks to which Master Chi appears as a delightful character. As a matter of fact, he is still the object of popular religious worship—a fact which may owe something to the popularity of the humorous romance.

[1] See Bowra, *op. cit.*, pp. 489–92.

The kind of humour shown in Chinese chivalric romances is largely good-natured, not directed against chivalry itself. As for satire, there is no masterpiece of parody in Chinese comparable to *Don Quixote*, only occasional satire. In the well-known eighteenth-century novel, *Unofficial History of the Forest of Scholars* (*Ju-lin Wai-shih*, translated into English as *The Scholars*), the following incident occurs: a self-styled knight-errant called Iron-armed Chang swindles two gullible young men out of five hundred taels of silver and leaves a bag which he says contains the head of his enemy. It turns out to be a pig's head.[1]

Finally, with regard to drama, Western chivalric literature seems less rich than Chinese in this respect. It is a pity that the heroes of mediaeval chilvaric romances did not appear on the stage, and one wonders why the exploits of crusading knights were not thought fit subjects for dramatic treatment in addition to miracles and mysteries during the Middle Ages. True, some of the Arthurian knights did belatedly come into their own in Wagner's music-dramas, but in spite of his ideal of combining music with poetry, these are in actual fact esteemed for their music rather than their language, and are therefore not true analogies with Chinese drama. When we turn to the Elizabethan and Jacobean dramatists, again we are disappointed at their apparent lack of interest in the theme of chivalry. Shakespeare did not devote any of his plays to chivalry, though there are numerous references in them to chivalric ideals and practices,[2] such as Edgar's challenge to Edmund to a combat in *King Lear*. Also, the behaviour of some of Shakespeare's other characters, though they are not knights in the Western sense, would be considered chivalrous by Chinese standards: such is the action of Antonio in *The Merchant of Venice*, and of the other Antonio (in *Twelfth Night*) who saves the life of Sebastian and entrusts the latter with his purse; and Friar Lawrence's attempt to help Romeo and Juliet, as I have had occasion to remark once before, is strangely similar to that of the knight-errant Ku Hung to bring about the reunion of the lovers Wang Hsien-k'ê and Liu Wu-shuang.[3] But all in all these are only casual

[1] See *The Scholars* (tr. Yang Hsien-i and Gladys Yang, Peking, 1957), pp. 189–98. I am indebted to Professor J. R. Hightower of Harvard University for calling my attention to this episode.

[2] See W. H. Scholfield, *op. cit.*, pp. 190–263.

[3] See above, pp. 99, 185.

instances, not full studies, of chivalry. As for Elizabethan and Jacobean revenge plays, at first sight they may appear to have something in common with Chinese chivalric plays which are also often concerned with revenge, but they are in fact quite different. These plays, from *The Spanish Tragedy* to *The Revenger's Tragedy*, are mainly concerned with personal vendetta, while the Chinese ones usually involve avenging the wrongs of others. Even when the knights in Chinese plays seek personal revenge, this is carried out as a protest against social injustice and oppressive government, which is not the case with Elizabethan revenge plays. Perhaps the nearest equivalent in Western literature to Chinese chivalric Dramatic Romances is Corneille's *Le Cid*, with its noble sentiments, its elevated style, and its preoccupation with the feelings of the principal characters rather than their deeds. Although its central theme—the conflict between love and honour—finds no parallel in Chinese chivalric drama, since love plays no important part there, the insistence on the point of honour and the conviction that revenge is a sacred duty would be readily understood by Chinese heroes and heroines. Indeed, Chimène's demand for her father's revenge and her refusal to marry her lover are somewhat similar to Thirteenth Sister's determination to avenge her father's death and her resolution never to get married,[1] though the latter is fortunate enough not to be in love with her father's killer.

The above comparisons are no doubt haphazard and superficial, though (let me reiterate my hope) they might stimulate other scholars to carry out more thorough comparative studies between Chinese and Western chivalry. Ignorance has also bid me refrain from comparing the Chinese *hsia* with the Japanese *samurai*. However, the differences I pointed out between Chinese and European knights may to some extent apply here too, in so far as the *samurai* were a caste who supported the feudal system instead of being rebels against it. In fact, the *hsia* seem to have more in common with the *rōnin* than the *samurai*.

In the foregoing pages I have ranged over several fields. If I am charged with not having adopted a sufficiently strict definition of 'knight-errantry', I can only cry *mea cupla*. But if this book has provided an opportunity to discuss certain aspects of Chinese civilization and certain types of Chinese literature which would

[1] See above, pp. 128–9.

otherwise have remained largely unknown to Western readers, then this might atone for my sins of excessive zeal and lack of discrimination and perhaps even (dare I hope?) appease my would-be critics.

ADDITIONAL NOTES

For explanation of abbreviations see Bibliography

1. The meaning of *yu* in *yu-hsia* 游俠

Professor Shih-hsiang Ch'en of the University of California suggested to me that perhaps the word *yu* here should be taken to mean *yu-li*—離 ('isolated' or 'displaced') rather than 'wandering'. However, I have not been able to find any example of such usage in pre-Han or Han texts. Professor Ch'en wondered why the knights should be called 'wandering' since some of them obviously had homes. This difficulty, I think, can be resolved by saying that they were so called not because they necessarily had no home but because they were ready to travel around for the sake of others, as for example Chu Chia did for Chi Pu or Kuo Hsieh did habitually (see above, pp. 36–9), not to mention being obliged to move or fleeing from the law.

2. The word *yi* 義

This word has been translated in various ways. E.g. the word in *Lun Yü*, II, 24, is translated as 'what is right' (Legge, Waley I), and 'the right' (Soothill, Lyall); in VII, 3, as 'righteousness' (Legge), 'righteous man' (Waley I), 'recognized duty' (Soothill), and 'the right' (Lyall); in XII, 20, as 'righteous' (Legge), 'right' (Waley I, Lyall), and 'justice' (Soothill). In the present book, the word is translated as 'altruism' when used in the sense understood by the knights-errant, but rendered into various other words according to the context and the speaker.

3. The term *shao-nien* 少年

This term, which normally means simply 'youth', in the *Shih Chi*, *Han Shu*, and *yueh-fu* songs often carries the implication of 'lawlessness'. Masubuchi (p. 90) therefore translated it as 'hooligans'. Since this may be a little too strong, I have used 'unruly youths' instead.

4. Nature (*tzŭ-jan*) and human nature (*hsing*)

In saying that the knights-errant practised the Taoist principle of following Nature, I do not mean that they necessarily shared the Taoist view of human nature. In fact, the knights' conception of human nature seems to have been more Confucian than Taoist: their actions suggest that they believed in the essentially moral character of human nature. I am indebted to Professor W. Theodore de Bary of Columbia University for bringing this point to my notice.

5. Bronze pillar or wooden pillar?

Some editions of the *Shih Chi* has 銅柱 ('bronze pillar') instead of 桐柱 ('pillar of *t'ung* wood'). Since the historian explicitly discounted exaggerated rumours about Ching K'o's attempt to assassinate the King of Ch'in, it seems unlikely that he believed in the legend that the knight's dagger hit a bronze pillar and struck fire, as described in the *Yen Tan Tzŭ* (see above, p. 84), if indeed the legend already existed in the historian's time.

6. *Pao-piao*

The word *piao* is written 鏢 or 鑣 and is generally understood to be a kind of weapon resembling a dart. Thus, *piao-k'ê* means 'traveller armed with *piao*'. But it seems strange to call the profession of armed escorts *pao-piao* or 'protecting the *piao*', since the *piao* was not the object but the means of protection. Perhaps we should adopt the second form of writing *piao* and take it in its original sense of 'horse's bit', in which case *pao-piao* would mean 'protecting the horse' (by synecdoche). Another possibility, suggested by my friend Mr. Chang Hsüan, is that *piao* should be written 標, meaning 'sign' or 'mark', and *pao-piao* means 'protecting the trade mark', since the armed escorts used to display a flag bearing the sign of their firm.

7. 'Pear-blossom spear' (*li-hua ch'iang*)

The *Tz'ŭ Yuan* quotes Ch'en Jen-hsi's *Pa-pien Lei-tsuan* (*c.* 1626): 'The wife of Li Ch'üan, *née* Yang [who lived at the end of Sung] said that for twenty years her "pear-blossom spear" had no match.' To this may be added Lu Feng-tsao's remark that the way of using the spear was handed down from Madam Yang and was known as 'pear-blossom spear' (*chüan* 8, p. 4b). The second reference is significant since it explicitly says 'way of using the spear', whereas in the first quotation the phrase could be taken to mean a kind of spear.

8. *Ch'uan-ch'i* 傳奇

This term has four different meanings: (*a*) At first it was used to designate tales in classical prose of the T'ang and Sung periods, and is still used in this sense sometimes. (*b*) In the classification of oral tales told in Sung times, it was confined to romantic love stories. (*c*) Since Southern Sung, the term has been applied loosely to any kind of dramatic writing. (*d*) Since Ming times, it has come to mean specifically long Dramatic Romances which developed from Yuan Southern Drama but also absorbed elements of Northern Drama.

9. *Pien-wen* 變文

I have adopted Sun K'ai-ti's interpretation of the terms *chuan-pien* 轉(囀)變 and *pien-wen* (Sun K'ai-ti II, p. 1). This is also the way Waley explains *pien-wen* (Waley III, p. 245), though he does not mention Sun. Other scholars prefer to explain *pien* as 'change, popularize', and *pien-wen* as 'changed writing' or 'popularization' (e.g. Cheng Chen-to I, p. 588; Bishop, p. 3; Ch'en Shou-yi II, p. 323). The interpretation of *pien* as 'the unusual' seems to me better because it can be applied equally well to the analogous term *pien-hsiang*: if *pien* means 'the unusual', then *pien-hsiang* means 'pictures of the unusual', which makes perfectly good sense, whereas if we take *pien* as 'change', *pien-hsiang* would have to mean 'changed pictures', but what pictures were changed? Cheng Chen-to's suggestion that *pien-hsiang* means 'changing Buddhist scriptures into pictures' (Cheng Chen-to II, Vol. 1, p. 190) seems forced and grammatically improbable. It should also be noted that strictly speaking the term *pien-wen* should not be applied to the texts of all kinds of popular recitals but only to those relating episodes. (See Hsiang Ta, pp. 305–7.)

10. Classification of Sung story-tellers

Our knowledge on this subject is derived from five sources: (*a*) Meng Yuan-lao's *Tung-ching Meng-hua Lu* (*c.* 1127), (*b*) Kuan-yuan Nai-tê-weng's *Tu-ch'eng Chi-sheng* (1235). (*c*) Wu Tzŭ-mu's *Meng-liang Lu* (*c.* 1274). (*d*) Chou Mi's *Wu-lin Chiu-shih* (*c.* 1274). (*e*) Lo Yeh's *Tsui-weng T'an-lu* (*c.* 1278). They differ considerably from each other. The discrepancies among the first four have been described by Sun K'ai-ti (II, pp. 16–21) and Bishop (pp. 7–9). However, all four mention the *ho-sheng*, which was probably a kind of performance involving play on words (Sun K'ai-ti II, pp. 23–5), after fiction proper, popularizations of history, and explanations of Buddhist sutras. The last book, discovered in Japan about 1941, does not mention the *ho-sheng*, nor does it state that there were four kinds of story-tellers. Since the statement that there were four kinds of story-tellers is found only in sources (*b*) and (*c*), and the passage in question in (*c*) was taken from (*b*) anyway, we may question its accuracy. Two questions, then, remain: were there indeed *four* categories of story-telling? and if so, was *ho-sheng* the fourth one?

11. Subdivision of fiction proper

This also caused some confusion due to the ambiguities of the first four sources mentioned in the preceding note. But thanks to the discovery of the *Tsui-weng T'an-lu*, this confusion has been cleared up. This book makes it clear that fiction proper was subdivided into eight categories, as described in my main text, not four or five, as previously thought (Sun K'ai-ti II, p. 21; Bishop, p. 9). See Lo Yeh, pp. 3–4; T'an Cheng-pi, pp. 13–37.

12. The tomb inscription of Chê K'ê-ts'un

The text of this inscription has been published by Mou Jun-sun (pp. 219–20, rep. fr. TWH No. 2). Chang Cheng-lang (in SYLC, pp. 207–23) uses the same inscription as ground for suggesting that Sung Chiang's capitulation in 1121 was merely pretended and that he never took part in the campaign against Fang La. But the evidence that Sung did play a considerable part in the campaign is too weighty to be dismissed as airily as it has been by Chang in his obvious efforts to paint Sung Chiang as a revolutionary hero who never helped to suppress other rebels. It is much more likely, as Mou suggests, that Sung Chiang was captured and killed after he had helped to suppress Fang La's rebellion, either because he himself rebelled again out of resentment that he had not received just reward, or perhaps because he was framed by other officers who were jealous of him and despised him as a former 'bandit'.

13. Stories about Liang-shan heroes mentioned in the *Tsui-weng T'an-lu*

Under 'public cases' is listed a story called '*Shih-t'ou* Sun Li' or 'Sun Li of the Stones', which presumably dealt with the robbery of the rare stones described in the *Hsüan-ho Yi-shih*, where Sun Li is mentioned as one of the twelve men sent to guard the stones. Under 'swords' is a story '*Ch'ing-mien Shou*' or 'Blue-faced Beast', which is the nickname of Yang Chih. Under 'clubs' are two stories, 'Wu Hsing-chê' or 'Wu the Mendicant Friar', and 'Hua Ho-shang' or 'The Tatooed Monk', i.e. Wu Sung and Lu Chih-shen respectively. Since the texts of these stories (if they were ever written down) are not extant, we do not know whether these stories formed part of the basis of the *Hsüan-ho Yi-shih* or dealt with different episodes about the same heroes.

14. The identification of Shih Nai-an with Shih Hui

Evidence for this is found in the *Ch'uan-ch'i Hui-k'ao Piao-mu* (*c.* 1720, reprinted in CKHLC, Vol. 7), which states, 'Shih Hui was styled Nai-an' (p. 249). Though this is not indisputable proof, it shows that the identification is not merely Wu Mi's conjecture, as Ho Hsin (p. 27) alleged. The identification has been accepted by Sun K'ai-ti (III, p. 181). The basis for stating that Shih Hui lived before 1330 is Chung Ssŭ-ch'eng's *Lu-kuei Pu* (preface 1330), which lists Shih among dramatists who were no longer alive but whom Chung had known personally.

15. The so-called tomb inscription of Shih Nai-an

Ch'en Chung-fan (in SYLC, p. 121) pointed out two blunders in the so-called tomb inscription: (*a*) The 'inscription' says that Shih passed the *chin-shih* examination in the year *hsin-wei* of the Chih-shun period (i.e. 1331), but no examination was held that year. (*b*) The 'inscription' states that Shih served as magistrate of Ch'ien-t'ang district, but his name does not appear in the list of successive magistrates in the district gazetteer. Ho Hsin (pp. 29–31) also raised objections to the 'inscription'. Moreover, this 'inscription' is only recorded but does not exist on stone, as does the tomb inscription of Chê K'ê-ts'un.

16. The date of the *Shih-kung An*

The date of the first edition of this romance is usually given as 1838, but according to Kê Hsien-ning (p. 193) there is an earlier edition bearing the date 'Third Year of Chia-ch'ing' (i.e. 1798), published by the Wen-tê T'ang of Amoy.

17. The date of the *Hao-ch'iu Chuan*

Lu Hsün (p. 202) listed the work among Ming novels, but Sun K'ai-ti (III, p. 140) thinks it probably belongs to early Ch'ing. It seems Sun is right, for at the beginning of the book we read, 'In the previous dynasty, in Ta-ming, Pei-chih-li. . . .' If the work was written in Ming times, then 'previous dynasty' would be Yuan, but the place name 'Pei-chih-li' only came into existence under Emperor Ch'eng-tsu of Ming. This shows the work must belong to the Ch'ing period. George Soulié de Morant's dating of the romance as a fourteenth-century work is wide of the mark.

18. The meanings of *kung-tiao* 宮調

This term has three different meanings: (*a*) The word *kung* refers to the keynote of a given tune, and *tiao* refers to the mode in which it is written. To understand this, we have to go back to the original meaning of *Kung*. This is the ancient name of the first note of the pentatonic scale: *Kung*, *Shang*, *Chiao*, *Chih*, *Yü*, or the first of the seven notes of the heptatonic scale: *Kung*, *Shang*, *Chiao*, *Pien Chih*, *Chih*, *Yü*, *Pien Kung*. (*Pien Chih* has been explained as meaning '*altered Chih*' or 'changing into *Chih*'. Since *Pien Chih* is a semi-tone lower than *Chih*, the second explanation seems more plausible. The same applies to *Pien Kung*. See GDMM, Vol. II, p. 229). These are shifted according to the key used; they correspond, respectively, to *do*, *ray*, *me*, *sol*, *lah*, and *doh*, *ray*, *me*, *fah*, *sol*, *lah*, *te* in the tonic sol-fa system. At the same time, the twelve fixed notes supposedly based on pitch-pipes, called the twelve *lü*, are arranged in an ascending series and correspond to the black and white keys of the keyboard. (For the names of the twelve *lü* in Chinese and English, see Levis, p. 64.) The actual pitch of the fundamental pitch-pipe used in ancient China is not known for certain (see Wang Kuang-ch'i, pp. 39–40), but for convenience's sake we may take the fundamental note *Huang-chung* ('Yellow Bell') as corresponding to, but not identical with, C. Thus, when a tune has *Huang-chung* as its keynote, it is said to have *Huang-chung* as its *kung*, as if we were to say, 'C is *doh*'. Further, the tune can be written in one of the five possible pentatonic modes, or one of the seven possible heptatonic modes (see Levis, pp. 72–3). This is referred to as its *tiao*. Both the key and the mode of a tune are indicated. Thus, a tune which has *Huang-chung* as its keynote and written in the *Kung* mode is designated '*Huang-chung*, *Kung*', which is really an abbreviation of '*Huang-chung kung*, *Kung tiao*' ('*Huang-chung* key, *Kung* mode', or 'C key, *doh* mode'). Since there are twelve keys, there can be 60 key-mode combinations (*kung-tiao*) using the pentatonic scale (12 × 5), and 84 key-mode combinations using the heptatonic scale (12 × 7). These have existed more in theory than in practice, though Emperors Wu of Liang and T'ai-tsung of T'ang are said to have used the 84 key-mode combinations. In Yuan and Ming drama, only nine key-mode combinations were actually used, though works on drama often misleadingly give the number as more than nine. (*b*) In a narrower sense, *Kung tiao* means 'the *Kung* mode', i.e. one of the five possible pentatonic modes, or one of the seven possible heptatonic modes. (*c*) To add to the confusion, in popular usage the key-mode combination of a tune is not referred to by the names of the key and mode involved, as it should be, but by a single 'popular name' (*su-ming*). For instance, a tune with *Huang-chung* as keynote and in the *Kung* mode should be called, as we have seen, '*Huang-chung, Kung*'; but in fact it is commonly called *Cheng Kung* ('Proper *kung*'), while, to make matters worse, '*Huang-chung kung*' is used as the popular name for the key-mode combination *Wu-yi, Kung*. In this popular usage, a key-mode combination which involves the *Kung* mode is called such-and-such a *kung*, all other combinations are called such-and-such *tiao*. Therefore, when Chinese works on dramatic music refer to the numbers of *kung* and *tiao* used in drama, they mean the numbers of key-mode combinations which involve the *Kung* mode and those which do not. To clarify the confusion, I suggest that in romanization the word *kung* should be written with a small k when used in the sense of 'key', and hyphenated with *tiao* (sense (*a*)); written with a capital K and not hyphenated with *tiao* when used in the sense 'the *Kung* mode': *Kung tiao* (sense (*b*)); written with a small k and not hyphenated with any other word when used in the sense 'a key-mode combination involving the *Kung* mode' (sense (*c*)), e.g. *Huang-chung kung*; 5 *kung*, 4 *tiao*.

19. Numbers of tunes used in Yuan Northern and Southern Drama

Modern authorities differ on the numbers of tunes used in Yuan Northern and Southern Drama, since they based their statistics on different sources and used different criteria. Wang Kuo-wei (p. 69) gave 335 tunes for Northern Drama and 543 for Southern. His figure for the former was based on Chou Tê-ch'ing's *Chung-yuan Yin-yun* (1324), and Chu Ch'üan's *T'ai-ho Cheng-yin P'u* (1398), though at the same time he admitted that this figure included tunes found only in Dramatic Lyrics (*san-ch'ü*) but not in extant plays, in which the number of tunes used did not far exceed 230. His figure for the latter was based on the *Nan Chiu-kung P'u* of Shen Ching (1553–1610). Chou Yi-pai (pp. 198, 236) gives 400 and 229 tunes, discounting overlappings, for Southern and Northern Drama respectively, based on extant plays. Aoki Masaru (tr. Wang Ku-lu, pp. 554–5) gives 450 for Southern Drama, based on the *Shih-san-tiao P'u* which he believes to be a Yuan work edited by Chiang Hsiao (*fl.* 1544), but does not give any figure for Northern Drama. Now, if we take the figure for Northern Drama from the *Chung-yuan Yin-yun* and the *T'ai-ho Cheng-yin P'u*, the criterion would seem to be too wide, for this figure includes tunes found only in Dramatic Lyrics but not in drama proper. If, on the other hand, we take the figure based on extant plays, the criterion might be too narrow, for tunes known by name but not found in extant plays could have been used in plays now lost. The probable number, then, would seem to be over 230 but not more than 335. As for Southern Drama, I am inclined to accept Aoki's figure, being based as it is on a work of probable Yuan origin, while Wang's figure, based on a later work, must have included tunes not used in pre-Ming Southern Drama, and Chou's figure, based on extant plays alone, is again not inclusive enough.

20. Chief accompanying instruments in Yuan Northern and Southern Drama

Assertions by modern writers on the subject are to be taken with caution, for the fact is we do not know for certain what the chief instruments were. Wang Kuang-ch'i (p. 175) states that the three-stringed *san-hsien* was the chief instrument in Yuan Northern Drama and the horizontal flute (*ti*) was that in Southern Drama. Chou Yi-pai (pp. 225, 231, 294) says the same thing about Northern Drama but thinks the four-stringed *p'i-pa* was the main instrument in Southern Drama before it was replaced by the flute. Aoki (Wang Ku-lu, pp. 499–500) is of the opinion that Northern Drama used the *p'i-pa* and Southern Drama the vertical flute (*hsiao*). Among recent Western writers on Chinese music, Laurence Picken agrees with Wang Kuang-ch'i in saying that the main instrument in Southern Drama was the 'cross-flute' and that in Northern Drama was 'a string instrument' (NOHM, Vol. I, pp. 114–15). Peter Crossley-Holland asserts the opposite: that the chief Northern instrument was the flute and the Southern one the 'lute' (GDMM, Vol. II, p. 243)—a statement either based on an authority of which I am ignorant or due to some confusion.

21. *T'o-po* 脫剝 (*or* 膊)

In translating this term as 'stripping down to the waist' I am following Miss Feng Yuan-chün (pp. 370–2). However, it is doubtful if Yuan players in this type of play always did strip to the waist, in view of the fact that sometimes women acted in such plays. (See above, p. 159.)

22. Numbers of extant and lost pre-Ming Southern plays

Ch'ien Nan-yang (p. 8) gives the following statistics: extant plays, 15; completely lost and known by title only, 33; plays of which excerpts have been gleaned from various sources, 119. But he is unaware of the unique texts of pre-Ming Southern Drama preserved in the *Feng-yueh Chin-nang* collection. According to my study (J. J. Y. Liu II, pp. 79–107), this collection includes five pre-Ming Southern plays and two excerpts, all of which are unique texts. One of the two excerpts is from a play listed by Ch'ien among those totally lost. Thus, his figures should be emended as follows: extant plays, 20 (15 + 5); lost and known by title only, 32 (33 − 1); plays of which excerpts exist, 120 (119 + 1).

23. Ling Meng-ch'u's triology

According to Ch'i Piao-chia (p. 171), Ling first wrote a play with

Hung-fu as protagonist, then another with Li Ching as protagonist, finally yet another one with Curly Beard as chief character. Fu Hsi-hua II only lists the first and third, which are extant, but not the second, which is lost. See also Wang Ku-lu, p. 367.

24. Dramatic Romances about Hung-fu

According to Lü T'ien-ch'eng (p. 328), there were three Dramatic Romances about Hung-fu, by Chang Feng-yi, Chin-*ch'i*(?) Wai-han 近齊外翰, and Chang T'ai-ho respectively. Fu Hsi-hua (III, p. 193) quoted the passage from Lü and emended (rightly, I think) the second name to Chin-*chai* Wai-han — 齋 — —. The play by Chang Feng-yi we have discussed; the other two are listed by Fu as no longer extant. However, since Feng Meng-lung stated that the first part of his *Nü Chang-fu* was adapted from 'the two texts of Chang Po-ch'i (i.e. Chang Feng-yi) and Liu Chin-ch'ung', Chin-chai Wai-han (a name not mentioned elsewhere) could be the pen-name of Liu Chin-ch'ung (not mentioned anywhere else either, to my knowledge). If that is the case, the scenes in Part I of *Nü Chang-fu* which are not from Chang's play should be from the play by Liu (i.e. Chin-chai Wai-han?), which Fu supposed lost. As for Part II of *Nü Chang-fu*, Feng said that this was adapted from the texts of Chang Po-ch'i and Ling Ch'u-ch'eng (i.e. Ling Meng-ch'u). A comparison with Ling's *Ch'iu-jan Weng* (described above on p. 167) shows that one scene of *Nü Chang-fu* is taken from it. The other scenes which are neither from the *Ch'iu-jan Weng* nor from Chang's play could be from either of the other two plays of Ling's trilogy (see preceding note), but since I have not seen the one with Hung-fu as protagonist, I cannot determine whether they are from this play or from the lost one with Li Ching as protagonist.

25. The author of the *Shuang Hung Chi*

In various bibliographies the play is given as by Keng-sheng-tzǔ 更生子 or Keng-sheng-shih — — 氏 (see Fu Hsi-hua III, p. 399), but in the Wan-li edition of the text (facsimile reprint, KHT), the author is given as Yü Hang, Keng-sheng-shih (or, Yü-hang, Keng-sheng-shih?) 禹航 — — —. This presents two possibilities: (*a*) Yü is the author's surname, Hang his personal name (*ming*), and Keng-sheng his courtesy name (*tzŭ*) or informal style (*hao*). (*b*) Yü-hang and Keng-sheng (or Keng-sheng-tzǔ) are both given names, while the surname is not mentioned. So far I have not been able to identify either Yü-hang or Keng-sheng with a known Ming writer. I know of no writer of the period with the name Yü-hang. As for Keng-sheng, two men had this courtesy name. One was Ch'ien Su (*fl.* 1368), a staunch Confucianist (Chiao Hung, ch. 115, p. 23a; Liu Feng, Ch. 8, p. 3a); the other was Ku Ch'i-lun (*fl.* 1578), who wrote poetry (SCTT, Ch. 178, p. 107). Neither is likely to have written the play, which must belong to a later date since it incorporated passages from *The K'un-lun Slave* by Mei Ting-tso (1549–1615). In the absence of any positive identification, I am inclined to think that Yü Hang is the author's real name.

Additional Notes

26. Attempts to Confucianize the Liang-shan heroes

One example is the affixation of the label *chung-yi* ('Loyal and Upright') to the title *Shui-hu*. This in fact may have been due to a confusion between legends about the Liang-shan heroes and those about the guerillas who fought against the Tartars in North China at the end of the Northern Sung period, and who were given the name Chung-yi Chün, 'Loyal and Upright Forces' (see Chang Cheng-lang, pp. 218–23). Whether the Ming editors of the *Shui-hu* realized this or not, they used the label to indicate that the Liang-shan rebels were at heart loyal to the imperial Sung house. In this way, *yi* lost much of its meaning as understood by the heroes themselves and became identified with the Confucian sense of the word.

BIBLIOGRAPHY

Note: This bibliography is in two parts, each subdivided into two sections. Part I consists of works in Chinese. In Section A, works are listed by author, and when two or more works by the same author are listed, they are placed in chronological order, with numbers attached to the author's name (e.g. Feng Yu-lan I, Feng Yu-lan II, etc.). In Section B, works are listed by title, preceded by an abbreviation if such has been used in the above pages. Works in this section include anonymous works, works by several hands, journals, anthologies, collecteana (*ts'ung shu*), as well as Confucian classics, ancient philosophical works, and standard histories. The names of the authors or compilers of some of these are known, but they are listed here because it is more common to refer to them by their titles (e.g. the *Confucian Analects* is listed as *Lun Yü*, not under K'ung Tzŭ; *History of the Han Dynasty* under *Han Shu*, not Pan Ku). Similar arrangement is followed in Part II, which consists of works in Western languages. In the Additional Notes and the list of Sources and References, except when it seems necessary to mention the full title of a work, works listed in Section A of either Part are referred to by author, and in the case of two or more works by the same author, the attached numbers are added; while those in Section B are referred to by title or abbreviation. The bibliography consists only of works cited or specifically referred to; other works consulted and general reference books are not included.

Part I

Section A

Aoki Masaru 青木正兒. See Wang Ku-lu

Chang Cheng-lang, 'Sung Chiang *K'ao*' 張政烺，宋江考 (SYLC)

Chao Yeh (first century), *Wu Yueh Ch'un-ch'iu* 趙曄，吳越春秋 (SPPY)

Ch'ao Ch'ung-chih (twelfth century), *Ch'ao Chü-tz'ŭ Hsien-sheng Shih-chi* 晁冲之，晁具茨先生詩集 (HHT)

Ch'en Ch'en (*c.* 1590–1670), *Shui-hu Hou-chuan* 陳忱，水滸後傳 (rep. Hong Kong, 1959)

Ch'en Yin-k'o, *Yuan Po Shih Chien-cheng Kao* 陳寅恪，元白詩箋証稿 (Peking, 1955)

Cheng Chen-to I, *Chung-kuo Wen-hsüeh Shih* 鄭振鐸，中國文學史 (Peiping, 1932)

—— II, *Chung-kuo Su Wen-hsüeh Shih*, — — 俗 — — — (Shanghai, 1938)

Ch'i Piao-chia (1602–45), *Yuan-shan-t'ang Ch'ü-p'in* and *Yuan-shan-t'ang Chü-p'in* 祁彪佳，遠山堂曲品 — — — 劇 — (ed. Huang Shang, Shanghai, 1955)

Chia Tao (777–841), *Ch'ang-chiang Chi* 賈島，長江集 (TSCC)

Chiao Hung (1541–1620), *Kuo-ch'ao Hsien-cheng Lu* 焦竑，國朝獻徵錄

Ch'ien Mu, *Hsien-Ch'in Chu-tzŭ Hsi-nien* 錢穆，先秦諸子繫年 (2nd edn, Shanghai, 1936)

Ch'ien Nan-yang, *Sung Yuan Hsi-wen Chi-yi* 錢南揚，宋元戲文輯佚 (Shanghai, 1956)

Chou Mi, *Wu-lin Chiu-shih* 周密，武林舊事 (*c.* 1274; rep. WCT)

Chou Yi-pai, *Chung-kuo Hsi-chü Shih* 周貽白，中國戲劇史 (Shanghai, 1954)

Chu Ch'üan, *T'ai-ho Cheng-yin P'u* 朱權，太和正音譜 (1398; rep. together with Chung Ssŭ-ch'eng below)

Chung Ssŭ-ch'eng, *Lu-kuei Pu* 鍾嗣成，錄鬼簿 (1330; rep. Shanghai, 1957)

Feng Meng-lung (1574–*c.* 1645), *Mo-han-chai Ting-pen Ch'uan-ch'i* 馮夢龍，墨憨齋定本傳奇 (rep. Peking, 1960)

Feng Yu-lan I, *Chung-kuo Chê-hsüeh Shih* 馮友蘭，中國哲學史 (Shanghai, 1934)

—— II, *Chung-kuo Chê-hsüeh Shih Pu*, — — — — — 補 (Shanghai, 1936)

—— III, *Hsin Shih Lun* 新事論 (Kunming, 1939)

Feng Yuan-chün, *Ku-chü Shuo-hui* 馮沅君，古劇說彙 (revised edn, Peking, 1956)

Fu Hsi-hua I, *Yuan-tai Tsa-chü Ch'üan-mu* 傅惜華，元代雜劇全目 (Peking, 1956)

—— II, *Ming-tai Tsa-chü Ch'üan-mu* 明代 — — — — (Peking, 1958)

—— III, *Ming-tai Ch'uan-ch'i Ch'üan-mu* — — 傳奇 — — (Peking, 1959)

Han Yü (768–824), *Ch'ang-li Hsien-sheng Chi* 韓愈，昌黎先生集 (SPPY)

Ho Ching-ming (1483–1521), *Ho Ta-fu Chi* 何景明，何大復集 (Ch'ien-lung ed.)

Ho Hsin, *Shui-hu Yen-chiu* 何心，水滸研究 (Shanghai, 1954)

Hsia Po-ho (*fl.* 1368), *Ch'ing-lou Chi* 夏伯和，青樓集 (SMYA)

Hsiang Ta, *T'ang-tai Ch'ang-an yü Hsi-yü Wen-ming* 向達，唐代長安與西域文明 (Peking, 1957)

Hsü Wei (1521–93), *Hsü Wen-ch'ang Wen-chi* 徐渭，徐文長文集 (1614)

Huan-chu-lou-chu, *Shu-shan Chien-hsia* 還珠樓主，蜀山劍俠 (rep. Hong Kong, no date)

Huang-fu Mei (ninth century), *San-shui Hsiao-tu* 皇甫枚，三水小牘 (YTTK)

Kao Ch'i (1336–74) I, *Ch'ing-ch'iu Shih-chi* 高啓，青邱詩集 (SPPY)

—— II, *Fu-tsao Chi* 鳧藻集 (SPPY)

Kao Shih (700?–765), *Kao Ch'ang-shih Chi* 高適，高常侍集 (SPTK)

Kao Shih-ch'i, *T'ien-lu Chih-yü* (1690) 高士奇，天祿識餘 (rep. KST)

Kê Hsien-ning, *Chung-kuo Hsiao-shuo Shih* 葛賢寧，中國小說史 (Taipei, 1956)

Ku Ying (1310–69), *Yü-shan P'u Kao* and *Yü-shan Yi-kao* 顧瑛，玉山璞稿，— — 逸 — (ed. Pao T'ing-po, 1772; rep. TSCC)

Kuan-yuan-nai-tê-weng, *Tu-ch'eng Chi-sheng* 灌園耐得翁，都城紀勝 (1235; rep. WCT)

Lao Kan, '*Lun Han-tai ti Yu-hsia*', 勞幹，論漢代的游俠 (TWH, No. 1 1950)
Li Meng-yang (1472–1529), *K'ung-t'ung Chi* 李夢陽，空同集 (HSC)
Li Po (701–62), *Li T'ai-po Ch'üan-chi* 李白，李太白全集 (SPPY)
Li T'ien-yi, '*Jih-pen So-chien Chung-kuo Tuan-p'ien-hsiao-shuo Lüeh-chi*' 李田意，日本所見中國短篇小說略記 (THH, No. 2, 1957)
Liu Feng (*fl.* 1544), *Hsü Wu Hsien-hsien Tsan* 劉鳳，續吳先賢贊 (YMST)
Liu Yi-ch'ing (403–44), *Shih-shuo Hsin-yü* 劉義慶，世說新語 (SPPY)
Lo Hsiang-lin, *T'ang-tai Wen-hua Shih* 羅香林，唐代文化史 (Taipei, 1955)
Lo Pin-wang (seventh century), *Lo Ch'eng Chi* 駱賓王，駱丞集 (TSCC)
Lo Yeh, *Tsui-weng T'an-lu* 羅燁，醉翁談錄 (*c.* 1278; rep. Shanghai, 1957)
Lu Chi (261–303), *Lu Shih-heng Chi* 陸機，陸士衡集 (SPPY)
Lu Feng-tsao, *Hsiao Chih Lu* 陸鳳藻，小知錄 (1804; rep. 1873)
Lu Hsün (Chou Shu-jen), *Chung-kuo Hsiao-shuo Shih-lüeh* 魯迅（周樹人），中國小說史略 (Peking, 1925; rep. 1952)
Lu Yu (1125–1210), *Chien-nan Shih-kao* 陸游，劍南詩稿 (SPPY)
Lü T'ien-ch'eng, *Chü P'in* 呂天成，曲品 (1610; rep. with Chung Ssŭ-ch'eng)
Meng Ch'i, *Pen-shih Shih* 孟棨，本事詩 (886; rep. YMST)
Meng Chiao (751–814), *Meng Tung-yeh Shih-chi* 孟郊，孟東野詩集 (SPPY)
Meng Yuan-lao, *Tung-ching Meng-hua Lu* 孟元老，東京夢華錄 (*c.* 1127; rep. TSCC)
Ming-chiao-chung-jen, *Hsia-yi Feng-yueh Chuan* (also called *Hao-ch'iu Chuan*) 名教中人，俠義風月傳（即好逑傳）(ed. 1863)
Mou Jun-sun, *Chu-shih-chai Ts'ung-kao* 牟潤孫，注史齋叢稿 (Hong Kong, 1959)
P'ei Ch'i (*fl.* 362), *Yü Lin* 裴啓，語林 (YSCY)
P'ing-chiang Pu-hsiao-sheng (Hsiang K'ai-jan), *Chiang-hu Ch'i-hsia Chuan* 平江不肖生（向愷然），江湖奇俠傳 (rep. Hong Kong, no date)
—— II, *Hsia-yi Ying-hsiung Chuan* 俠義英雄傳 (rep. Hong Kong, no date)
Shih Yü-k'un, *San-hsia Wu-yi* 石玉崑，三俠五義 (1879; rep. Shanghai, 1959)
Su Shih (1036–1101), *Tung-p'o Hsien-sheng Shih* 蘇軾，東坡先生詩 (SPTK)
Sun K'ai-ti I, *Jih-pen Tung-ching so-chien Chung-kuo Hsiao-shuo Shu-mu T'i-yao* 孫楷第，日本東京所見中國小說書目提要 (Peiping, 1931)
—— II, *Su-chiang, Shuo-hua, yü Pai-hua Hsiao-shuo* 俗講說話與白話小說 (Peking, 1956)
—— III, *Chung-kuo T'ung-su Hsiao-shuo Shu-mu* 中國通俗小說書目 (Peking, 1957; revised edn.)
Sun Sheng (*c.* 302–73), *Chin Yang-ch'iu* 孫盛，晋陽秋 (HYK)
T'an Cheng-pi, *Hua-pen yü Ku-chü* 譚正璧，話本與古劇 (Shanghai, 1957)
T'an-meng Tao-jen, *P'eng-kung An* 貪夢道人，彭公案 (*c.* 1891; rep. Hong Kong, no date)
T'ao Ch'ien (365–427), *Ching-chieh Hsien-sheng Chi* 陶潛，靖節先生集 (SPPY)

T'ao Hsi-sheng, *Pien-shih yü Yu-hsia* 陶希聖，辯士與游俠 (Shanghai, 1933)
Ts'ao Chih (192–232), *Ts'ao Tzŭ-chien Shih Chu* 曹植，曹子建詩注 (ed. Huang Chieh, Peking, 1957)
Tu Fu (712–770), *Tu Shih Hsiang-chu* 杜甫，杜詩詳注 (ed. Ch'iu Chao-ao, 1693; facsimile rep.)
Tuan Ch'eng-shih (ninth century), *Yu-yang Tsa-tsu* 段成式，酉陽雜組 (SPTK)
Wang Ch'eng (twelfth century), *Tung-tu Shih-lüeh* 王偁，東都事略 (rep. no date)
Wang Ku-lu (tr.), *Chung-kuo Chin-shih Hsi-ch'ü Shih* 王古魯譯，中國近世戲曲史 (revised edn, Peking, 1958)
Wang Kuang-ch'i, *Chung-kuo Yin-yueh Shih* 王光祈，— — 音樂史 (1931; rep. Hong Kong, 1962)
Wang Kuo-wei (1877–1927), *Wang Kuo-wei Hsi-ch'ü Lun-wen Chi* 王國維，— — — 戲曲論文集 (Peking, 1957)
Wang Shih-chen (1634–1711), *Yü-yang-shan-jen Ching-hua Lu* 王士禛，漁洋山人精華錄 (WYWK)
Wang Wei (699–759), *Wang Yu-ch'eng Chi Chu* 王維，王右丞集注 (ed. Chao Tien-ch'eng, SPPY)
Wen-k'ang, *Erh-nü Ying-hsiung Chuan* 文康，兒女英雄傳 (1878; rep. Hong Kong, no date)
Wu Ching-tzŭ (1701–54), *Ju-lin Wai-shih* 吳敬梓，儒林外史 (rep. Peking, 1954)
Wu Tzŭ-mu, *Meng-liang Lu* 吳自牧，夢梁錄 (*c.* 1278; rep. WCT)
Yang Yin-liu, *Chung-kuo Yin-yueh Shih-kang* 楊蔭瀏，中國音樂史綱 (Shanghai, 1953)
Yü Hsin (513–81), *Yü Tzŭ-shan Chi* 庾信，庾子山集 (SPPY)
Yü Wan-ch'un, *Chieh Shui-hu* 俞萬春，結水滸 (1851; rep. no date)
Yuan Mei (1716–98), *Hsiao-ts'ang-shan-fang Shih-chi* 袁枚，小倉山房詩集 (in *Sui-yuan San-shih-liu-chung*, 1892)

Section B

BSS Basic Sinological Series (see *Kuo-hsüeh Chi-pen Ts'ung-shu*)
CLC *Chi-ku-kê Liu-shih-chung Ch'ü* 汲古閣六十種曲 (ed. Mao Chin, 1599–1659; rep. Peking, 1958)
Chi-kung Huo-fo 濟公活佛 (current edn, no date)
Chin Shu 晋書 (ES)
CTC *Ch'ing-jen Tsa-chü Ch'u-chi* 清人雜劇初集 (ed. Cheng Chen-to, no date)
Ch'ing Shih 清史 (Taipei, 1961)
CTT *Ch'ü-hai Tsung-mu T'i-yao* 曲海總目提要 (ed. Tung K'ang, Shanghai, 1928)
CTTP *Ch'ü-hai Tsung-mu T'i-yao Pu-pien* — — — — — — 補編 (ed. Pei-ying, Peking, 1959)
Ch'uan-ch'i Hui-k'ao Piao-mu 傳奇彙考標目 (*c.* 1720; rep. CKHLC)

	Chuang Tzŭ (Chi-chieh) 莊子集解 (ed. Wang Hsien-ch'ien, BSS)
	Ch'üan Ch'en Shih 全陳詩 (CHSCNS)
	Ch'üan Chin Shih — 晋 — (CHSCNS)
CHSCNS	*Ch'üan Han San-kuo Chin Nan-pei-ch'ao Shih* 全漢三國晋南北朝詩 (ed. Ting Fu-pao, Shanghai, 1916)
	Ch'üan Pei-Chou Shih — 北周 — (CHSCNS)
	Ch'üan San-kuo Shih (CHSCNS)
	Ch'üan Sung Shih — 宋 — (CHSCNS)
CPC	*Chui Pai Ch'iu* 綴白裘 (ed. Wang Hsieh-ju, Shanghai, 1940)
CKHLC	*Chung-kuo Ku-tien Hsi-ch'ü Lun-chu Chi-ch'eng* 中國古典戲曲論著集成 (Vol. VII, Peking, 1959)
ES	*Erh-shih-wu Shih* 二十五史 (Hong Kong, 1959)
HHT	*Hai-shan Hsien-kuan Ts'ung-shu* 海山仙館叢書 (ed. P'an Shih-ch'eng, 1849)
	Han Fei Tzŭ 韓非子 (SPPY)
	Han Shu 漢書 (ES)
	Hsin T'ang Shu 新唐書 (ES)
	Hsin Yuan Shih 新元史 (ES)
	Hsüan-ho Yi-shih 宣和遺事 (*c.* 1280; rep. Shanghai, 1954)
	Hsün Tzŭ 荀子 (SPPY)
	Hou Han Shu 後漢書 (ES)
	Hsiao Wu-yi 小五義 (1889; rep. Hong Kong, no date)
	Hsü Hsiao Wu-yi 續 — — — (1889; rep. Hong Kong, no date)
	Huai-nan Tzŭ 淮南子 (SPPY)
HYK	*Huang-shih Yi-shu K'ao* 黄氏逸書考 (ed. Huang Shih, 1893)
HSC	*Hung-cheng Ssŭ-chieh Chi* 弘正四傑集 (1896)
KST	*Ku-chin Shuo-pu Ts'ung-k'an* 古今說部叢刊 (ed. Wang Wen-ju, Shanghai, 1910)
KHT	*Ku-pen Hsi-ch'ü Ts'ung-k'an* 古本戲曲 — — (Peking, 1957–?)
KYMT	*Ku-pen Yuan Ming Tsa-chü* 孤本元明雜劇 (Peking? no date)
	Ku Wen Yuan 古文苑 (TSCC)
(BSS)	*Kuo-hsüeh Chi-pen Ts'ung-shu* 國學基本叢書 (Shanghai, 1936)
	Lao Tzŭ (Ho-ku) 老子覈詁 (ed. Ma Hsü-lun, Peking, 1923)
	Lieh Tzŭ 列子 (SPPY)
	Lun Yü 論語 (SPPY)
	Meng Tzŭ 孟子 (SPPY)
	Mo Tzŭ 墨子 (SPPY)
	San-kuo Chih 三國志 (ES)
SMT	*Sheng Ming Tsa-chü* 盛明雜劇 (ed. Shen T'ai, *c.* 1630; rep. Peking, 1958)
	Shih Chi 史記 (ES)
	Shih-kung An 施公案 (1798; rep. no date)
SMYA	*Shuang-mei-ying-an Ts'ung-shu* 雙梅景闇叢書 (ed. Ye Tê-hui, 1914)
	Shui-hu 水滸 (120-chapter version, Shanghai, 1934)

SHC *Shui-hu Hsi-ch'ü Chi* — — 戲曲集 (Vol. I, Shanghai, 1957; Vol. II, 1958)

SYLC *Shui-hu Yen-chiu Lun-wen Chi* — — 研究論文集 (Peking, 1957)

Shuo Fu 說郛 (ed. T'ao Tsung-yi, fourteenth century, ed. 1647)

SCTT *Ssŭ-k'u Ch'üan-shu Tsung-mu T'i-yao* 四庫全書總目提要 (WYWK)

SPPY *Ssŭ-pu Pei-yao* 四部備要 (Shanghai, 1927–35)

SPTK *Ssŭ-pu Ts'ung-k'an* — — 叢刊 (Shanghai, 1920–35)

Sung Shih 宋史 (ES)

TPKC *T'ai-p'ing Kuang-chi* 太平廣記 (rep. 1934)

TWH *T'ai-ta Wen-shih-chê Hsüeh-pao* 台大文史哲學報 (Taipei)

Tsa-chü San-chi 雜劇三集 (ed. Tsou Shih-chin, seventeenth century, rep. Peking, 1958)

THH *Tsing Hua Hsüeh-pao* 淸華學報 (New Series, Taipei)

TSCC *Ts'ung-shu Chi-ch'eng* 叢書集成 (Shanghai, no date)

Tun-huang Pien-wen Chi 敦煌變文集 (ed. Wang Chung-min and others, Peking, 1957)

WYWK *Wan-yu Wen-k'u* 萬有文庫 (Shanghai, 1929–?)

Wen Hsüan 文選 (WYWK)

WCT *Wu-lin Chang-ku Ts'ung-pien* 武林掌故叢編 (1883)

Yen Tan Tzŭ 燕丹子 (SPPY)

YCH *Yuan Ch'ü Hsüan* 元曲選 (ed. Tsang Mao-hsün, sixteenth century; rep. Peking, 1961)

YSCY *Yü-han Shan-fang Chi Yi-shu* 玉函山房輯佚書 (ed. Ma Kuo-han, 1884)

YCLH *Yuan-chien Lei-han* 淵鑑類函 (1710; rep. 1883)

YMST *Yuan Ming Shan-pen Ts'ung-shu* 元明善本叢書 (Shanghai, 1937)

YFSC *Yueh-fu Shih-chi* 樂府詩集 (ed. Kuo Mao-ch'ien, *c.* 1100; rep. SPPY)

YTTK *Yun-tzu-tsai-k'an Ts'ung-shu* 雲自在龕叢書 (ed. Miao Ch'-üan-sun, 1891)

Part II

Section A

Acton, Harold (tr.), 'Lin Ch'ung Yeh Pen' (THM, Vol. IX, No. 2, 1939)

Archer, William, *The Old Drama and the New* (London, 1923)

Ariosto, Lodovico, *Orlando Furioso* (Florence, 1948)

Arlington, L. C. and Acton, H. (trs.), *Famous Chinese Plays* (Peiping, 1937)

Auerbach, Erich, *see* Trask.

Bibliography

Baker, Sir Richard, *Theatrum Triumphans* (London, 1670)

Bedford-Jones, H. (tr.), *The Breeze in the Moonlight* (New York, 1926)

Bishop, J. L., *The Colloquial Short Story in China* (Harvard, 1956)

Bowra, C. M., *Heroic Poetry* (London, 1952)

Buck, Pearl S. (tr.), *All Men Are Brothers* (New York, 1933)

Caxton, William (tr.), *Ordre of Chyualrye* (Early English Texts Society, London, 1926)

Chaucer, Geoffrey, *Canterbury Tales* (ed. V. F. Hopper, Brooklyn, 1948)

Ch'en Shou-yi I, 'Thomas Percy and His Chinese Studies' (CSPSR, Vol. XX, 1936–7)

—— II, *Chinese Literature, a Historical Introduction* (New York, 1961)

Corneille, Pièrre, *Le Cid* (ed. F. M. Warren, Boston, 1829)

Crump, J. I., 'The Elements of Yuan Opera' (JAS, Vol. XVII, No. 3, 1958)

Davis, Sir John F. (tr.), *The Fortunate Union* (London, 1829)

Delza, Sophia, *Body and Mind in Harmony*: T'ai Chi Ch'üan (New York, 1961)

Dickinson, J. (tr.), *Policraticus* (PMR)

Edwards, E. D., *Chinese Prose Literature of the T'ang Period*, Vol. II (London, 1938)

Frith, Henry (tr.), *Chivalry* (London, 1891)

Gautier, Léon, *see* Frith

Giles, Lionel, *Six Centuries at Tun-huang* (London, 1944)

Graham, A. C. (tr.), *The Book of Lieh Tzŭ* (London, 1961)

Hsia, C. T., 'Comparative Approaches to *Water Margin*' (YCGL, No. 11, 1962)

Ho, Ping-ti, 'Records of the Grand Historian: Some Problems of Translation' (PA, XXXVI, 2, 1963)

Irwin, R. G., I, *The Evolution of a Chinese Novel*: Shui-hu-chuan (Harvard, 1953)

—— II, '*Water Margin* Revisited' (TP, Vol. XLVIII, Livr. 4–5, 1960)

Jackson, J. H. (tr.), *Water Margin* (Shanghai, 1937)

Joseph, B. L., *Elizabethan Acting* (Oxford, 1951)

Legge, James (tr.), *The Chinese Classics* (rep. Hong Kong, 1960)

Levis, J. H., *The Foundations of Chinese Musical Art* (Peiping, 1936)

Liao, W. K. (tr.), *Han Fei Tzŭ* ,Vol. II (London, 1959)

Liu, James J. Y., I, *Elizabethan and Yuan* (London, 1955)

—— II, 'The *Feng-yueh Chin-nang*: a Ming collection of Yuan and Ming plays and lyrics preserved in the Royal Library of San Lorenzo, Escorial, Spain' (JOS, Vol. IV, Nos. 1–2, 1957–8)

—— III, 'The Knight Errant in Chinese Literature' (JHKBRAS, Vol. 1, 1961)

—— IV, *The Art of Chinese Poetry* (London and Chicago, 1962)

Lull, Ramon, *see* Caxton

Malory, Sir Thomas, *Le Morte d'Arthur* (ed. Sir Edward Strachey, London, 1906)

Masubuchi, Tatsuo, 'The *Yu-hsia* and the Social Order in the Han Period' (AHA, Vol. III, No. 1, 1952)

Morant, George Soulié de (tr.), *La brise au clair de lune* (Paris, 1925)
Mote, F. W., I, 'Confucian Eremitism in the Yuan Period' (CP)
—— II, *The Poet Kao Ch'i* (Princeton, 1962)
Nivison, David, 'Protest Against Conventions and Conventions of Protest' (CP)
Painter, Sidney, *French Chivalry* (Great Seal Books, New York, 1961)
Percy, Thomas (ed.), *Hau Kiou Chuaan* (London, 1761)
Ritson, Joseph, *Robin Hood* (London, 1887)
Ruhlmann, Robert, 'Traditional Heroes in Chinese Popular Fiction' (CP)
Salisbury, John of, *see* Dickinson.
Schofield, W. H., *Chivalry in English Literature* (Harvard, 1925)
Scott, A. C., *The Classical Theatre of China* (London, 1957)
Shakespeare, W. *The Arden Shakespeare* (revised edn).
Sidney, Sir Philip, *An Apologie for Poetrie* (ECE)
Soothill, W. E. (tr.), *The Analects of Confucius* (London, 1937)
Spenser, Edmund, *Works* (variorum ed., Baltimore, 1932–49)
Trask, W. R. (tr.), *Mimesis* (Princeton, 1953)
van Gulik, R. H., *Hsi K'ang and his Poetical Essay on the Lute* (Tokyo, 1941)
Waley, Arthur (tr.), I, *The Analects of Confucius* (London, 1938)
—— II, *The Poetry and Career of Li Po* (London, 1950)
—— III, *Ballads and Tales from Tun Huang* (London, 1960)
Wang, C. C., *Traditional Chinese Tales* (New York, 1944)
Yang, Hsien-i and Gladys (trs.), I, *The Fisherman's Revenge* (Peking, 1957)
—— II, *The Scholars* (Peking, 1957)
Yang Lien-sheng, 'The Concept of *Pao* as a Basis for Social Relations in China' (CTI)
Zucker, A. E., *The Chinese Theater* (Boston, 1925)

Section B

AHA	*Annals of the Hitotsubashi Academy* (Tokyo)
CSPSR	*Chinese Social and Political Science Review* (Peiping)
CTI	*Chinese Thought and Institutions* (Chicago, 1957)
CP	*The Confucian Persuasion* (Stanford, 1960)
ECE	*Elizabethan Critical Essays* (Oxford, 1904)
ECCP	*Eminent Chinese of the Ch'ing Period* (Washington, 1944)
GDMM	*Grove's Dictionary of Music and Musicians* (5th edn, London, 1954)
JAS	*Journal of Asian Studies*
JHKBRAS	*Journal of the Hong Kong Branch of the Royal Asiatic Society*
JOS	*Journal of Oriental Studies* (Hong Kong)
NOHM	*New Oxford History of Music*, Vol. I (London, 1957)

PA	*Pacific Affairs*
	The Penguin Book of Chinese Verse (Baltimore, 1962)
PMR	*The Portable Medieval Reader* (New York, 1961)
THM	*T'ien Hsia Monthly* (Shanghai)
TP	*T'oung Pao* (Leiden)
YCGL	*Yearbook of Comparative and General Literature* (Indiana)

SOURCES AND REFERENCES

Page	Line	
xi	6	F. W. Mote I (CP, pp. 202–40)
xi	7	D. Nivison (*Ibid.*, pp. 177–201)
xi	10	James J. Y. Liu III (JHKBRAS, Vol. 1, pp. 30–41)
xii	21	W. K. Liao, p. 297
xii	22	R. Ruhlmann (CP, pp. 170–3)
xii	22	A. C. Graham, p. 172
xii	22	Ping-ti Ho (PA, XXXVI, 2, p. 180)
2	7	Feng Yu-lan II, pp. 31–2, 59
2	9	Lao Kan (TWH, No. 1, pp. 238–9)
2	14–23	T'ao Hsi-sheng, pp. 74, 31
2	29–41	Lien-sheng Yang (CTI, p. 294)
3	3	Masubuchi (AHA, Vol. III, No. 1, p. 100)
3	23	*Han Shu*, *chüan* 92 (p. 0591 in the whole volume)
3	30	Masubuchi, p. 96
3	33	*Shih Chi*, ch. 122 (p. 0265)
4	29–31	Feng Yu-lan III, pp. 77–8; quoted in English in Yang p. 296
5	17	*Shih Chi*, ch. 120 (p. 0262)
6	10	*Han Fei Tzŭ*, ch. 19, p. 8b; cf. Liao, p. 297
6	34	*Huai-nan Tzŭ*, ch. 18, p. 21b
7	12	*Han Shu*, *loc. cit.*
7	28	Lien-sheng Yang, p. 306
7	note 1	*Lieh Tzŭ*, ch. 8, pp. 10b–11b
8	18	*Lun Yü*, XIII, 20; quoted in Yang, *loc. cit.*
9	6	Feng Yu-lan II, pp. 36–8
9	11	*Lun Yü*, XV, 19
9	13	*Ibid.*, I, 14; VI, 9
9	15	*Meng Tzŭ*, VI, 2
10	7	*Han Fei Tzŭ*, ch. 19, p. 4b; cf. Liao, p. 285
10	16	Ch'ien Mu, p. 83
10	18–30	Feng Yu-lan II, pp. 31–4
10	31–7	*Ibid.*, pp. 49, 58
11	30	*Ibid.*, pp. 39–41
12	11	Feng Yu-lan I, pp. 114–15; II, p. 44
12	22	Lao Kan, p. 241
13	1–5	*Chung Tzŭ*, 8 (p. 50)

Page	Line	
13	11–14	*Lao Tzŭ*, 51
13	14–18	*Chuang Tzŭ*, 10 (p. 56)
14	5–9	*Shih Chi*, ch. 130 (p. 0281)
14–7		*Ibid.*, ch. 124 (p. 0269)
15	note 2	*Chuang Tzŭ, loc. cit.*
16	note 2	*Hsün Tzŭ*, ch. 1, p. 1b
17–25		*Shih Chi*, ch. 77 (pp. 0200–1)
25–34		*Ibid.*, ch. 86 (pp. 0213–4)
25	note 4	Yang Yin-liu, p. 66
26	note 1	*Han Fei Tzŭ*, ch. 4, p. 10
35–6		*Shih Chi*, ch. 124 (p. 0269); ch. 100 (p. 0231)
37	1–16	*Ibid.*, ch. 124 (p. 0269); ch. 11 (p. 0042)
37	17–26	*Ibid.*, ch. 101 (p. 0232)
37–40		*Ibid.*, ch 124 (p. 0269); ch. 112 (p. 0251)
41	8–35	*Han Shu*, ch. 92 (p. 0592)
41	37	Lao Kan, pp. 244–7
42	18–36	*Hou Han Shu*, ch. 59 (p. 0761)
43	1–8	*Ibid.*, ch. 54 (p. 0748)
43	9–32	*San Kuo Chih, Wu Chih*, ch. 9 (p. 1050)
43–4		*Ibid.*, *Wei Chih*, ch. 18 (p. 0972)
44	12–19	*Ibid.*, ch. 20 (p. 0979)
44–5		P'ei Ch'i, p. 3a; Liu Yi-ch'ing, ch. 2B, p. 31; *Chin Shu*, ch. 43 (p. 1201)
45	3–15	*Chin Shu*, ch. 69 (p. 1265)
45	16–30	Sun Sheng, pp. 23b–24a; *Chin Shu*, ch. 62 (p. 1249); Liu Yi-ch'ing, ch. 3A, p. 31b.
45–6		*Hsin T'ang Shu*, ch. 85 (p. 3888)
46	12–27	*Ibid.*, ch. 122 (p. 3957)
46	28–32	*Ibid.*, ch. 202 (p. 4102)
46	32	Li Po, ch. 31, p. 5a
46	33–4	*Ibid.*, ch. 26, p. 20b
47–8		YCLH, ch. 311, quoting Liu Chung-ta's *Hung Shu*, which was destroyed during the Ch'ing period.
48	6–19	*Sung Shih*, ch. 261 (p. 5201)
48–9		*Ibid.*, ch. 273 (p. 5231); Wang Ch'eng, ch. 29, pp. 6b–7a
49	5–22	*Sung Shih*, ch. 440 (p. 5610)
49–50		YCLH, ch. 311, quoting P'an Yung-yin's *Sung-pei Lei-ch'ao*
49	note 1	*Sung Shih*, ch. 183 (p. 4937)
50	9–25	*Ibid.*, ch. 464 (p. 5663)
50	26–32	*Ibid.*, ch. 462 (p. 5659)
50–1		*Hsin Yuan Shih*, ch. 136 (p. 7053)

Page	Line	
51–3		*Ming Shih*, ch. 285 (p. 7792); Kao Ch'i II, ch. 4, pp. 1a–b
53	13	*Ch'ing Shih*, ch. 539 (p. 5991)
53	28	Kao Shih-ch'i, ch. 2, p. 38
56	19–33	*Wen Hsüan*, ch. 2, p. 34
57	3	*Han Shu*, ch. 66 (p. 0524)
57–8		Ts'ao Chih, pp. 69–70
58–9		YFSC, ch. 67, p. 4b; *Ch'üan Chin Shih*, ch. 2, pp. 2a–b
59–60		*Ch'üan Sung Shih*, ch. 4, p. 5b
60	17–25	*Ch'üan Pei-Chou Shih*, ch. 2, p. 22a; Yü Hsin, ch. 4, p. 40a
60–1		*Ibid.*, ch. 1, p. 14b
61	18–34	*Ch'üan Ch'en Shih*, ch. 4, pp. 14a–b
61	35	Lu Chi, ch. 6, p. 2b
62	12–22	YFSC, ch. 67, p. 3b
62–3		*Ibid.*, ch. 66, p. 4a; Wang Wei, ch. 14, p. 2a
63	4–10	YFSC, ch. 66, p. 5a
63	11–15	*Ibid.*, p. 6a; Tu Fu, ch. 10, p. 53a
63–4		YFSC, ch. 66, p. 9a; Kao Shih, ch. 5, p. 5
64–5		Li Po, ch. 3, p. 31a
65	20–8	*Ibid.*, ch. 6, p. 7a
66	1–32	*Ibid.*, ch. 6, pp. 14b–15a
66	note 1	Hsiang Ta, pp. 80–6; Lo Hsiang-lin, pp. 221–47
67	2–6	Li Po, ch. 6, p. 8a
67	10	Hsiang Ta, p. 39
67	11	Ch'en Yin-k'o, p. 53
67	15	YFSC, ch. 63, p. 1a
67	31–9	*Ibid.*, ch. 67, p. 3b; Meng Chiao, ch. 1, p. 6b
68	18–22	Chia Tao, ch. 1, p. 2
68	note 1	Su Shih, ch. 2, p. 5
69	1–25	Lu Yu, ch. 9, pp. 7a–b
70	4–16	*Ibid.*, ch. 4, p. 9a
70	19–20	*Ibid.*, ch. 16, p. 16a
70–1		Ch'ao Ch'ung-chih, ch. 4, p. 4a
71	7	*Ku Wen Yuan*, ch. 2, p. 58
71	10	*Chuang Tzŭ*, 10 (p. 60)
71	35–8	YCLH, ch. 311, gives this poem as by Ku Ying, though it does not appear in his collected poems.
72–3		Kao Ch'i I, ch. 1, pp. 17a–b
73	28–36	Li Meng-yang, ch. 12, p. 4b
74	4	Han Yü, ch. 20, p. 1a
74	13–23	Ho Ching-ming, ch. 6, p. 1a
74–5		Hsü Wei, ch. 4, p. 23a

Page	Line	
75	18	Wang Shih-chen, ch. 1, p. 2
75	20	Yuan Mei, ch. 1, pp. 5a–b; 6b; 7b
75–6		*Ch'üan Chin Shih*, ch. 2, pp. 2a–b
76	8	*Lun Yü*, VII, 2
76	17–29	Wang Wei, ch. 6, p. 1a
76	35	*Chin Shu*, ch. 48 (p. 1211)
77	4–8	Li Meng-yang, ch. 31, p. 12a
77	15–25	*Ch'üan San-kuo Shih*, ch. 3, p. 9b
77–8		*Ch'üan Chin Shih*, ch. 4, p. 11a
78–9		T'ao Ch'ien, ch. 4, pp. 11b–12a
78	note 3	*Huai-nan Tzŭ*, ch. 20, p. 21a
79	30–4	Lo Pin-wang, ch. 4, p. 73
80	6–18	Ho Ching-ming, ch. 6, p. 8a
82–5		*Yen Tan Tzŭ, passim.*
85–6		Chao Yeh, ch. 9, pp. 6a–b
87–8		TPKC, ch. 193, pp. 1a–4b
88–9		*Ibid.*, ch. 194, pp. 1a–3a
89–90		*Ibid.*, ch. 194, pp. 5b–8a
90–1		*Ibid.*, ch. 195, pp. 1a–3b
92		*Ibid.*, pp. 5a–b; Tuan Ch'eng-shih, ch. 9, pp. 3b–4a. I have collated the two texts and found certain variant readings. Since both contain obvious misprints, I have sometimes followed the one, sometimes the other.
93–4		*Ibid.*, ch. 195, pp. 5b–6a; Tuan Ch'eng-shih, ch. 9, pp. 4a–b. Collation as above.
94–6		*Ibid.*, ch. 195, pp. 7a–b, given as from the *Yuan Hua Chi*, though not in the *Shuo Fu* edition of this work.
96–7		*Ibid.*, ch. 194, pp. 5a–b. Above note also applies to this tale.
97	21	*Ibid.*, ch. 196, pp. 5a–6a
97–8		*Ibid.*, ch. 196, pp. 3a–4a. The story is not in the extant edition of Huang-fu Mei's *San-shui Hsiao-tu.*
98–9		*Ibid.*, ch. 485, pp. 4b–6b
99	2–13	*Ibid.*, ch. 486, pp. 5a–9a
99	13–18	*Ibid.*, ch. 487, pp. 1a–7a
101–6		*Tun-huang Pien-wen Chi*, Vol. I, pp. 58–71
107	8–19	Lo Yeh, pp. 3–4
109	11–21	*Hsüan-ho Yi-shih*, pp. 41–4
115	7–10	Sun K'ai-ti II, p. 16; Bishop, p. 8
118	4–6	*Sung Shih*, ch. 316 (p. 5333)
118	15	Li T'ien-yi (THH, No. 2, p. 79)
130–4		Huan-chu-lou-chu, Vol. II, ch. 1, pp. 3–5

Page	Line	
136	33–5	Chou Yi-pai, p. 560
144	9–10	*Ibid.*, p. 236
145–6		Chu Ch'üan, p. 135
146		Hsia Po-ho, pp. 3b, 4a, 5b, 7a, 8b, 10b, 11a
148	11–18	Lü T'ien-ch'eng, p. 313
150	11–35	Ch'ien Nan-yang, pp. 241, 181, 13
151	8–10	Fu Hsi-hua I, pp. 19, 23, 80, 89, 90, 120, 122–4, 129, 133, 139, 167–8, 307, 331–2, 341, 355, 366–7
151	23–31	YCH, pp. 687–704; SHC, Vol. I, pp. 1–15
152–7		YCH, pp. 1518–31; SHC, Vol. I, pp. 33–45
154	note 1	Tu Fu, ch. 9, p. 51a
158–9		SHC, Vol. I, pp. 80–94; KYMT, Vol. II (no pagination)
159	28	Chou Yi-pai, p. 281
159	36	Hsia Po-ho, pp. 5b, 7a, 8b
160–3		SHC, Vol. I, pp. 95–114
163	19–23	*Ibid.*, pp. 115–26
163–4		*Ibid.*, pp. 208–24
164–6		SMT, Vol. I, ch. 21
166	12	Fu Hsi-hua II, p. 111
166–7		SMT, Vol. I, ch. 22
167	7–8	Fu Hsi-hua II, pp. 22, 108
167–8		SMT, Vol. II, ch. 22
168–9		*Ibid.*, ch. 11
170	9–27	*Tsa-chü San-chi*, ch. 7
170	33–4	Fu Hsi-hua II, pp. 207, 230, 265
171	4–16	CTC, No. 10
171	17–30	SHC, Vol. I, pp. 225–8
171–2		*Ibid.*, pp. 229–33
172–7		SHC, Vol. II, pp. 1–98
177	15	*Ibid.*, pp. 101–57
177	20	CTTP, p. 38
177–80		SHC, Vol. II, pp. 159–230; CLC, Vol. X
180–2		SHC, Vol. II, pp. 231–97; CLC, Vol. IX
182	4	Fu Hsi-hua III, p. 229
182	6	*Ibid.*, p. 477
182	9–17	SHC, Vol. II, pp. 301–55
182–3		*Ibid.*, pp. 357–434
183	1–2	CPC, Vol. II, pp. 150–6
183	5–10	*Ibid.*, Vol. I, pp. 164–75; Vol. III, pp. 69–80; Vol. VIII, pp. 169–80
183	19	CLC, Vol. III
183	23	Meng Ch'i, pp. 1a–b

Page	Line	
184	18	Fu Hsi-hua III, pp. 193, 400
184	20	Feng Meng-lung, Vol. I
184–5		KHT, series II, No. 52
185	23	CLC, Vol. III
185	25	*Ibid.*, Vol. IV
185–6		*Ibid.*, Vol. XII
186–7		*Hsin T'ang Shu*, ch. 117 (p. 3945)
187–8		KHT, series III, No. 2
189	16	Fu Hsi-hua III, pp. 436–7, 512, 508; Wang Ku-lu, p. 355; Chou Yi-pai, p. 779; CTT, ch. 23, 25, 30, 33; CTTP, pp. 134, 137; Ch'i Piao-chia, p. 85
206	7	Wu Ching-tzŭ, ch. 12–13. The episode is based on the *Kuei-yuan Ts'ung-t'an*, quoted in TPKC, ch. 238.

GLOSSARY

ch'ang-k'ao wu-sheng 長靠武生 (Peking Theatre) military man in full armour
chê 折 (Northern Drama) act
ch'en tzŭ 襯字 (Northern Drama) 'padding words', i.e. additional words
cheng-ming 正名 (Northern Drama) title
cheng-mo 正末 (Northern Drama) male lead
cheng-tan 正旦 (Northern Drama) female lead
chia-men 家門 (Southern Drama) prologue
chia-t'ou tsa-chü 駕頭雜劇 (Northern Drama) plays about royalty
chiang-shih 講史 (in oral recital) popularization of history
chieh 介 (Southern Drama) word indicating action
chih-chi 知己 an appreciative friend
chieh-yi 節義 (Dramatic Romances) plays about chastity and justice
ch'ih-chien ma-ch'an 叱奸罵讒 (Northern Drama) plays about scolding wicked officials
ch'in 琴 seven-stringed zither
ching 淨 (drama) choleric man
ch'ing-lou 青樓 house of singing girls
chou 州 prefecture
ch'ou 丑 (drama) clown
chu 筑 zither played with a stick
chu-ch'en ku-tzŭ 逐臣孤子 (Northern Drama) plays about exiled officials and orphaned sons
chu-kung-tiao 諸宮調 story-telling combined with singing, using tunes in various keys and modes
ch'u 齣 (Southern Drama) scene
ch'ü 曲 lyrics or sung passages in drama; dramatic poetry
chuan-pien see Additional Note 9
ch'uan-ch'i see Additional Note 8
chün 郡 prefecture
chün-ch'en tsa-chü 君臣雜劇 (Northern Drama) plays about kings and officials
chung-ch'en lieh-shih 忠臣烈士 (Northern Drama) plays about loyal officials and martyrs
chung-hsiao 忠孝 (Dramatic Romances) plays about loyalty and filial devotion
erh-huang 二黃 see *pi'-huang*
feng-ch'ing 風情 (Dramatic Romances) plays about romantic love
feng-hua hsüeh-yueh 風花雪月 (Northern Drama) plays about romantic love
fu 符 tally signifying authority

fu-mo 副末 (drama) second male lead
hao-hsia 豪俠 (Dramatic Romances) plays about knights-errant
hsi-p'i 西皮 see *p'i-huang*
hsi-wen 戲文 Southern Drama
hsiao 簫 vertical flute
hsiao-mo 小末 (Northern Drama) juvenile lead
hsiao-shuo 小說 fiction proper
hsiao-yi lien-chieh 孝義廉節 (Northern Drama) plays about filial devotion, justice, integrity, and chastity
hsieh 俠 see *yu-hsia*
hsieh 挾 to force
hsieh-tzŭ 楔子 (Northern Drama) induction
hsien 縣 district
hsien-fo 仙佛 (Dramatic Romances) plays about Taoist immortals and Buddhist gods
hu-ch'in 胡琴 two-stringed fiddle
hua-chü 話劇 modern drama without music
hua-lien 花臉 or *hau-mien* 花面 see *ching*
hua-pen 話本 story-teller's prompt book
hua-tan 花旦 (drama) flirtatious female
hui 回 session, chapter (in prose romance)
hui-yen 慧眼 (Buddhism) 'wisdom eye'
hung 鴻 wild swan
jang 讓 (Confucianism) yielding, deferring, or 'one-downmanship'
jou 猱 ape
k'ai-ch'ang 開場 see *chia-men*
kan-pang 杆棒 (story telling) tales of chivalry involving use of clubs
k'ang 炕 brick bed
karate 唐手，空手 (Japanese) empty-handed combat
k'ê 科 (Northern Drama) word indicating action
k'ê 客 guest, knight retained by patron
kuei-yuan tsa-chü 閨怨雜劇 (Northern Drama) plays about plaintive ladies
K'un-ch'ü 崑曲 K'un-shan style of singing used in Dramatic Romances
kung 公 duke, lord, term of respect for old men
kung-an 公案 (story-telling) 'public cases', i.e. detective stories
kung-ming 功名 (Dramatic Romances) plays about official honours
kung-tiao see Additional Note 18
li 里 Chinese mile (about one-third of a mile)
lin-ch'üan ch'iu-ho 林泉邱壑 (Northern Drama) plays about recluses
ling-kuai 靈怪 (story-telling) tales about the miraculous
lien-huan t'u-hua 連環圖畫 comic strips
lu-lin tsa-chü 綠林雜劇 (Northern Drama) plays about outlaws
mo 末 (drama) male character. See also *cheng-mo*, *fu-mo*, *hsiao-mo*, *wai-mo*
mu-chih-ming 墓誌銘 inscription on stone buried in tomb
Nan-hsi 南戲 Southern Drama
pai 白 (drama) spoken monologue
pao-piao see Additional Note 6

Glossary

pei-huan li-ho 悲歡離合 (Northern Drama) plays about sadness and joy, partings and reunions
p'i-huang 皮黃 *hsi-p'i* and *erh-huang*, the two main styles of singing in the Peking Theatre
p'i-pa 琵琶 four-stringed lute (*biwa* in Japanese)
p'i-p'ao ping-hu 披袍秉笏 (Northern Drama) plays about kings and officials
pien-shih 辯士 sophists, men who specialized in persuasion
pien-wen see Additional Note 9
p'ien-wen 駢文 Parallel Prose, a kind of euphuistic prose
pin 賓 (drama) spoken dialogue
p'u-tao 朴刀 (story-telling) tales of chivalry involving use of swords
p'u-tao kan-pang 朴刀杆棒 (Northern Drama) plays about chivalry. Cf. *p'u-tao* and *kan-pang*
rōnin 浪人 (Japanese) 'wandering men', e.g. unemployed samurai
san-hsien 三絃 three-stringed lute (*samisen* in Japanese)
shen-hsien 神仙 (story-telling) tales about gods and immortals
shen-hsien tao-hua 神仙道化 (Northern Drama) plays about becoming gods and immortals
shen-t'ou kuei-mien 神頭鬼面 (Northern Drama) plays about Buddhist and Taoist gods
sheng 生 (Southern Drama and Peking Theatre) male character
sheng 省 province
shih 士 men of special skill
shu 恕 (Confucianism) forgiveness, consideration for others
shuo-ching 說經 popular explanation of Buddhist scripture
su-chiang 俗講 popular Buddhist preaching
sumo 相撲 (Japanese) wrestling
t'ai-chi-ch'üan 太極拳 style of boxing
tan 旦 (drama) female character. See also *cheng-tan*, *hua-tan*, *t'ieh-tan*
t'ang-mu-yi 湯沐邑 'bathing place', i.e. temporary fief
ti 笛 horizontal flute
t'i-mu 題目 (Northern Drama) subject
t'ieh-tan 貼旦 (Northern Drama) additional female character
t'o-po tsa-chü see Additional Note 21
tsa-chü 雜劇 'mixed plays', i.e. Northern Drama
tuan-ta wu-sheng 短打武生 (Peking Theatre) military men in short dress
t'uan-yuan 團圓 (Southern Drama) reunion, happy ending
tz'ŭ 詞 Lyric Metres
tz'ŭ-ku 茨菰 name of plant
wai-mo 外末 or *wai* (drama) extra or super
wen-hsi 文戲 (Peking Theatre) civil plays
wu-ch'ou 武丑 (Peking Theatre) military clown
wu-hsi 武戲 (Peking Theatre) military plays
wu-sheng 武生 (Peking Theatre) military man
wu-shih 武士 military expert
yang-sheng 養生 (Taoism) preserving one's life
yao-shu 妖術 (story-telling) tales about witchcraft

yen-fen 烟粉 (story-telling) tales about female ghosts
yen-hua fen-tai 烟花粉黛 (Northern Drama) plays about courtesans
yen-yi 演義 popularization of history in fiction form
yi see Additional Note 2
yin-chü lo-tao 隱居樂道 (Northern Drama) plays about recluses
yu-hsia or *hsia* knight-errant
yueh-fu 樂府 Music Department songs of the Han period; later imitations; also applied loosely to Lyric Metres and dramatic poetry.

INDEX

Index

Made in the USA
Las Vegas, NV
24 October 2024

087f709d-4afe-44a3-8ee1-b4fb49018713R01